*"Small Stakes No-Limit Hold'em...*has set the standard for what a poker book should be and is by far the most definitive no-limit hold'em strategy guide to date."
Andrew Brokos, thinkingpoker.net

"Miller and Co. are established authors with a strong sense of how to communicate both beginner and advanced ideas, and those skills are on display in this book...This book fills a critical gap – providing recreational to intermediate players with the tools they need to be competitive in modern online no-limit games."
Chris Grove, parttimepoker.com

"Small Stakes No-Limit Hold'em is the best no-limit book I've read; the knowledge is worth thousands of dollars to full-time mid-stakes players."
ML4L – high stakes No-Limit cash game player

"Small Stakes No-Limit Hold'em is a well-written, high-level discussion of no-limit hold'em that does a masterful job of explaining difficult, complex concepts with clarity and precision."
Martin Harris, pokernews.com

Small Stakes
No-Limit Hold'em

Ed Miller   Sunny Mehta   Matt Flynn

Dimat Enterprises, Inc.

Publishing Today's Best Poker Books

pokerbooks.InternetTexasHoldem.com

About Dimat Enterprises, Inc.

Our Mission

To publish today's best poker books and grow the game we all love.

Our Pledge

To Our Customers: Dimat is committed to the publication of outstanding poker books that combine cutting-edge content and strategy with clear instruction from today's leading players.

To Our Authors: Dimat treats our authors with respect and professionalism, providing top-notch publishing services while offering some of the best royalty rates in the industry. Cover, paper quality, readability, and graphics are expertly handled to make your book shine.

ABOUT THE AUTHORS

Ed Miller: Noted Poker Authority

Ed Miller is one of the world's best-known and respected poker educators. He's authored five books: *Small Stakes Hold'em* (2004), *Getting Started In Hold'em* (2005), *No-Limit Hold'em: Theory and Practice* (2006), *Professional No-Limit Hold'em* (2007), and now *Small Stakes No-Limit Hold'em*.

He is a lead instructor for StoxPoker video poker training and a regular columnist for Card Player magazine. He also writes an online poker advice column at his website, www. notedpokerauthority.com.

Ed has earned his reputation for excellence by consistently producing some of the clearest and easiest-to-apply poker instruction available anywhere. His mantra is Poker Made Simple, and his contributions to *Small Stakes No-Limit Hold'em* will make poker simple for you.

Sunny Mehta: The Professional

Sunny Mehta plays a lot of no-limit hold'em. He has been successfully making a living as a no-limit hold'em cash game pro for over five years. He has played as high as $25-$50 and won at every level he's tackled.

During the time spent writing *Small Stakes No-Limit Hold'em*, Sunny played hundreds of thousands of hands in the games the book is written about, $1-$2 6-max online no-limit. Many poker books are written by people who haven't played the games or the stakes they're writing about. Not this book! Sunny knows small stakes games intimately well. He knows how the opposition plays. He knows what works and what doesn't. And he's not holding back.

Matt Flynn: Practical Theorist

Matt Flynn cut his teeth in high-stakes no-limit long before the poker boom and loves the intricacies of the game. He is our resident expert in no-limit theory. Want to know how to stop getting exploited or how much to bet on the flop? Matt has your answer.

Matt contributed some of the most advanced material in *Small Stakes No-Limit Hold'em*. He teaches you to balance your betting lines to keep your play unpredictable and hard to exploit. He teaches you how to determine the right bet sizes, both from a theoretical perspective and from experience as a seasoned and highly successful player.

With an incredible math background and degrees from Harvard, Stanford, and Duke, Matt has provided the book with a solid theoretical grounding. So you're not just learning a few tricks that happen to work today. You're learning a system that will beat no-limit games long into the future.

ACKNOWLEDGMENTS

First and foremost, we thank the delightful Anna Paradox for her careful and kind editing. Anna was most helpful in shaping the manuscript and keeping a keen eye not only on what we wrote, but also on what we did not write. Any editor can see the former, but not many see the latter. If you need a good editor, poker or otherwise, she is your huckleberry. She can be reached at www.annaparadox.com.

We thank Mark Roh for his friendship, careful review of the manuscript, and perpetually cheerful willingness to help whenever he was needed. Scott Roh contributed his math and programming savvy to create the dominance chart for big card hands. Thank you, Scott! Professor Lars Stole of the University of Chicago was most helpful with the game theory discussions in the text. Several people helped review the manuscript, including Cero Zuccarello, Piotr Lopusiewicz, Marc Crawford, Elaine Vigneault, and Mimi Miller. Thanks to Jason Hughes for designing the cover art.

Ed would like to thank Elaine, Mom, and Dab. Your love and support is with me in every word. Also thanks to Sunny and Matt for being just foolish enough to complete this journey along with me.

Sunny would like to thank his family and friends for their constant support, as well as his coauthors for their combination of intelligence and diligence.

Matt thanks most of all Theresa, Sean, and Ryan for their continued support and affection. Last book for a long time, I promise! Thanks to my family and friends. Thanks to my coauthors for their persistence and especially their easygoingness. Thanks to Tommy and Alex for teaching me how to play back in the day. And thanks to all my acquaintances in the pokerverse who have made it interesting, especially the Raleigh cast of characters.

CONTENTS

INTRODUCTION

Do you one day envision yourself playing no-limit hold'em for a living? Or do you hope to turn your poker hobby into a lucrative side income? If you do, then you're in the right place. In the coming pages we will arm you with the most important concepts and insights to make your dream a reality. We'll show you how a pro crafts a strategy and then adjusts it to maintain an edge over the competition. And we won't hold back.

But you have to be prepared for a challenge. Small stakes no-limit isn't for wusses anymore. A few years ago, all you needed to win was a little common sense and some patience. The legions of weak players would practically beat themselves. These days the Internet is full of smart, motivated players battling it out for $20 and $50 pots. You can beat them and enjoy the spoils (which can be more than enough to let you quit your job). But you'll have to work, and you'll probably have to change the way you play (and think) in some fundamental ways.

We're not going to waste your time and money rehashing common sense advice you've heard a hundred times before. There's no filler in this book. From the very beginning, we are going to attack your weaknesses. We want to find the places where you mess up. We want to find the opportunities you miss. We want to find the decisions you think about the wrong way. And we want to help you fix them.

This book is example-driven. We teach many critical ideas through hand examples, most of which were taken from the authors' actual play in small stakes games. We've selected hands that improve over the way a typical small stakes regular would play the hand. Some of our plays should surprise you. If you finish this book having never once said to yourself, "Wow, I would never have played the hand like that!" then we haven't done our jobs.

Chances are you won't learn everything here the first time you read the book. It may take several readings before you'll be able to incorporate most of the new ideas into your game. But if you're serious about becoming an excellent no-limit player, the effort will be worth it.

PART 1: FRAMEWORK

64 Squares

Once upon a time, there was a young boy (hint: he's one of the authors of this book) who had a strong inclination for chess. He had an excellent mentor who would frequently set problems for him to solve. If the boy was having trouble finding the right move on a particular problem, the mentor always prompted him with the same advice.

"Sixty-four squares," he would say.

There are 64 squares on a chess board, and the mentor was reminding the boy that to find the best move, he couldn't safely ignore any of them. Any piece, any square could, potentially, be the right one.

When you play a lot of chess, you see the same moves and patterns over and over again. The knights go here, the bishops go there, these pawns thrust forward in attack, and so forth. Anyone who gets to be decent at chess learns to recognize these patterns of play and can replicate the usual moves as they arise. Great players, however, see these patterns, and they also see more. They see the usual moves and they see unusual ones, and they evaluate both. Typically the usual moves end up being best, but sometimes they don't. Sometimes the unusual moves turn out to be brilliant. Great players make these brilliant moves while average players are stuck in the usual rut.

You can't look at only half the board. You won't consistently make the best moves if you play blind to many of them from the very start.

The 64 Squares principle applies just as well to no-limit hold'em. All reasonable players know that they should usually fold T4o or that they shouldn't go too crazy holding two pair when a possible flush is on board. These are decent rules of thumb. But too many players allow these rules of thumb (and others like them) to rigidly define the way they play. And so they miss brilliant play after brilliant play.

This is how typical small stakes regulars play. They develop a basic game plan, and they more or less stick to it. They play a nitty game. They fold all the marginal and bad preflop hands. Every pot they play, they focus on making a big hand. If they make one, they bet and raise to try to make money. If they don't, they might fire a half-hearted bluff, or they might just give up. If they make a medium-strength hand, they try to get it to showdown without putting too much in the pot. The strategy is simple: make money off the big hands and avoid paying off with second-best hands.

The nitty regulars are marginally successful. In small stakes games, enough players will pay off their big hands to keep them going. But they don't see all 64 squares. They pass up opportunity after opportunity because, though profitable, these opportunities don't fit their game plan. Indeed, they don't even notice these opportunities as they arise. They've trained themselves not to.

If you want to be a great no-limit player, you must remove those blinders. It's harder than it sounds. In everyday life, our subconscious brains are constantly eliminating options for us, options they assume aren't worth considering. To play great no-limit, you need to consider all the options. This book will, among other things, help you to see all 64 squares as you play. We'll show you numerous examples where we go beyond the usual play to find the best play. And soon enough, you'll find yourself making plays you would never have seen before.

Showdown Equity And Steal Equity

Let's apply the 64 Squares principle to no-limit hold'em. A poker hand, much like a chess game, can take an extraordinarily large number of paths. For example, you hold pocket threes under the gun. One possible path the hand can take is:

You fold, the next player raises, and everyone else folds.

Another is:

You raise the pot, and only the big blind calls. The flop comes 6♥6♦5♣. You bet half the pot, and your opponent folds.

Change one minor thing about that last example, perhaps a board card or your bet size, and the hand has taken a different path. But you need not be overwhelmed by the possibilities. Fortunately, we don't have to consider each possible path individually to succeed. We just need an overall plan that generates a profit on average over all possibilities.

There are only two ways to make money in no-limit hold'em.

When you really get down to it, there are only two ways of making money in no-limit hold'em. They are:

1. Make the best hand.
2. Steal the pot.

All of your profit derives from one of those two methods, or more precisely, a combination of the two.

By "make the best hand," we are referring to your expectation from winning at showdown. Pot equity, showdown equity, showdown value, implied odds, implied equity, and numerous other poker terms fall into this category. Just to keep it simple, we'll talk about a hand's potential to win money at showdown as its *showdown equity*.

By "steal the pot," we are referring to your expectation from winning the pot before showdown. Fold equity, folding equity, steal equity, and so forth are the relevant terms here. We'll talk about a hand's potential to win money before showdown as its *steal equity*.

Every hand has both showdown equity and steal equity. For example, say you have 87s on the button. You might win by making two pair and winning at showdown. Or, you might win by raising before the flop, betting the flop with no pair, and having your opponents fold. The showdown equity and the steal equity work together to make the hand profitable.

This logic applies to every starting hand: even pocket aces have both showdown equity and steal equity. While most of the hand's value consists of showdown equity, it does also have some steal equity. For instance, if you have black aces, and by the river there are four diamonds on board, you might launch a big bluff to try to force your opponent off of a medium-sized flush. Certainly pocket aces is a profitable starting hand even if you never bluff with it, but it's more profitable if, when the situations arise, you take advantage of steal equity.

In both of the previous examples, the showdown equity and steal equity combine to make the hand profitable. With the 87s, if you concentrate on just one type of equity and ignore the other, the hand won't be profitable. With aces you have so much showdown equity that you can ignore the steal equity and still be profitable (though you shouldn't ignore it). In many cases, however, the two equities combined are still not enough to make the hand profitable. For example, say you have 7♦2♠ under the gun. You have showdown equity and steal equity. After all, you can flop a full house, or you can raise and win the blinds. However, due to your weak hand and poor position, usually these equities will be relatively small—too small to justify risking money to take advantage of them.

♦ All hands have two kinds of equity: showdown equity and steal equity.

♦ When the combined equity is worth more than what you have to risk to play on, the situation is profitable.

♦ When the combined equity is too small to justify the risk, fold.

Using Equities To Make Decisions

How do I plan to make money in this situation?

Every time you act, ask yourself that question. To answer, evaluate both your equities.

As we said before, every hand situation has two main components of value: showdown equity and steal equity. A hand is worth playing when the combination of these two components is worth more than what you risk to play it. You fold 72 preflop because, while the hand has both showdown equity and steal equity, it doesn't have *enough* to justify the risk.

Before you play a hand, think about why you're playing it. Are you relying mostly on your chance to make the best hand, as you would with big pocket pairs? Or do you need to steal frequently to make the hand profitable, as you would with a small suited hand on the button?

Few hands can be played solely to make the best hand. One common error many players make is that they focus too narrowly on showdown equity with hands like suited connectors, small suited aces, and other speculative hands. With these hands they try to see a cheap flop and hope to catch a monster. If they miss, they usually don't bother trying to steal. They just fold. Unfortunately, these speculative hands don't connect with the board often enough to have good showdown equity. Unless your opponents are exceptionally loose, these hands *rely on steal equity to be profitable*. If you won't frequently make money from stealing, your default play should be to fold them.

If your hand relies significantly on stealing, remember that fact as the hand proceeds. It does not mean you should try to steal every time. But if you don't take advantage of steal situations, you'll turn a profitable hand into an unprofitable one.

If your hand relies significantly on showdown equity, remember that not all such hands play the same way. Contrast KT with 44. With KT you'll frequently make medium-strength pair hands. To make the hand profitable, you have to extract one or two bets from weaker hands while avoiding paying off better hands. With 44 you'll infrequently make monster hands. To make the hand profitable, you have to induce your opponents to pay you off those rare times you hit your hand. Thus, these two hands, even though they both rely on showdown equity, will profit in different situations and require different plans.

Now suppose you open for a raise on the button with **T♣8♠** in a 100bb $1–$2 game. Only rarely will **T♣8♠** make a good hand. You rely largely on stealing to make the hand profitable. So, you decide to plan around stealing. Where will your stealing profit come from? Either you could win the blinds without a fight or steal the pot postflop. Before you play a hand to steal, consider where your steal equity will come from. Do you expect simply to steal the blinds often enough to profit? Or do you rely on frequent postflop steals to supplement the blind steals? Before you put one chip in the pot, you should have a rough idea about how frequently, and at what points in the hand, you need to steal to show a profit.

Remember the questions you should ask yourself at every decision: How do I plan to make money in this situation? What is my showdown equity? What is my steal equity? Which one will be more likely to make me money? And how should I plan my play to make the most of the equity I have?

Stealing

Stealing well is critical to no-limit success. Yet most small stakes regulars focus mainly on making hands and give stealing relatively little thought. This undue emphasis on making hands condemns most small stakes regulars to only marginal success. They win lots of money in pots that go to showdown, but they lose nearly as much in pots that don't go to showdown, and their overall winrates hover near zero. If you suffer from this problem, we're going to fix it.

Stealing and making the best hand can overlap considerably. For example, say you have 9♦8♦ and completely miss a flop of A♣J♥4♣. You should immediately think, "Can I steal?" However, if your lone opponent has 7♥6♥, you actually have the best hand.

Frequently everyone misses the flop or makes a weak hand, and it becomes a game of chicken: whoever blinks first, loses. Say you have that 9♦8♦ and the flop comes A♣J♥8♣. Now you have third pair. But unless your opponents check it through to the river and your weak hand holds up, you'll rarely win at showdown. You should prefer to take the pot down earlier. We think of such situations as stealing, even if your weak hand happens to be best.

Marginal hand situations often rely on stealing to be profitable. If you can't steal in these situations, either because you're out of position, you aren't comfortable stealing, or your opponents won't cooperate, you should normally play tightly preflop. For example, suppose you are in early position and one or two tough, aggressive opponents are likely to enter the pot behind you. You should fold speculative hands like **8♠7♠** and **A♣7♣**, because they depend heavily on stealing to be profitable.[1]

Playing speculative hands in early position is a common and major leak. You should play very tightly in early position unless you can steal well, or it's a loose game where large preflop raises are uncommon.[2] In a 10-handed game, that means folding everything under the gun except pairs, AK-AJ, and KQ. If you don't read hands well, you may be better off folding AJ and KQ, and even AQo. This may sound absurd if you're used to loose, easy games. However, in tougher games, playing speculative hands out of position is a disaster for players who don't steal a decent share of the missed pots.

When your steal equity is low, you should play much tighter preflop *regardless of position*. That rule isn't just for weak players. In tough games, for example, you will often find yourself playing against opponents who call on the button with a very broad range of hands and then use position to steal well postflop. If you run into one of these opponents and cannot hold your own, then you should play tightly preflop even from the cutoff in a 6-handed game.

The rule of thumb is simple:

Avoid playing speculative hands unless you expect to have significant steal equity.

---

[1] We are assuming your opponents won't routinely pay off a couple bets with middle pair or routinely pay off big those few times you make a strong hand. Throughout this section, we assume the game isn't loose or passive or deep-stacked enough that you can play speculative hands purely on make-a-hand value.

[2] Unless you can make money from stealing, large preflop raises increase the cost of playing any speculative hand.

Here is the more general case:

> If you have low steal equity, you need high showdown equity to play. Otherwise you should fold.

Here is how that applies to early position play:

> If you are out of position and cannot steal effectively, fold unless you have a pair, the likely best big card hand, or you expect to get paid enough when you hit to cover your preflop costs.

On the other hand, if you're good at stealing from out of position, many marginal hand situations become profitable. Here's the bottom line. Play tight or learn how to steal.

What Makes Stealing Likely To Succeed

If you're like most players, you've tried to bluff a crazy player who calls with anything. It doesn't work. You cannot steal if they will not fold.

Several basic factors help you steal. They include:

♦ Position.
♦ Stacks deep enough that opponents aren't likely to commit with one pair.
♦ Fewer players, making running into a big hand less likely.
♦ Nonaggressive or timid opponents.
♦ An image conducive to stealing.

If you have enough of these factors, you have steal equity and should consider playing to steal. If you don't have these factors and won't be stealing, you should avoid even suited connectors and other reasonably attractive preflop hands.

Here are some hand examples:

1. Position. You have **7♣6♣** on the button in a tough 6-handed $1–$2 online game with $200 (100bb) stacks. One player raises to $6. You are very unlikely to have the best hand. But you are in good shape to steal. You reraise to $24. Everyone folds. Or, alternatively, your opponent calls and checks to you on the flop. You bet $35. He folds.

Sometimes that opponent will reraise you, or one of the blinds will play, or you will get checkraised on the flop. However, as long as that doesn't happen often, you profit from stealing. Making a good hand with your 7♣6♣ is only a backup plan.

Now replay the hand out of position. You have 7♣6♣ under the gun in a tough $1–$2 online game with 100bb stacks. You raise to $6. The cutoff calls. You miss the flop, as you will most of the time. You make a continuation bet of $12. Your opponent calls. Is he calling to bluff you on the turn? Is he calling with a real hand? You don't know. You might fire a second bluff on the turn or checkraise with nothing, but that can get expensive. Throughout the hand, your opponent will be able to exploit knowing your action before you know his.

Alternatively, suppose the cutoff reraises you preflop to $24. Should you reraise him back? Perhaps occasionally, but if you make a habit of it, your opponent will wise up and you'll lose money.

2. Stacks deep enough that opponents are unlikely to commit with one pair. You have $400 (200bb) in a moderately tough 6-max $1–$2 game. You open for $6 from the cutoff with T♥9♥. The big blind reraises to $18. You call, planning to outplay him postflop. The flop comes K♠J♠4♣, giving you a gutshot straight draw. Your opponent checks. You bet $30. He checkraises all-in. Belatedly you realize that he started the hand with only $60, so his all-in is just $12 more. You are getting 9–to–1 on your money with two cards to come, so you call. He has K♣Q♠. You got all-in as almost a 6–to–1 dog.

What went wrong? Preflop, each player put 9bb into the pot. Your opponent had only 21bb behind. There was little chance he would fold top pair if he hit. Indeed, in aggressive games, he would be hard pressed to fold second pair, especially if you will often bet the flop if he checks. All he has to do is checkraise all-in to profit on average.

The preflop raise from the cutoff with **T♥9♥** is fine. Calling the raise to 9bb from a player with a 30bb stack is horrible. Folding or reraising are the only reasonable options, and usually you should fold.

Now replay the hand with deeper stacks. This time, you both start with $400. You raise to $6 with **T♥9♥** from the cutoff. The big blind makes it $18 and you call. The flop comes **K♠J♠4♣**. He bets $30. If you play back at him now or on the turn, he'll be in a difficult situation. He has just top pair, and the stacks are deep.

Suppose you call the $30 flop bet. The pot then becomes almost $100. Meanwhile, your opponent has top pair, is not committed, and has two streets left to play. If he checks, you have an excellent steal opportunity. Suppose he checks and you bet $70. That bet puts him to a tough decision. If he calls, he's put a third of his stack in when not committed, and he is at your mercy on the river. Your bet forces him to guess for big money.[3]

Deeper stacks make it easier to steal because opponents won't want to risk their entire stack as often.

3. Few enough players that you aren't likely to run into a big hand. In a 6-handed $1–$2 online game, you have **A♦5♦** under the gun. Should you play? Assuming you'll come in for a raise, one consideration is how frequently you will get reraised preflop. If someone makes a big reraise, you will be forced to fold or put in far too much money out of position with a mediocre hand. (This assumes reraising back on a bluff isn't profitable.) Fortunately for you, your opponents in this game happen to be relatively tight and will usually only reraise with

---

[3] This bet puts approximately a third of the stacks in, forcing the opponent to a stack decision. If he calls, you can put him all-in on the turn or river. Since he is not committed, he will be at your mercy. So, the $70 bet threatens him with much more than just a $70 loss.

AA-JJ, AK, and the occasional suited connector or other hand. The chance any one opponent holds such a hand is roughly 1 in 30. The chance one or more of your five opponents has a reraising hand is roughly 1 in 6. Overall, about one-sixth of the time you raise with a small suited ace under the gun, you will fold without seeing a flop.

This is a tremendous hurdle to overcome. You'll have to steal very often to make up for it. For most players in such a $1–$2 6-handed game, playing A♦5♦ under the gun is a significant leak.

Now suppose it's folded to you on the button with A♦5♦ in the same game. With just two players remaining, the chance of getting reraised drops to about 1 in 15. Once fewer players remain, the chance you'll run into a big hand drops dramatically.

4. Nonaggressive or timid opponents. In a 6-handed online $1–$2 game, you raise from the button to $7 with A♥9♥. The big blind reraises. He is not aggressive, so he likely has a big hand. You fold.

Alternatively, the small blind calls. He is a timid player. The flop comes Q♠7♥6♣, giving you ace-high. He checks. You bet $10. You will take the pot down often on the flop. If he calls, he'll almost always have top pair or better, so you can shut down and wait for another opportunity.

A more aggressive opponent might reraise out of the blinds preflop with many different hands. Or, he might checkraise you with air on the flop. Both actions normally reduce your earn from stealing.

5. An image conducive to stealing. In a $1–$2 game, you have played few hands in the last two hours, and no one has reason to think you're on tilt. You raise to $6 first to act from the cutoff with 5♠4♠. Only the button calls. The flop of K♣J♦9♣ misses you completely. You check, the button bets $8, and you checkraise to $24. He thinks about it briefly, then folds.

Now let's change the backstory. You have played many hands in the last two hours and just took a bad beat for your stack. You raise to $6 with 5♠4♠. The button calls. The flop comes K♣J♦9♣. You check, he bets $8, and you checkraise to $24. He thinks briefly, then calls. Your wild play has made him much more likely to call. Unfortunately, you still have no idea whether he has a big hand or is calling to see what you do. He might even be calling with nothing just to bet big on the turn because he is tired of you pushing him around. Either way, you are less likely to win the hand.

Often a tight image makes it easier to steal. However, other images can also help. For example, say you get all-in several times in a short period. Opponents may tighten up preflop because they don't want to face your aggressive betting when they hit a pair.

These are basic concepts about stealing. None is absolute. For example, you might find it easier to steal out of position if your opponents may think you have a big hand. Or it might be easier to steal from an aggressive opponent if he folds when you apply pressure. In general, however, stealing is easier when you have position, deeper stacks, fewer potential opponents, nonaggressive opponents, and an image conducive to stealing.

When evaluating steal equity, keep in mind that most successful steals happen when no one flops top pair or better. In these situations, the player who makes the last bet usually wins. If you play chicken well, you gain more value from stealing. That's one reason a good loose aggressive player can do so well against weak-tight opponents, particularly in shorthanded games.

With this basic primer on equity and stealing under your belt, you're now ready to move on.

PART 2: BEATING ONLINE $1–$2 6-MAX GAMES

Introduction

This next part is focused on a quite specific topic: how to beat an online $1–$2 6-max no-limit game. Why did we choose to focus on this game? In fact, why did we choose to focus so narrowly on any one game? And if you intend to play a game other than online $1–$2 6-max, how relevant will this book be to you?

Here are the short answers to those questions. This game provides an ideal platform to teach the most critical no-limit concepts. If you can learn to crush an online $1–$2 6-max no-limit game, then you can handily beat 99 percent of all no-limit games in the world. So this book is highly relevant to the vast majority of no-limit players, whether you play live games or online, shorthanded games, full-ring, or even heads-up. Learn these ideas, apply them to your game, and you will destroy the competition.

And now for the slightly longer answers.

The Threshold For Professional Play

We want you to play poker at a professional level. That's our goal. Online $1–$2 6-max represents a critical threshold for professional players. Good $1–$2 pros make a good living—$10,000 per month or more even with a relatively relaxed playing schedule. So when we teach you to beat an online $1–$2 6-max game, we've taught you to play at a professional level.

If you prefer playing live, you're in for a real treat. Taking someone who can beat an online $1–$2 6-max game and putting them in a typical $1–$2 or $2–$5 live game is like taking a professional football player and putting him in a game full of 14-year-olds. The pro will run absolutely rampant.

This book teaches an aggressive style. If you play online, you'll be playing against a fair number of players who have seen this approach before and who can fight back. But if you play live, often none of the players at the table will have any clue how to defend themselves against you. You can pick them all apart. Anyone who can make a living playing online $1–$2 6-max can also make a living playing $2–$5 or $5–$10 live no-limit.

Developing A Robust Strategy

You can beat easy no-limit games with a limited, simple strategy. Nut peddling, for instance, will beat most small stakes live games and some online microlimit games. It's easy. Just play tight preflop, wait until you hit the flop, and get your money in. Don't bluff much, and don't worry too much about what your opponents have. Rely on your hand strength to give you a long term edge.

Limited strategies will succeed at low levels, but not at higher levels. Good players can beat nut peddlers simply by refusing to pay off their good hands and stealing most of the other pots.

Limited strategies like nut peddling don't work well at online $1–$2 6-max. If you hope to generate a meaningful edge, you have to adopt a more complete strategy. You have to bluff and play hands for value. You have to read hands. You have to adjust to your opponents. You have to exploit others while you avoid getting exploited.

This book teaches a more robust strategy. Current online $1–$2 6-max is arguably the smallest game where most opponents play well enough that you need an advanced strategy to succeed. So that's the game we chose.

Applying Our Lessons To Your Game

After reading this book, some of you will jump directly into the online $1–$2 6-max game we use in most of our examples. And some of you will choose a different game. You might play a lower limit or a higher one. You might play a 9- or 10-handed game instead. Or you might play in a loose live game where six players limp in every hand.

Many of the ideas from this section will apply to your no-limit game, even if yours appears at first to be a very different type of game from the one we describe. Basic ideas like leveraging position, running bluffs, playing for value, and isolating bad players can be used to good effect in nearly every no-limit game on the planet. Indeed, we chose this particular game because it's an excellent one for teaching practical no-limit ideas that are useful across a broad spectrum of games.

Get Ready To Rock

This section will teach you how to defeat an online $1–$2 no-limit 6-max game. It may take you a little time to work all of these ideas correctly into your game, but once you do, you will be a force to be reckoned with. Let's get started.

Stealing Blinds And Playing Position

Blind stealing is the cornerstone of any successful 6-max strategy. It's the absolute bedrock of a winning player's game. We're not speaking in theoretical terms either. The difference between a break-even player and a modestly successful pro is one blind steal per 100 hands. And you'll see the results very quickly because it's a source of consistent profit.

Blind stealing simply means raising preflop in an attempt to win the pot immediately. But what does it mean to blind-steal better than you currently do? There are two basic variables:

1. Stealing range
2. Raise size

You can choose to steal with a hand or you can pass on it. And you can raise to various amounts. You can adjust both of these variables to optimize your blind-stealing strategy.

Stealing Range

For now, let's talk about stealing from the button, since it's the canonical stealing situation. We'll talk about stealing from the cutoff and small blind later in the section.

The top factor for determining your stealing range is how tightly your opponents in the blinds play. If you have two tight opponents in the blinds, often 100 percent of your hands will be profitable to open. You can get a sense of how tight your opponents are by looking at their "Fold To Steal In Big Blind" stat in a tracking program such as PokerTracker or Hold'em Manager.

The Fold To Steal (FTS) stat gives you a rough idea of how often your opponents fold from the blinds when someone opens from the cutoff or button. For typical players in $1–$2 6-max games, this stat ranges from about 50 percent up to about 90 percent. Most players fall between 65 percent and 85 percent.

For example, if a player has a FTS percentage of 80 percent, it means that you can expect them to fold to your button open roughly 80 percent of the time. It's only a rough estimate because the stat includes open raises from positions other than the button and because your opponents will adapt their strategies for different situations and opponents. Always remember that tracker stats measure your opponents' average tendencies over a wide range of situations and opponents, and they may not accurately reflect how your opponents will play against you in this particular situation. Having said all that, if your opponent has a FTS stat of 80 percent, you can expect them to play fairly tightly against your button opens.

The Range War

We refer to "ranges" over and over again in this book. If you need a brush-up on the general concept of a hand range, review "The REM Process" we presented in *Professional No-Limit Hold'em: Volume 1*. The general premise of REM is that in any given hand, you should formulate a hand range for each opponent, calculate your equity against their ranges, and then maximize your expectation. Range, Equity, Maximize.

In this book we delve deeper into not only your opponents' ranges, but also your own range. By that we mean the range of hands you take certain actions with, as well as the range of hands your opponents perceive you to have when you take certain actions. You can think of no-limit hold'em as being a big range war. It's always your range versus their ranges.

Assume the players in the small and big blinds both have FTS stats of 80 percent. They might play AA-22, AK-AT, KQ-KJ, some suited connectors, and the occasional suited ace, suited one-gapper, and unsuited connector. That's a 20 percent range, which corresponds to an 80 percent Fold To Steal.

As a rough estimate, if you raise from the button you can expect to win the blinds about 64 percent of the time ($0.8 \times 0.8 = 0.64$). In practice you'll probably succeed somewhat less often than that, so let's round that number down to 60 percent.

Say you open raise to $6 (three times the big blind). You're risking $6 to win $3, so if you were to succeed more than 67 percent of the time, your steal would show an immediate profit. By "immediate profit" we mean that even if you turbo-mucked your hand (without seeing the flop) as soon as an opponent called your steal, you'd still make money over time on the steal attempt.

We estimated that a steal will succeed about 60 percent of the time, so you fall short of an immediate profit. Fortunately, however, you won't be turbo-mucking your hands when called. You'll see a flop, and, even if your hand is trashy, you'll have the advantage of position. In practice it's not difficult to steal a few pots after the flop, and that's all you need to do to make the entire hand profitable.

So if both blind players fold to a steal about 80 percent of the time or more, you can reasonably open any hand on the button and expect to make a profit.

If both blind players fold to a steal about 80 percent of the time or more, you can reasonably open any hand on the button and expect to make a profit.

You can steal profitably with any hand. But that doesn't mean that you should necessarily try to steal at every opportunity. If you pound on tight players too relentlessly, some of them will start to play back at you. You don't want otherwise tight players to adjust to your stealing by starting to 3-bet (reraise) with weak hands. So mix it up a little bit. Show your opponents that you can fold your button every once in a while, preferably when you have an offsuit trash hand.

But don't fold too often. Steal most of the time. And if the blind players are even tighter, folding to a steal up to 90 percent of the time, then don't give them any room to breathe. When players are ultra tight from the blinds, it generally indicates that they're playing a limited, nut-peddling strategy, and they aren't likely to adjust to your steals. So rob them blind.

In a typical $1–$2 6-max game, you'll frequently find two tight players in the blinds, and therefore you'll often be in a situation where you can profitably open any two from the button.

Raise Size

All else equal, you'd like to raise as little an amount as you can get away with when you are stealing. After all, a smaller raise means that you're risking less for the same reward. But all else isn't equal. Different raise sizes will change the dynamics in two areas:

1. Folding frequency
2. Postflop expectation

Theoretically speaking, your opponents should fold more often against big opening raises and less often against small ones. If you raise to $4, the big blind has to call $2 to have a chance to win $7 (your $4 raise and the $3 from the blinds). If you raise to $8, the big blind has to call $6 to have a chance to win $11 (your $8 raise and the $3 from the blinds). Clearly the odds offered in the first scenario are more generous, and therefore the big blind should play with a wider range of hands.

In practice, however, typical players don't adjust their playing ranges the way they should. Many players, especially tight players, will fold a good portion of their hands from the blinds regardless of game conditions. For example, a lot of players will virtually never play a hand like Q♠7♠ from the big blind against a raise, no matter who raised, how much the raise was, or from what position.

Small steal raises pay off against the many players who don't adjust their blind ranges for the size of the bet.

Against players who play roughly the same strategy against a small or a large steal raise, raise small.

The story doesn't end there, however. Postflop expectation is also important for determining the size of your steal raises. What do we mean by postflop expectation?

Let's say you have a very tight player in the big blind. If you open-raise on the button, he'll fold 90 percent of his hands whether you raise to $5 or $10. But the 10 percent of the time he plays, he 3-bets to $24.

Against this player you should steal 100 percent of your hands from the button. Because he folds so often, your raise will show an automatic profit. But when he does pick up a hand, you'll usually be facing a large 3-bet with a hand that's not strong enough to continue. So you have virtually no postflop expectation against this player: Either you steal the blinds, or he 3-bets you and you have to fold. You'll rarely see a flop.

When you have a low postflop expectation, you should choose a small raise size. Why risk $10 when $5 will do the job just as well?

With little postflop expectation, choose a small steal raise size.

Now let's say the big blind plays very differently. He folds 80 percent of the time and calls 17 percent. With the best 3 percent of his hands, he 3-bets to $24. Against this player your steals won't win immediately as often, but you'll usually see a flop when your steal fails. You have some postflop expectation. Even with a stinker of a hand like 9♣4♠, you will sometimes win with a continuation bet or another well-timed bluff.

The more postflop expectation you have, the more reason you have to make a larger steal raise. Indeed, if you expect to win much more than your share of the pots postflop, you should make as large a raise as you think your opponent will still call. Since you have the advantage, the more money that goes in the pot, the more you win on average.[4]

Note that we're not suggesting that you make big raises with your good hands and small raises with your bad ones. In an online $1–$2 6-max game, you should generally choose one steal raise size and use it whether you have seven-deuce or pocket aces. If you raise more with good hands and less with bad ones, you give away too much information about your hand strength.

> Do not adjust your steal raise size based on the strength of your hand. Use the same fixed raise size for all hands in your range.

Your postflop expectation is determined in large part by how your opponents play. Let's take the player who folds 80 percent of the time, calls 17 percent of the time, and 3-bets 3 percent of the time. When he calls, you'll know that he likely has a medium-strength hand—strong enough to call, but not strong enough to 3-bet.

Let's also assume that this player plays a passive strategy after the flop. He'll check nearly every flop, and he'll fold if he misses. If he catches something like a draw or a pair, he'll usually call one bet. If the turn doesn't improve his hand, he'll check again and fold his weak draws and pairs. So if he calls

---

[4] This advice to make larger preflop raises assumes you won't tend to win small pots and lose big ones after the flop. In most practical blind-stealing situations, that assumption is a reasonable one.

both the flop and turn, he'll usually have either a strong draw or top pair or better.

This postflop strategy (or one similar to it) is common enough to have its own name—it's the *fit or fold* strategy. The player sees a flop, and if his hand doesn't fit sufficiently well with the board, he folds. Note that the player who employs this strategy does little to no hand reading. He is concerned only with his own hand strength, not with yours or anyone else's.

The fit or fold strategy is extremely and easily exploitable. It loses to a strategy of raw aggression. Just keep betting and, the vast majority of the time, a fit or fold opponent will end up folding. The small number of times the fit or folder makes a hand, you'll tend to lose a bigger pot than those you steal. However, choosing moderate bet sizes and practicing basic hand reading will give you a big postflop edge over a fit or folder.

Here's the bottom line. If a player tends to defend his blinds by 3-betting rather than calling, you should choose a small bet size. If a player tends to defend his blinds by calling rather than 3-betting, and then uses a fit or fold strategy after the flop, you should choose a large bet size. Since you'll steal so many pots postflop, you benefit from starting with a larger pot.

Choose small steal-raise sizes against players who like to 3-bet. Choose large steal-raise sizes against players who like to call and then play fit or fold.

When in doubt about your opponent's tendencies, default to a small raise size. It's less exploitable.

Return To Stealing Range

We have already argued that you should steal with 100 percent of your hands against sufficiently tight players in the blinds. But we didn't talk about how to adjust your stealing range when your opponents aren't sufficiently tight. We'll talk about that now.

Say the two players in the blinds will defend often enough that you won't show an automatic profit by stealing even if you raise to just $5 or $4.50. Furthermore, assume that they will never flat call your steal raise. If they defend, they will 3-bet to about $24.

Few blind players in real games will follow this strategy. If they did, each of these players would be 3-betting with nearly 25 percent of their total hands. But, for the sake of argument, let's assume you have two very loose and 3-bet happy opponents in the blinds. How should you adjust?

Clearly you shouldn't steal with 100 percent of your hands any longer. Too often you'll raise your trash, face a 3-bet, and have to fold. So fold your offsuit trash.

Against a frequent 3-bettor, instead of folding to the 3-bet, you can sometimes play back by calling and making a play postflop or by 4-betting as a bluff.

We'll discuss these options in depth in the "3-Betting Light and the 3-Bet, 4-Bet, 5-Bet Game" chapter. For now, just know that when your opponents defend against steals by 3-betting with a wide range of hands, you'll react by tightening up and 4-bet bluffing sometimes.

In practice, you won't usually come up against players who 3-bet as often as 25 percent of the time. Even players who like to 3-bet to defend will usually fold frequently enough to make stealing profitable.

> When stealing against players who often 3-bet when they defend, choose a small bet size and trim the worst offsuit hands from your range.

If your opponents defend often, but they usually call rather than 3-bet, then your stealing range depends on how your opponents play postflop. If they play a fit or fold strategy, then you can steal aggressively—with potentially up to 100 percent of your hands against sufficiently compliant opponents. Fit or fold players don't take your hand strength into account, and they usually end up folding by the river. So it doesn't really matter much what hand you have since you'll win so many pots against them without a showdown.

> Against players who defend often, but who usually defend by calling and who play fit or fold postflop, choose a large bet size and open with most of your hands.

Now let's talk about the real calling stations. They call preflop with a wide range of hands, and they don't like to fold postflop either. As you might imagine, stealing becomes a relatively weak strategy against a calling station. These players force you to tighten up a bit.

Say the big blind player will call roughly 70 percent of the time you open from the button. You should stick to opening a range of hands that you can often play for value postflop, something like:

22+, A2s+, K2s+, Q7s+
JTs-54s, J9s-75s, J8s-96s
A2o+, K9o+, Q9o+, J9o+,T9o[5]

This range comprises about 40 percent of your total possible hands. It's a flexible range—whether a particular hand is profitable or not will depend on the specifics of how your opponent tends to play. Calling stations force you to pass on steals with weak hands, but they more than compensate you by paying off your good hands after the flop.

Calling stations force you to tighten up your stealing range. But against them you can choose larger raise sizes and value bet more aggressively after the flop.

When you have two very different opponent types in the blinds, you'll usually be forced to play the more conservative of the two associated strategies. For instance, if you have a fit or folder with an 80 percent Fold To Steal (your associated strategy: 100 percent open, big raise size) and a frequent 3-bettor (your associated strategy: tighter open, small raise size), you should protect yourself against the 3-bettor by tightening up a bit and using a small raise size.

---

[5] Large hand ranges can be difficult to conceptualize, and it's a challenge to write them out in an intuitive way. We've settled on a three-line format. Line one lists pocket pairs and suited hands with a specific high card. Line two lists suited connectors. Line three lists offsuit hands. A plus sign indicates all better hands of the same type. So 55+ indicates all pocket pairs 55 and better, and Q7s+ indicates all suited hands containing a queen that are Q7s and stronger. Thus, one could read this range as, "Any pocket pair, any suited ace, any suited king, any suited queen Q7s or better, no-gap suited connectors down to 54s, one-gap suited connectors down to 75s, two-gap suited connectors down to 96s, any offsuit ace, and offsuit kings, queens, jacks, and a ten with at least a nine kicker."

Button Stealing Summary

When you're opening from the button, you want to steal with as many hands as you can get away with. When both of the blinds are quite tight, you can steal with up to 100 percent of your hands. You should perhaps fold a hand here and there to avoid making your strategy too obvious, but you can open nearly every time.

When your opponents tend to defend by calling and then playing a fit or fold strategy postflop, you can also open nearly all of your hands. This is true even if they defend fairly frequently. You'll win often enough by stealing pots postflop that the overall play will be profitable. When your opponents are playing fit or fold, you should make large raises so the pots you steal are worth more.

When your opponents defend fairly tightly, but they respond aggressively to your steals by 3-betting or by calling and playing back postflop, you can still steal with a fairly wide range. You might want to dump your worst offsuit trash, but you can steal with most other hands profitably. Choose a small raise size to minimize your exposure to your opponents' aggression. If your opponents 3-bet too often, you will have to incorporate some 4-bet bluffing into your strategy to keep your button steals profitable.

Calling stations force you to severely curtail your button stealing. Since they call preflop and don't give up easily postflop, you can't play bad hands profitably. But your better hands will be more profitable against these players. So if a calling station is in one of the blinds, you should make large raises with somewhere around 40 percent of your hands.

Finally, if your two opponents call for two very different strategies, choose the more conservative option.

Stealing From The Cutoff

The cutoff is a tempting position to steal from, but it is nowhere near as good as the button. You have an extra player to contend with, and he has position and an incentive to play.

Don't try to steal with offsuit trash from the cutoff. Conditions have to be nearly perfect to make it profitable, and they rarely are.

If you have three tight and compliant players behind you, try opening with approximately the 40 percent range from the calling station discussion above:

22+, A2s+, K2s+, Q7s+
JTs-54s, J9s-75s, J8s-96s
A2o+, K9o+, Q9o+, J9o+, T9o

If one of your opponents is aggressive or loose (particularly the button), drop the weak hands from this range. So against two reasonably tight players and one troublesome player in the big blind, perhaps open a range like this:

22+, A2s+, K9s+, Q9s+
JTs-54s, J9s-T8s
A2o+, KTo+, QTo+, JTo

This range represents approximately 30 percent of your hands.

If the troublesome player is on the button, you can trim some of the weaker hands such as A7o-A2o from this range.

Again, these ranges are all flexible, and they depend on your situation. We just want to point you in the right direction to come up with your own hand ranges.

You shouldn't steal nearly as aggressively from the cutoff as you do from the button. If all of your opponents are tight, you can open up to about 40 percent of your hands. If there's a troublesome player behind you, tighten up to about 30 percent or possibly 25 percent of your hands.

Because you are stealing into three players, usually you should default to a conservative raise size.

Stealing From The Small Blind

When everyone folds to you in the small blind, you're in an interesting situation. Unlike stealing from the button or the cutoff, you're going to play the hand out of position if you get called. This fact can alter your strategy dramatically.

Say you raise to $6. You're risking $5 beyond your $1 small blind, and you hope to win the $3 in blind money. If the play succeeds more often than 5 times out of 8 (62.5 percent), you'll show an automatic profit.

Some players in the big blind fold far too often in these blind versus blind situations. Indeed, a fair number of players will fold more often than 62.5 percent of the time. Against these players you should raise 100 percent of your small blinds.

> If the big blind folds more than about 60 percent of the time, open every hand from the small blind.

Here's where it gets complicated. Say there's a fairly good player in the big blind. You decide to open 100 percent of your hands from the small blind. The good player will respond by defending nearly all of his hands. He might 3-bet with 35 percent of his hands, call with 50 percent, and fold only the worst 15 percent. He can play so loosely because he has position and because you're playing every hand.

Against this loose defending strategy, raising all of your hands would be disastrous. You have to tighten up. Depending on how strongly and aggressively your opponent plays postflop, you might tighten up to about the 30 percent range from the discussion about stealing from the cutoff:

22+, A2s+, K9s+, Q9s+
JTs-54s, J9s-T8s
A2o+, KTo+, QTo+, JTo

So, like stealing from the cutoff, you have to play fairly tightly when conditions are bad for stealing. But, unlike stealing from the cutoff, you can open 100 percent of your hands when the big blind is tight. Because your strategy from the small blind can vary so much, pay close attention to the player on your left and know which strategy you'll employ before you get into a blind versus blind situation.

Putting It All Together

Because online 6-max games tend to play fairly tightly preflop, blind stealing is extremely important. Indeed, an aggressive blind stealing strategy can improve a player's overall winrate by 1.5bb/100 ($3 per 100 hands in a $1–$2 game) over a tight or weak strategy.[6] A good percentage of your opponents will play tightly enough from the blinds that you can profitably open 100 percent of your hands from the button and from the small blind. Stealing from the cutoff is more dangerous, so even under good conditions you should typically avoid opening trash from the cutoff.

When your opponents defend their blinds by calling then playing a fit or fold strategy postflop, you can steal with a wide range of hands and rely on taking pots away postflop. When your opponents are looser, more aggressive, and less willing to fold, you have to tighten up on your stealing. But often you'll be compensated for the lack of stealing opportunities against these players by making more money on your good hands.

---

[6] How much is aggressive button stealing worth? Poker success can be measured in big blinds per 100 hands. Suppose you are a solid winning player in $1–$2 who makes 4bb/100 hands. You open 30 percent of your button hands (e.g., 22+, A2s+, KTs+, QTs+, JTs-54s, J9s-64s, A9o+, KTo+, QTo+, JTo-54o). A little less than half the time you have the button it is folded to you. So in a 6-handed game, about 8 times per 100 hands it will be folded to you on the button. You raise 30 percent of those hands, or about 2.4 hands per 100.

Now suppose you expand your raising range to 80 percent of your hands. Of the times it is folded to you on the button, you are now raising an extra 50 percent of hands. This is 4 extra hands per 100. Against blinds who fold 80 percent of their hands to a 2.25bb raise, you win immediately roughly 64 percent of the time. This nets 0.15bb per steal attempt not including any money you make when you get called or reraised. You win 0.15bb and *freeroll on postflop play*. Now suppose you are against blinds who do not 3-bet often. Say of the 36 percent of the time either blind calls or reraises, they reraise 12 percent of the time. Even if you fold every time they reraise, 24 percent of the time you will see a flop with 5 or 5.5bb in the pot. If you win just 1bb of that on average, you net an additional 0.25bb per hand. This is a quite conservative total of 0.4bb per hand. At 4 extra hands per 100, the successful pro earns an extra 1.6bb/100 by expanding his button opening range from 30 percent to 80 percent of hands against tight blinds. This yields a 40 percent increase in overall earn.

Stealing from tight blinds is a tremendous source of profit. It is also an easy strategy that does not require great play to be successful.

Profiling Opponents Using Stats

If you play online, you should use tracking software. It is tremendously useful, and there's really no reason not to. As of the time of this writing, the two most popular tracking software options are PokerTracker and Hold'em Manager.

These programs gather all of your hand histories automatically. After the software has digested all the hands you have played and stored them in a database, it slices and dices all that information in numerous useful ways. It tells you how much money you and any of your opponents have won or lost in hands you have tracked. It tells you what percentage of the time you see the flop, how often you raise, how often you play from two seats off the button, and so forth.

Some time ago, the tracking software packages added a heads-up display (HUD). This allows you to superimpose the statistics of your choice for each player in your game over the table as you play. So if, for instance, you wanted to know what percentage of the time each of your opponents sees the flop, you could tell the HUD to show that statistic, and then you'd see that percentage next to the name of each player inside the table window.

Using these statistics in combination with a HUD allows good players to play many tables at once. Instead of watching each hand intently to get a read on their opponents, a HUD user can display a few telling statistics and gain immediate insight into each player's style. In this chapter we'll talk about a few important statistics and how you can use them to profile your opponents. Even if you don't want to play with a HUD, learning to profile opponents using stats is an extremely useful skill.

The Three Basic Stats

If you read any online poker strategy discussion group, you'll see people using three basic stats to offer a quick outline of their opponents' play. All major tracking programs will calculate these stats for every player in your database. These stats are:

1. Voluntarily Put Money In The Pot Percentage
2. Preflop Raise Percentage
3. Aggression Factor

The first two stats measure only preflop play, while the third measures a player's aggression over all streets.

Voluntarily Put Money In The Pot Percentage (VP$IP) measures the percentage of hands a player plays preflop, excluding hands where the player checks from the big blind, but including hands where the player limps in or raises and then folds to a raise or reraise. This stat measures how tight or loose a player plays.

In a 6-max game, this stat generally ranges from 10 percent to 80 percent. A player with a 10 percent VP$IP plays exceedingly tightly, likely playing only pocket pairs and perhaps AK and AQ. A player with an 80 percent VP$IP is extremely loose and plays nearly every hand.

Most online 6-max players tend to fall in a range between about 15 and 30. Players with a VP$IP over 40 tend to be loose and bad players, so you can use the stat to aid in your table selection. For example, if you were choosing between two tables, one where everyone had a VP$IP under 25, and one where two of the players were over 50, you'd want to choose the table with the two loose players.

Preflop Raise Percentage (PFR) measures the percentage of hands a player raises preflop. PFR is never higher than VP$IP, because every time a player raises preflop, they are voluntarily putting money in the pot as well.

Most good players have a PFR within a few percentage points of their VP$IP. For instance, a solid player might have a VP$IP of 24 and a PFR of 20 (written 24/20 from now on). This indicates that the player raises most of the time that he plays a hand, only occasionally limping in, cold-calling a raise, or calling from the blinds.

Aggression Factor (AF) measures how often a player takes an aggressive action (bet or raise) versus a passive one (call). Checks and folds are ignored for the purposes of calculating AF.

This stat, unlike the previous two, is calculated using actions on all four betting rounds. (Some formulae exclude preflop play and include only the three postflop rounds.) It is calculated as a ratio—the number of aggressive plays divided by the number of passive ones. Because it's a ratio, the values can range from 0 (if the player in question has never bet or raised) to infinite (if he has never once called).

In practice a player with an AF between 0 and 1 is fairly passive, tending to call more often than bet or raise. And a player with an AF of 4, 5, or more, is quite aggressive, betting and raising far more frequently than calling.

AF can be a difficult stat to interpret correctly. First of all, a high AF is more significant for a player with a high VP$IP than it is for a player with a low one. If you play 50 percent of your hands and you still bet and raise 4 times more often than you call, you are necessarily betting and raising with a wide range of very weak hands. Whereas, if you play only 15 percent of your hands, betting and raising 4 times more often than calling doesn't suggest nearly as reckless a style.

Also, AF measures play across all betting rounds, and therefore two players with an AF of 3 could play very different styles—one, perhaps, focusing on flop aggression, while the other focuses on river aggression.

In recent years this stat, once a staple of player profiling, has lost some of its importance because newer versions of tracking software packages have provided easier to interpret stats based on street-by-street play. Nevertheless, you will still often see this stat used as one of the three basic stats to describe an opponent's style.

Using Stats To Profile Opponents

Poker players can adopt any of a vast number of possible strategies. They can play tight and aggressively preflop, aggressively on the flop, and back off on the turn and river. Or they can play tight and passively preflop, passively on the flop, hyper-aggressively on the turn, and back off on the river, and so forth.

Strategies are composed of numerous variables and, theoretically speaking, players could mix and match these variables at will to create their unique strategies.

In practice, however, no-limit players tend to adhere more or less to one of a handful of strategic archetypes. Out of all the vast possiblities, the overwhelming majority of players tend to fall into one of just a relatively few categories.

We aren't going to speculate on why this happens. But we're going to take for granted that it does and show you how to draw fairly reliable conclusions about an opponent's entire approach to the game by looking at just a few stats.

We have developed these profiling methods through experience and observation. Again, there's no underlying reason why this sort of profiling has to work. It just does, at least in today's online \$1–\$2 6-max games.

We said above that AF is losing importance, and it's for good reason. Therefore, we use just VP\$IP and PFR to define our profiles.

Let's look at some stats-based profiles. Note that these numbers are specific for 6-max play. In full ring play, expect all archetypes to play a few points tighter due to the extra seats in early position. Also make sure your HUD is using only 6-max data when it compiles stats for your opponents. If you play both 6-max and full ring games, your stats might be tainted with data from full ring play.

The Setminer: 9/7

The setminer's stats are extremely tight and aggressive. A typical stat set might be 9 for VP\$IP and 7 for PFR, henceforth written 9/7. Obviously, an individual player might differ from this standard by a point or two in either of the stats. A setminer plays an exceedingly rigid strategy: wait for pocket pairs preflop, and maybe (if feeling frisky) take a flyer on AK. After the flop, try to get all the money in with a set or overpair and fold otherwise.

Setminers will usually open the pot for a raise, but will sometimes flat call a raise with a small pocket pair. Thus, expect their PFR to be two or three points less than their VP$IP. After the flop they do very little calling because they fold their marginal hands.

The formula for beating a setminer is simple. Don't play big pots with them unless you have the nuts, or can at least beat their likely set. Steal their blinds with wild abandon. When they do see a flop, most likely they will have a small or medium pair and will miss their set. So make a continuation bet on nearly every flop. Usually they'll be in the mood to fold. When they don't fold, surrender to any resistance.

Setminers don't make a lot of money, but their strategy can be profitable, particularly in microstakes games. Often they make up for their relatively small edges by playing massive numbers of tables simultaneously. Because of their tendency to play up to 24 tables, don't expect them to surprise you much. They have almost no time to think about any of their plays. Just keep stealing their blinds.

The Nit: 13/9

Setminers turn into nits when they're all grown up. Nits take a general approach that's similar to the setminer, but they play a few more hands preflop such as KJ and JTs on the button in unraised pots. Because they play more big card hands than the setminer, they'll hit the flop more often (though not as hard on average), and they'll generally be more willing to get all-in on the flop without a set.

Your general strategy against the Nit should be roughly similar to your strategy against the Setminer. Don't pay them off in big pots, and steal, steal, steal.

Nits don't build big pots without big hands. If a Nit bets the flop and turn and then shoves all-in on the river, you almost never have a tough decision. Either you have the nuts, or you fold because he has them.

One of the authors (who shall remain unnamed for dignity's sake) once played the following hand against a nit (stats: 12/9).

It was a $1–$2 6-max game. The nit had $200, and the author had him covered. The nit opened in the cutoff for $7, and the author called on the button with **A♠K♥**. The big blind also called.

The flop came **A♥5♣3♣**. The nit bet $18 into the $22 pot, and the author called. The big blind folded.

The turn was the **T♣**. The nit bet $58 into the $76 pot, and the author called.

The river was the **6♦**. The nit shoved all-in, $117 into the $192 pot, and the author called.

What mysterious, entirely unknowable hand did the nit hold? He had **K♣J♣**—the second-nuts. Who could have guessed?

Without a flush, most nits would slow down on the river. Even with a set of aces, most nits would play the river cautiously in fear of a flush. Top pair/top kicker is often a good enough hand to play for stacks in an online 6-max game. But in this particular hand, the decision to play for stacks by calling the final river bet was horrendous because the nit would never make that bet with a hand worse than AK. Indeed, the hand was botched from beginning to end.

What's the moral of this story? There are two. First, do not pay off nits in big pots. If they seem to want to get the money in, they have a very good reason to do so. Get out of their way. Second, everyone screws the pooch once in a while. Next time you do something really dumb, remember this hand and cut yourself a break.

Nits, like Setminers, are quite vulnerable to stealing. Since they won't get their money in without a big hand, and they will rarely catch a big hand, you can steal the majority of the pots you play against them. Steal their blinds and lean on them after the flop. You won't beat them in the big pots, but you can swipe most of the small ones from them.

The Nitty Tight-Aggressive (TAG): 17/13

The Solid TAG: 21/17

The Loose TAG: 24/20

Most of the winners in online $1–$2 6-max games play a TAG style. These styles can range from a fairly nitty 17/13 style to a looser 24/20 style. Unlike the Setminer and the Nit, no simple strategy will beat these players. You can't just avoid their big hands and steal their blinds like you can with the Setminers and Nits because TAG players tend to steal back.

You can assume that players with TAG styles are trying to play well. They've likely read a few books (perhaps this one), and they think about their play. That doesn't mean they play well. Many TAGs make plenty of mistakes. Numbers such as 17/13 and 24/20 just describe preflop play. Some TAGs play a serviceable preflop strategy, but end up lost once the flop comes. If you master the ideas in this book, you should be able to find the weaknesses of your TAG opponents, both before and after the flop, and exploit them.

Having said that, avoid games where all of your opponents play a TAG style. Even if you can beat TAGs, if you look around you can usually find games with at least one weaker player whom you can beat for more profit.

The Thinking Loose-Aggressive (LAG): 29/24

Thinking LAG players can win a lot of money also. Indeed, if you play roughly as we describe in this book, you'll likely end up with stats that place you in this category. One main difference between a Thinking LAG and a TAG player is that Thinking LAGs take more shots at stealing the blinds. For instance, if you try to steal the blinds as often as we suggested in the first section, you'll almost certainly end up with stats that are looser than the TAGs you play with.

As with the TAGs you play against, most of your Thinking LAG opponents will have weaknesses. For instance, you can frequently convince them to try to steal pots that they have no actual chance to steal. And also, as with the TAGs, no simple strategy will beat Thinking LAG players.

Nearly all players who consistently make money will play one of the preceding styles. In other words, we just finished talking about the good players. Now let's talk about the bad ones.

The Wet Noodle: 22/7

This player type can have stats that vary considerably. Generally, players of this type will have a VP$IP stat in the high-teens or low- to mid-twenties. So they aren't outrageously loose preflop. But their aggression numbers—PFR in particular—fall considerably below those of stronger players.

These players limp into a lot of pots, frequently from out of position. This tendency is what causes their VP$IP numbers to be significantly higher than their PFRs. After the flop they tend not to get out of line too often. They might semibluff a good drawing hand or put in a modest raise with a hand like top pair/weak kicker sometimes. But they generally don't leverage position well, and they are unlikely to try any multistreet bluffs.

They can vary in their willingness to call down with weak made hands. Sometimes they will tend to play tightly, releasing most weak hands to big turn and/or river bets. And sometimes they will get frustrated by aggressive play and call down lightly.

It's easy to get an edge on a Wet Noodle. They limp in too often from out of position. You punish that error by making isolation raises from the cutoff and button with a wide range of hands when they limp in front of you. So if they limp in for $2, you should make it $11 (give or take a few dollars) on the button with any hand you would consider playing. You'll be playing most of your hands against them with the advantage of position, and that fact alone will give you a strong edge.

Overall, Wet Noodles are not dangerous opponents. You can play most of your hands against them with position, and they don't fight back enough with postflop aggression.

The Totally Clueless: 65/7

If you find a player with a very high VP$IP (higher than 40) combined with a low PFR (lower than 15), you have yourself a Totally Clueless player. Games build around these players. They limp in with trash from out of position, and they call isolation raises. Then they blunder through the postflop streets looking for boneheaded and amusing ways to squander their buy-ins.

If you see one of these players sitting with a full stack or more, grab a seat, preferably on their left. We'll talk about how to win the most from these players in the chapter "Isolating Bad Players."

The Crazy LAG: 53/39

Crazy LAG players differ from Thinking LAG players (outlined above with the example stats 29/24) in two substantial ways. First, Crazy LAGs tend to play looser preflop, wading into many pots with trash hands from out of position. Second, their postflop aggression is more haphazard and generally reflects poor hand reading skills.

These players make profitable opponents. They share a common thread with the Wet Noodles and the Totally Clueless: they are far too willing to play hands from out of position. As such, you can isolate them from the button and cutoff and gain a consistent advantage that way.

Against Crazy LAGs, the main pitfall you must avoid is folding too often postflop. Generally, Crazy LAGs will have high postflop aggression to go along with their high VP$IP. They will often get all-in on the flop with top pair/no kicker, middle pair, or sometimes even worse. This is particularly true when they are playing with less than a full stack. They will launch large but sometimes hopeless bluffs at the slightest provocation.

If you play weakly, checking decent hands and then folding them to pressure, you won't perform well against Crazy LAGs. Adopting a fit or fold strategy will have you folding far more often than necessary or prudent. But you can use their craziness to your advantage by pushing good hands like top pair with a decent kicker farther than you normally might. And you can intentionally show weakness with made hands to try to induce wild bluffs.

Don't Jam A Square Peg Into A Round Hole

Don't categorize your opponents too zealously. These labels are meant as an aid to get you started profiling using stats. They aren't rigid. There is no real dividing line where one label ends and another begins. Many players will fall between two (or more) categories. Typically you can assume that a player between categories will show some characteristics of each type.

Beyond The Basic Stats

The basic stats are extremely useful for instant profiling. Using just these numbers, you can roughly classify any opponent into one of the above groups, and you can make educated guesses about their hand ranges, bluffing frequencies, and more. And with a HUD, you can evaluate the profitability of any table instantly just by reviewing the basic stats of each player at the table. If you see a 60/12 player and a 49/33 player at a table, sit down. And if you see no one at the table with a VP$IP over 23, look elsewhere. (Or sit down and steal their blinds while you look elsewhere.)

But modern tracking software packages provide far more information than just these stats. They track preflop 3-betting percentages, continuation betting percentages, postflop folding percentages, and more. You can use these supplemental stats to gain even more insight into your opponents' style.

Throughout the book we will use both the basic stats and some additional stats to profile our opponents. So far we've just scratched the surface.

Examples

Using stats may be new to you, but it won't take long for you to translate numbers like 24/20 into a mental picture of an actual hand range. Here are a few simple examples to get you started. All examples are from a 6-handed $1–$2 game.

Example 1. The first three players fold, and you open for $5 on the button with Q♠8♠. The small blind calls with $100 behind. He is a 49/26. That puts him in our Crazy LAG category above. As a reference, a 49 percent preflop range looks something like this:

> 22+, A2s+, K2s+, Q2s+, J4s+, T6s+
> 98s-65s, 97s-86s, 96s
> A2o+, K5o+, Q7o+, J8o+, T8o+, 98o

The big blind calls with $195 behind. His stats are 11/9, so he's a Nit. His range in this situation is probably something like:

> 44+, ATs+, KTs+, QJs
> No suited connectors
> AJo+, KQo

The flop comes Q♥9♠4♣. The small blind bets $10 into the $15 pot. The big blind folds. What's your best play?

You are very likely ahead of the small blind. His preflop range was wide, and he could be leading into you with a host of hands you beat, including top pair/worse kicker, middle pair, a straight draw, bottom pair, and so forth. You should be happy to commit with top pair here, even though your kicker isn't very good. If you call his bet, the pot will be $35 and he'll have $90 left. You should just raise the flop and be willing to call a shove. You'll see a player like this get all-in with all kinds of garbage.

On the other hand, let's say on the same Q♥9♠4♣ flop, the action goes a little differently. Say the small blind checks, the big blind checks, and you bet $10. The small blind calls, and the big blind checkraises to $40. This is a completely different situation, even though your hand is the same. Your equity is much worse and the effective stacks are almost twice as large. The big blind's preflop range was tight to begin with, and his range for checkraising here is strong. The board is fairly dry (few draws), so he isn't likely to be semibluffing with a draw. (A nitty player would usually just call with jack-ten after a bet and a call.) His made hands all have you crushed—top pair/ better kicker, a set, maybe occasionally a strangely played AA or KK. Your best play in this spot is to fold.

Example 2. Effective stacks are $200. A Solid TAG opens for $7 in middle position. His stats are 22/20. The cutoff folds, and you are on the button with A♥T♥. The small blind is a 9/8 Setminer, and the big blind is a Totally Clueless 63/9. Your hand does okay against the TAG's range, and you have position. The setminer will probably fold, but you want to play as many hands as possible against the totally clueless player. You elect to flat call to encourage him to enter the pot with his wide range. The small blind folds, and the big blind calls.

The flop comes A♣6♦2♥. The big blind checks, and the preflop raiser bets $15 into the $22 pot. His stats indicate that he continuation bets 89 percent of the time. So for now, his range is fairly wide. He could be betting with a pocket pair below aces, top pair with a better or worse kicker than you, or a completely whiffed hand. Again, you do not want to encourage the big blind to fold. He could easily have a worse hand that he'll play on with, such as a weaker ace, an underpair, middle pair, or even bottom pair. You decide to flat call and see what develops on the turn. The big blind overcalls.

The turn is a **3♠**. Let's discuss a couple different scenarios.

If the big blind checks and the TAG makes a solid bet, you have two good options. One, you can strongly consider folding. Usually a TAG will not bet this turn into two people with many hands you beat. While his range for c-betting is wide, he'll rarely fire a second barrel with hands worse than top pair. A strong turn bet here usually means top pair with a good kicker, a set, or even possibly a straight (i.e., he bet the flop with 54 and made his gutshot on the turn). He'll almost always give up his pure bluffs, and he'll usually check the turn for pot control with top pair/weak kicker. This situation is slightly unusual because he himself might be adjusting his play to the weak big blind, so there is some chance he'll bet any ace here. Therefore, your other option is to flat call again with the intention of folding to a river bet from the TAG.[7]

On the other hand, if the big blind checks the turn and the TAG also checks, you should bet. A turn check from the TAG is usually a white flag, and it means you very likely have the best hand. You do not want to needlessly give both opponents a free card. Bet your hand for value. The big blind will often call with worse hands. He was your main target to begin with. And in fact, if he does call the turn and the TAG folds, you should probably bet the river for value as well.

Example 3. Effective stacks are $200. The first two players fold, and you open for $7 in the cutoff with **8♣7♣**. The button and small blind fold, and the big blind calls. His stats are 15/11. According to our categories, that puts him somewhere in between a Nit and a Nitty TAG. A 15 percent preflop range looks something like this:

---

[7] Note that this line only works well if your opponent won't often bluff or bet a weak ace on the river. That is likely the case here with the TAG.

22+, A7s+, KTs+, QTs+

JTs-T9s, J9s

ATo+, KQo

The flop comes 7♥6♦3♠. The big blind checks, and you bet $11 into the $15 pot. He checkraises to $44. Your move?

You have top pair, but it's a weak top pair, and your opponent is tight. His checkraising range is probably only overpairs and sets. You're in bad shape. Your default action here should be to fold.

Barreling

Betting the flop after raising preflop is known as a *continuation bet* or *c-bet*, and it is sometimes referred to as firing the *first barrel*. Following it up with another bet on the turn is known as firing the *second barrel*. Finally, another bet on the river would be the *third barrel*.

Firing these barrels at the right time to exploit your particular opponents' strategies is a critical tool for maximizing your profit. Before we talk about playing against specific opponents, however, we'll roughly outline what an optimal barreling strategy looks like.

A generic optimal strategy doesn't seek to extract the maximum against any specific opponent, but it does seek to guarantee that, no matter what strategy your opponents employ, you will perform reasonably well.[8] Therefore, it's a good strategy to fall back on against strong opponents, and it's a reasonable default way to play against unknown players.

Say you open raise and get called by the big blind. Your opponent checks the flop. You'll bet some hands and check others. Say you bet and your opponent calls and checks the

---

[8] For you game theory purists, when we say generic optimal strategy here, we mean a strategy that is robust against a broad range of opponents of varying skill. The best strategy against this range accounts for the middling and bad players, or "bounded-rationally players" in game theory terms. A Nash equilibrium against near-perfect players (or those with unlimited computational ability) may not work well against such opponents. Game theorists have not offered much practical advice in these situations without resorting to empirical work, assessing what does well in real world play. It is in this sense that a robust strategy is "generically optimal." If your opponents aren't generic—perhaps they are much better or worse than a typical range of opponents—then the generic optimal strategy may not work particularly well, and some adjustments may be needed.

turn. Again you'll bet some hands and check others. If your opponent calls and checks the river, you have one more bet or check decision.

So what's optimal play with these decisions? Calculating the optimal strategy for a full no-limit game is an impossible task. But by solving similar, but simpler, games, one can get a feel for what the strategy would look like without actually calculating solutions for every hand in every situation.

The optimal strategy looks roughly like this. We'll start with the river strategy and work backwards.

On the river, you'll bet your strong hands for value, and you'll bet enough of your busted hands as a bluff that your opponent will be forced to pay off some of your value bets or risk getting run over. You'll check down most modest-strength hands and try to win at showdown. Thus, from your opponents' perspective, your river betting range is polarized—either you have a very strong hand or a weak hand—as you'll tend to check hands of modest strength.

On the turn, you'll bet your good hands for value, and you'll bet enough bad hands for balance so that, again, your opponent will be forced to pay you off sometimes or risk getting run over. In general, you'll bet a larger proportion of your total hands on the turn than you will on the river for two reasons:

First, when your opponent calls preflop, on the flop, and on the turn, he shows a fair amount of strength. So, in turn, you need a stronger hand yet to bet the river profitably. On the turn your opponent has called only twice, so his range will be weaker on average, and you can bet more hands for value.

Second, betting can charge your opponent to draw on the turn, but drawing isn't a consideration on the river.

On the river you choose your worst hands—those that have little chance to win a showdown—to bluff with. That's because if you bluff with your medium hands, often when you "bluff out" your opponent, you would actually have won the showdown anyway, and you gain nothing. Bluffing with a terrible hand wins something when it's successful.

But on the turn, you don't necessarily want to bluff your worst hands. Often you want to choose decent drawing hands to bluff with and simply give up on your very worst hands. The obvious advantage to semibluffing (with a draw) rather than cold bluffing (with a totally busted hand) is that you have a chance to win if called when you're on a draw.

So on the turn you bet your good hands for value, you bet weak hands as bluffs to balance, and the weak hands you choose are usually those that have a chance to draw out if called. You mostly check behind medium hands and terrible hands with some big hands and draws for balance. And the overall percentage of hands you bet on the turn is significantly greater than on the river.

The logic on the flop is similar to that on the turn. You can bet even more hands for value because your opponent has called only preflop and therefore can have a wide and weak range. You also bet to charge your opponent to draw. Because you're betting more good hands, you bet more weak hands and draws also for balance.

So a basic outline of the generic optimal strategy is to bet a large percentage of hands on the flop, bet a smaller percentage on the turn—weighted toward betting good hands for value and betting some draws as semibluffs for balance—and bet a smaller percentage still on the river in a polarized fashion—strong hands and terrible hands for balance.

(Obviously, your opponent doesn't have to check and call every street. He can bet out or checkraise. These options would lead you to make adjustments to the strategy. But, perhaps surprisingly, these adjustments do not change the optimal strategy's basic form. They change decisions with hands on the borderlines, but the threat of getting checkraised isn't nearly reason enough to abandon the entire framework.)

This strategy leverages position and the no-limit structure to full effect. It makes it very difficult for your opponent to play modest made hands profitably. For instance, say your opponent has A5 on an A96 flop. If you play a decent range of hands preflop, your opponent will be the favorite to have the best hand. Unfortunately for him, he won't be able to convert that advantage to profit by the end of the hand, because he will have to run a gauntlet of three betting rounds where your betting ranges narrow progressively. So when your opponent has the best hand, you may bet the flop and check the turn and river. But when he has the worst hand, you may bet all three streets. He can't respond to this strategy by simply folding to the larger bets, because you bluff weak hands often enough to force him to choose between paying you off or abandoning hands with value. So even though he has the best hand on the flop more often than not, he tends to win small pots and lose big if he tries to get to showdown. That's the power of this generic optimal strategy.

The critical component of the strategy is that the big turn and river bets will usually be strong hands, but will be balanced by enough bluffs to deny your opponent the ability to simply lay down when you bet. Many, if not most, players go wrong because they do not bluff often enough on the turn and river to adequately balance their value bets. This flaw is extremely exploitable. For example, against someone who gives up too often on the turn, the player with A5 on an A96 flop can profitably call the flop continuation bet and hope the pot gets checked down. In fact, even just giving up too often on the river can be a critical error.

In response to the large number of players who give up too frequently, some fairly good players have adopted the counter strategy. With decent made hands, they call one or maybe two bets, hoping from that point to check it down. If their opponent follows through with a big bet, they just fold. This counter strategy works well against many players, but pays a heavy price against someone bluffing as we described above. It performs even worse against a strategy that includes more bluffs than the generic optimal strategy.

No matter your opponent, your barreling strategy will resemble this strategy. You'll bet more hands on the flop than you do on the turn and on the river. But depending on your opponents' mistakes, you can alter the strategy in different ways to further exploit them.

Before we begin, keep in mind that whenever you deviate consciously from the optimal strategy, you open yourself up to exploitation from an appropriately crafted counter strategy. For example, if you bluff more often than is optimal, then your opponent can exploit you by checking and calling more frequently with decent made hands.

> Deviate from the generic optimal strategy only consciously and only when it benefits you.

Principles For Continuation Betting

Continuation betting is a crucial aspect of any no-limit strategy. Whether to try a continuation bet after missing the flop can be a somewhat complex decision, but at its heart is a simple trade-off. By betting, you're more likely to win pots where your opponent flopped a weak hand. But you're also more likely to lose extra money in pots where your opponent flopped strong. You want to balance these two factors to make the most profitable strategy.

Principle 1: Just Do It

Very strong opponents require you to utilize a measured and nuanced continuation betting strategy. Fortunately, the vast majority of opponents you'll encounter at $1–$2 are not very strong. As a result, the basic continuation betting strategy for $1–$2 can be summed up thusly:

Just do it.

As we said before, the main trade-off for continuation betting is that, by betting you'll win more pots against bad hands, but you'll lose more money against good hands. Your typical opponents at $1–$2 (even the "good" ones) fold too frequently to pressure, and on top of that they don't win as much as they could with their strong hands. So by continuation betting against these players, you'll succeed more often than you should, and you'll lose less on average than you should when you get caught. Both factors make betting more attractive than it would be against a very strong opponent.

So we recommend you continuation bet frequently, and pull back on the aggression only against opponents who exploit your strategy. As a baseline, you could bet nearly every time in heads-up pots and perhaps 70–80 percent of the time in three-handed pots. In four-handed or more pots, you should be more measured, but you can still profitably make c-bets on many dry flops.

Example 1. Your 27/9 opponent limps under the gun, and you make it $10 on the button with A♠6♠. The blinds fold, and the limper calls.

The flop is J♦9♠8♦. Your opponent checks.

Bet about $15. This flop is coordinated and leaves you with few prospects to improve. It hits many of the hands your opponent might have limped in with. Overall this situation is relatively inhospitable for a continuation bet.

Yet we think you should bet anyway. The flop misses many of your opponent's hands, just as it also hits many of them. And often when your opponent has hit the flop and does call, he'll have hit the flop weakly, holding just a draw or a weak pair. Depending on the turn and river cards and action, you may be able to steal a fair percentage of pots on a later street. Your opponent plays weakly enough that you should try a continuation bet even in this relatively poor scenario.

Example 2. You open for $7 from under the gun with A♣Q♠. A tight, somewhat nitty player calls on the button. The big blind, a 38/14 player, also calls.

The flop comes J♣9♠4♠. The big blind checks.

Go ahead and try a continuation bet. A bet of about $12 into this $22 pot should work fairly well. Usually the nitty player will hold a pocket pair, or a suited ace or a connector, and many of those hands have missed this flop.

The loose player in the blind plays a lot of trash and therefore usually makes weak hands. If the nitty player folds, and the loose player calls, you will have position and often have a good opportunity to steal the pot later in the hand.

A slightly reckless continuation betting style gets the money in small stakes no-limit. Your opponents, by and large, won't make the adjustments necessary to exploit you. They'll struggle to cope with your aggression. And it's no big deal if you take it a little too far and throw out a dubious bet here and there. Your slightly over-aggressive style will earn you extra money on your good hands, and this benefit alone can be enough to pay for your mistaken bets. Overall, you're much better off continuation betting a little too often than not betting often enough.

Principle 2: Don't Use A Sledgehammer When A Slightly Smaller Sledgehammer Will Suffice

Overall, the strategy is not subtle: Bet the flop and dare your opponents to try to defend themselves. But you can employ a little subtlety in your bet sizing. You don't have to fire the pot every time it's your turn to bet. Often a smaller bet will work just as well.

Your opponents will often think in binary terms on the flop—either they hit the flop, or they didn't. If they are feeling like they didn't hit the flop, they may be willing to fold even to a very small bet. Whereas if they feel like they hit the flop, they may be likely to call a pot-sized bet, since in absolute terms, even pot-sized flop bets tend to be relatively small.

The result of this tendency for binary thinking on the flop is that half pot bets are often nearly as good at stealing the pot as larger bets.

Some scenarios in particular promote binary thinking. If the flop comes K22 rainbow, for instance, your opponents will either have strong hands, or they'll have "nothing." Only medium pocket pairs like 77 can fall into the ambiguous middle.

Thus, there's little reason to bet full pot on a dry flop like this one, even if you happened to flop a strong hand. Limiting your c-bets to half pot on dry flops like this one will have you winning nearly as often as a full pot bet would, while losing just half as much when things go wrong. In fact, smaller bets often work well too.

Another situation where binary thinking often takes hold is in pots that were 3-bet preflop. In these bloated pots, your opponents will often tend to evaluate their hands as either good enough to stack off with or not good enough. Since the pots are large compared to the remaining stacks, there's little room to maneuver, to chase a weak draw, or to employ any wait-and-see tactics like floating.

You can harness this binary "to commit or not to commit" thinking to your advantage when c-betting by choosing a small bet size. Sure, blasting a pot-sized $50 bet at a 3-bet pot will tend to get your opponents off their marginal hands. But firing $25 or $30 will often do the trick nearly as well. These bets are small compared to the pot, but they are large enough compared to the stack sizes that your opponents will usually revert to a fit-or-fold strategy.

When the pot is small compared to the starting stacks, and the board is fairly coordinated (also called a "wet" board), binary thinking begins to break down. The bets are relatively small, and many hands can catch a weak piece of the flop—gutshots, bottom pairs, overcards, backdoor flush draws, and so forth. So in these situations, you should tend to make somewhat larger continuation bets with an eye toward following up with a possible second barrel to force opponents off all their marginal flop calling hands.

Example 3. A 20/17 player opens from the button for $7. You 3-bet to $24 in the big blind with 3♣3♠. Your opponent calls. You know that this player tends to 4-bet with his premium hands, rarely choosing to trap with them. And you also know that he tends to adopt a fit-or-fold strategy postflop after calling a 3-bet.

The flop comes 9♠7♦2♦. You can bet about $25 into this $49 pot. That bet size should be enough to get your opponent off of his whiffed overcard hands like KQ. And if your opponent happened to catch a lucky set or big flush draw on you, you'll extract yourself from the situation without losing over a quarter of your stack in the process.

Principle 3: Back Off Against Strong Players

Occasionally you will come up against a player who will try to use your prolific continuation betting against you. Watch out for these signs:

A normally-aggressive player who starts to play a trapping game against you with hands like top pair or an overpair. For example, you 3-bet preflop, half-pot bet the flop, half-pot bet the turn, and shove the river, and the player calls and shows pocket aces. If this is a player who would typically put in action sooner with pocket aces, he may be adjusting to your aggression by trapping more often.

A player who begins checkraising the flop frequently against you. Generally speaking, the flop checkraise is a play used sparingly by most small stakes no-limit players. If one player seems to be checkraising you much more frequently than usual, there's a good chance he's trying to exploit your weak continuation bets.

A player who begins floating your bets frequently or raising with position either on the flop or on a later street. As with the previous sign, good players can add more floating to their games against a player who fires off too many c-bets.

If someone seems to be taking one of the above countermeasures against your continuation betting, you should bet fewer hands. In particular, consider the following guidelines:

Check more often when out of position than when in position. It's much easier for your opponents to exploit your loose continuation betting when they have position on you. If you 3-bet from the blinds and a tough player calls you (someone who is likely either to try to trap you or to try to steal the pot), you should frequently check the flop, and you should check with your bad and good hands alike. Checking bad hands saves money, and checking good hands reverses the trapping play on your opponents if they try to steal the pot after your show of weakness.

Against a good player, you can check more than half of your out of position hands on the flop. When you have position you should still be betting more than half of your hands. Also, when you do c-bet from out of position and are called, check the turn more with your made hands. This punishes floaters.

Check more often when the board connects well with your opponent's hand range. When TAG players call your preflop raises, you can make some assumptions about their hand ranges. They likely have a big card hand, a small or medium pocket pair, or a connected hand (usually suited). Therefore, your continuation bets will succeed less frequently on coordinated and big card flops, and you should be willing to check more often. As when out of position, you should also check some good hands on those flops to balance your range.

Be more willing to rebluff. Say you raise preflop, and a 26/24 opponent calls out of the blind. The flop comes K52 rainbow. He checks, you bet a little more than half-pot, and he checkraises half the pot. Sometimes (but not always) you should reraise as a bluff. Since the flop is dry and hits relatively few hands, your opponent can be testing you in this situation with nothing. By occasionally rebluffing, you help protect yourself from being outright exploited.

Also, when out of position, instead of continuation betting on a dry or semi-coordinated board, you could sometimes check with the intention of checkraising as a bluff. Deploying this play occasionally will prevent your opponent from showing an automatic profit by playing a "bet when checked to" strategy.

Earlier, we made the case for keeping bet sizes small when bluffing. But aggressive opponents will sometimes pounce on weak bets harder than strong bets. When this is the case, bet larger when you don't want your opponent to play back at you, and bet smaller when you do—at least until he begins to figure this pattern out.

Again, you shouldn't have to use these countermeasures too often when playing at $1–$2. Most players at that level aren't sophisticated enough to begin trapping you or bluffing and rebluffing you to defend themselves against your aggressive flop betting. But if you think you've found such a player in your game, you now know what to do about it.

igh Boards And Continuation Betting

In some ways, an ace is the ultimate scare card. It's obvious, and if you don't have one, it's very threatening. If you raise preflop and an ace flops, your opponents may think it likely you have an ace. This fact can work both for and against you.

Say you open preflop on the button with T♣9♣ and get called by an unknown big blind. The flop comes A♦7♣5♠. Your opponent checks. You should certainly continuation bet here against nearly all opponents. The big blind doesn't need a great hand to defend his blind against your button raising range, so a large percentage of his hands won't include an ace. If he holds a hand like Q♦T♠, he'll be concerned that you have an ace and that he's drawing slim. If the flop had been J♦7♣5♠, your opponent might choose to peel on the flop with his three-straight and overcard. But with the ace on board, usually he'll just fold.

So when your opponent begins the hand with a wide preflop range, he's more likely than usual to fold to a continuation bet on an ace-high flop, particularly a ragged ace-high flop.

However, when your opponent has connected with the flop, he's less likely than usual to let go to a flop bet. He's also less likely to fold on the turn. If he holds an ace, he's unlikely to fold on the flop or turn. Many players will routinely call two streets with any ace. And even those who usually fold weak aces to a second barrel will sometimes spike their kicker or decide to look you up, particularly if they think you're aggressive.

If your opponent doesn't hold an ace, but has connected with the flop in another way, he's also less likely to let go because he'll assume he has implied odds. Since you're the preflop raiser, you're marked with a possible ace. Someone with bottom or middle pair will often call the flop trying to spike two pair or trips and to win a big pot. Likewise, someone with a gutshot or other weak draw will often peel to try to outdraw you. These weak hands will likely fold if they miss when you bet the turn and river.

But it often doesn't pay to double and triple barrel ace-high flops when called on the flop. First, you will often be up against an ace, and most players with an ace will be loathe to fold. Second, your opponents looking to draw out on an ace want implied odds, and by double and triple barreling, that's what you're offering them. They think it's profitable to draw because if they hit, they can get you for turn and river bets. If you triple barrel them, they get what they want.

Triple barreling ace-high flops can set you up for a double whammy. You pay off your opponents who have aces, and you sometimes also pay off opponents looking for implied odds. This effect tends to make running big bluffs on ace-high flops unprofitable.

So when the flop comes ace-high and you've raised preflop, usually continuation bet because your opponents are unlikely to call unless they've connected fairly well with the flop. But if your opponent does call the flop and your hand is still garbage on the turn, usually give up.

When you've raised preflop, ace-high flops are prime candidates for a continuation bet. But if your flop bet is called and you still have garbage on the turn, continuing the bluff will usually be unprofitable.

Giving up on the turn with most of your garbage hands opens up a possible strategy to exploit you. Your opponent can call the flop with any pair or even king-high, and then fold if you bet the turn and take the free showdown if you give up. To balance your turn checks with garbage, you should sometimes also check the turn with decent hands. Weak aces and pocket pairs just below the ace are good hands to check back. If you check back a decent hand and your opponent checks the river, you can consider value betting. Your opponent might mistake your turn check for giving up on a bluff and look you up light. Finally, you should balance these value bets against thinking players by bluffing sometimes with the garbage hands you checked back.

To summarize, usually check the turn and river with nothing after getting called on an ace-high board. To punish opponents who try to get cheap showdowns on you, sometimes play your aces with a bet-check-bet pattern, extracting bonus value on the river. Against especially perceptive opponents who will decode the bet-check-bet line as strength, throw in the occasional bet-check-bet as a bluff. Against most players this final measure of balance is unnecessary.

For instance, say you're playing $1–$2 with $200 stacks. You open for $6 on the button with **T♣9♣** and an unknown big blind calls. The flop comes **A♦7♣5♠**. Your opponent checks, you bet $8, and he calls. (Your flop c-bets need not be large on ragged ace-high flops because your opponent can have few marginal hands. Either he's got something worth calling with or he's got nothing and he's worried about drawing dead to an ace.) The turn is the **4♦**. Your opponent checks, and you check. The river is the **Q♥**. Your opponent bets $16, and you fold.

Your opponent called your flop continuation bet and you didn't improve on the turn. Furthermore, if your opponent held a small straight draw on the flop or a suited connector that flopped bottom or middle pair, the turn card improved him. This is a straightforward situation to give up.

Now say you're playing the same game and open for $6 on the button with **A♣3♠**. The big blind calls, and the flop comes **A♦7♣5♠**. Your opponent checks, you bet $8, and he calls. The turn is the **T♦**. Your opponent checks. You can check this hand back sometimes to balance your checks when you're giving up. Then if your opponent checks again on the river, you can often bet 1/3 to 2/3 pot for value on the river, aiming to get calls from unimproved pocket pairs and sevens and fives. Since you checked back the turn, and since you often check back garbage on the turn, often they'll suspect a bluff and look you up.

If your opponent bets the river, you should call against some players and fold against others. It depends on their bluffing frequencies and willingness to bet less than an ace for value.

Above we noted that ace-high flops tend to be poor to double-barrel because you'll be giving value to aces and giving implied odds to drawing hands. One might then wonder, wouldn't that be the case on every flop? By double barreling, we're offering value to top pair and implied odds to drawing hands whether the top card is an ace or a ten. It's true, but ten-high flops have three factors that make continuing a bluff more attractive:

Opponents are more likely to peel light on ten-high flops than they are on ace-high flops. Someone with queen-jack or ace-eight might call a flop bet on a ten-high flop, whereas queen-jack and king-high are less likely to peel an ace-high flop. Your opponents will fold a larger percentage of their range on an ace-high flop, but their calling ranges will tend to be stronger and therefore less profitable to continue to bluff into. Players will call ten-high flops with a weaker range, and therefore future bluffs will tend to be more profitable.

Overcards are the natural scare cards for top pair. Overcards can come to a flopped pair of tens, but no overcards can come to a flopped pair of aces. Therefore, if you bluff a ten-high flop and get called by a ten, there's a good chance you'll catch a scare card later on and have a good bluffing opportunity. That is unlikely to happen on an ace-high flop.

Your bluffing hands will tend to have more equity when called on a ten-high flop than on an ace-high one. Say you have queen-nine and continuation bet a ten-high flop. If you get called by a ten, you have overcard outs. If you get called by an ace on an ace-high flop, you have almost no equity when called.

Aces On The Turn

You raise preflop with pocket deuces and get called by a blind. The flop comes ten-high and ragged. Your opponent checks, you bet, and he calls. The turn is an ace. This might seem at first like the ideal bluffing card. It's a decent bluffing card, but it's not ideal. There are two main problems:

As we mentioned before, people call ten-high flops fairly often with ace-high hands. These hands have now improved, but will still likely check to you.

Much of the time when someone calls out of position on a ten-high ragged flop, they will have flopped a pair. Since many people play ace-rag hands often, the turn will have made them aces up more likely than it might at first seem. For instance, on a T73 flop, you'll frequently be up against A7, A3, 87, or 76. You're unlikely to be up against 72 or 93.

Nevertheless, the ace will be scary to someone who holds just a smaller pair, and turn bluffs will succeed fairly often. You can also bluff a turn ace if you chose not to c-bet the flop. Your opponent will suspect that you checked behind on the flop with ace-high and then spiked your ace on the turn.

However, if you actually hold an ace, especially with a weak kicker, then often it's better to check it back on the turn rather than bet it. The reason is simple. The ace is a good bluffing card, meaning that your opponents will often suspect you have an ace and fold weaker pairs. So when you have an ace, they won't give you much action with weaker hands. On the other hand, you'll get plenty of action from bigger aces, aces up, and better. Since the turn bet will tend to get action mostly from better hands, and since a pair of aces will usually hold up if ahead, checking it on the turn frequently is the best play.[9]

With a big ace such as ace-king or ace-queen, checking the turn isn't as tempting. Big aces can extract value from tenacious opponents with bad kickers. Therefore, usually bet your big aces on the turn. However, against some players you can consider checking even big aces.

If you follow this strategy when an ace comes on the turn, then your turn play will become somewhat inverted. You'll be betting your weak hands as bluffs and checking back many of your aces. Against opponents who understand this, your inverted strategy is extremely exploitable, since they can bluff-raise your bets and refuse to pay you off when you check. To protect yourself from thinking players, rather than betting the turn as a bluff, you can employ a delayed bluff. Instead of betting the turn with your weak hand, check. Then if your thinking opponent checks the river, you bluff. This sequence will mimic how you'd play a weak ace. If you play your weak aces and some bluffs this way, then your opponent will either

---

[9] An exception is if you are playing a predictable opponent on a draw-heavy board. In that case you are better off betting the turn and folding to a checkraise.

have to pay off your aces sometimes or let your bluffs succeed sometimes.

While this delayed bluff balances your play against thinking players, beware of using it against unthinking players. An unthinking player won't deduce that you could bet weak hands on the turn ace, but check behind your aces. When you bet the turn ace, they'll think, "I guess he has the ace," and fold. But if you check it back on the turn, they'll think, "I guess he doesn't have an ace. Maybe my pair is good." If you try to bluff the river, these players will often call you with most pairs.

To summarize, after raising preflop and getting called on the flop, a turn ace represents a decent bluffing opportunity. It's only decent because, while it's easy for you to represent the ace, the card will often have improved your opponent's hand as well. If you actually hold an ace in your hand, particularly with a weak kicker, then checking it is often best against both bad and good players. Because an ace is your most obvious holding, you'll tend to get folds from weaker hands and action from better ones. If you get checked to again on the river, you can bet your ace for value. This sequence will improve your chance of getting action from weaker hands and sometimes allow you to get away against better ones (if your opponent makes a big river bet that is not likely to be a bluff). If you don't hold an ace, then against unthinking players you can just bet the turn as a bluff, representing the ace. Unthinking players won't know that you would often check it back if you actually held an ace. Thinking players, however, will know that your turn bet is fishy, and they can use that information to exploit you. So against thinking players, you can employ a delayed bluff by checking the turn and bluffing the river. This action mimics how you'd play a real ace and is therefore a more credible bluff.

Barreling Examples

64s On The Button: Firing A Second Barrel

You are in a 6-handed $1–$2 game with $200 effective stacks. The first three players fold to you on the button. You look down at **6♦4♦**. Both players in the blinds are tight and passive. Your chances of stealing the blinds are good, so you raise to $5. The small blind folds, and the big blind calls. He is a 19/6.

The big blind plays predictably preflop with big hands. He would likely have reraised with a big pocket pair and probably with ace-king. Since he didn't, you estimate his range to be medium and small pocket pairs, big cards, and maybe some suited connectors. You think he'd often fold suited connectors out of position, but you aren't sure, so you include it in his possible range.

The flop comes **5♦5♠3♣**, giving you an open-ended straight draw. The big blind checks, and you bet $6 into the $11 pot. He calls.

The turn is the **K♥**, and your opponent checks again. What should you do?

You should bet big. Players often check behind here because they think taking the free card is the right play. But it's not. The reason? Fold equity.

Consider your opponent's range for checkcalling a flop bet. His most likely hand is a medium or small pocket pair. He could also have a strong hand like a five or threes full, or he could have a weak hand like ace-high.

The king is a great card to bet because your opponent likely doesn't have one. He probably would have reraised preflop with ace-king, and—as a tight player—he probably would have folded king-high on the flop. The king is a scare card for all of his medium and weak hands.

Perhaps you might be asking, "What about my draw? I don't want to get blown off my hand!"

The value of your draw is far secondary to your fold equity. Your implied odds are weak because your opponent likely doesn't have much of a hand. And if he does have a strong hand, you may be drawing dead. Folding to a checkraise now may actually cost you less over the long-run than making your draw.

This is a good spot to fire a second barrel. Bet the pot or close to it.

Barreling In And Out Of Position

The hero opens for $7 from under the gun with 5♠5♥. The cutoff and button both call. The cutoff is new to the game, and the button is a decent if somewhat weak-tight 15/10 player. Effective stacks are $260, or 130bb.

The pot is $24, or 12bb. The flop is 7♦6♥3♣, making a gutshot for the pocket fives. The hero bets $18. The cutoff folds, and the button calls.

The turn is the K♣. What should the hero do now?

This is a great situation to fire a second barrel. Several things are going for you:

- ♦ The button is somewhat weak-tight.
- ♦ The button is a 15/10 so he is unlikely to have a king.

- The turn is a big overcard that could easily have given you top pair.
- You have a gutshot draw if behind, and a five will likely win it also.
- If you get raised, you can fold knowing that you're likely behind and have relatively little equity.

When an overcard comes on the turn, it's often a great time to fire a second barrel, especially if you raised preflop. Many of your opponent's flop calls will be made with marginal pairs, and the overcard could be just enough to convince them that they don't really want to take their shrinking pair to an expensive showdown.

Marginal pair-plus-draw hands are also attractive for making turn semibluffs. Several good things can happen when you play these hands hard:

- You could win the pot without a fight.
- You could get called by a drawing hand, the river could go check-check, and you could win a showdown.
- You could get called by a moderate made hand, hit your draw, and win even more on the river.
- You could get raised off your hand by a monster, saving you from a big loss.

The last point is the most subtle. When you have a combination marginal pair/marginal draw hand such as a small pair with a gutshot draw, your hand has decent equity against bigger pairs, but it can get into real trouble against two pair, a set, or a better draw.

If you're up against a set of sixes or sevens, for instance, instead of having six outs to a decent winner, you have four outs to the win but two outs to a big losing hand. Your draw loses the bulk of its value against strong hands, and it's these strong hands that rate to raise you on the turn. So if you get raised on the turn, often you're merely being warned that your hand had little value to begin with, and having to fold it is no big deal.

Here's another example of firing a second barrel on the turn with a marginal pair and draw. Both players involved in the hand start with $200.

Everyone folds to the 22/9 small blind who calls. The 25/23 big blind holds T♣8♦ and makes it $8 to go. This raise is a standard, positional one. Often it will win the pot immediately. If the small blind calls, the big blind will be fine, playing a decent hand with position.

The small blind does call, and the flop comes J♦8♥6♦, giving the big blind middle pair. The small blind checks, and the big blind bets $12. The small blind calls.

The turn is the 7♦, putting a three-straight and a three-flush on board. The small blind checks. The big blind now has second pair, a one-card gutshot, and a weak one-card flush draw. This collection of marginal draws and a marginal pair gives him strong reason to bet the turn. If he gets called, he has a number of outs against top pair. And if he gets checkraised, frequently he's drawing nearly dead, so he may not be missing out on much if he has to fold.

Ace-Jack Offsuit In The Small Blind

Stacks are $200. Everyone folds to you in the small blind, and you make it $8 with A♠J♥. The 29/8 big blind calls. He is a passive player and slightly on the loose side. Keeping in mind that this is a blind versus blind battle, and also that he views you as being fairly aggressive, you expect him to have a fairly wide range of hands here. That means pretty much anything playable, although he would probably have reraised with a premium hand.

The flop comes **Q♠8♣5♦**. You c-bet $12 into the $16 pot. He calls. The turn is the **K♦**. Should you check and give up, or should you fire again?

This is an excellent spot for a second barrel, and you should definitely bet again. Your opponent's range is weak. He flat called a likely blind steal preflop, and then he called your flop bet on a fairly dry board. His most likely hand is one weak pair or a gutshot. The overcard king is unpleasant for most of the hands in his range. You have good fold equity, and a big turn bet will take down the pot a high percentage of the time.

Players sometimes see the king on the turn and think, "Oh, I picked up a gutshot. And because it's a scare card, if I check, he'll probably check and let me draw to my straight for free." This is a classic example of overestimating implied odds and underestimating fold equity.

It's true that if you check the turn, he'll often check behind. So what? That just confirms what you already suspect, which is that his hand is weak. Even if you hit one of your meager four gutshot outs on the river, you don't stand to make very much money. Further, checking the turn makes it harder to steal the pot on the river when you miss. A checked turn means a smaller pot on the river, which makes it easier for him to call your bluff. Plus, by checking the turn you give *him* a free card to improve, which would give him another reason to call your river bet.

When your opponents' ranges are weak, think first about stealing and then about making the best hand. Even when you have some showdown equity, don't ignore your folding equity.

Ace-King Out Of Position: Turn Semibluff

Stacks are $200. Everyone folds to the 27/25 button, who raises to $6. The small blind folds, and you are in the big blind with A♥K♠. The button is a solid, aggressive player capable of opening on the button with a wide range, playing back at 3-bets, 4-bet bluffing, floating flops, and so forth. You reraise to $21 with the intention of getting all-in preflop if your opponent comes back over the top. But instead, your opponent calls. His range remains wide.

The flop comes 9♥5♥2♦. Here you should check sometimes and bet sometimes. This time you c-bet $35 into the $43 pot. Your opponent thinks for a few seconds and calls.

The turn is the 4♥. What should you do?

Your opponent's range is still wide. He could have a big hand like a set or a flush. He could also have called on the flop with a weak hand like pocket sevens or any nine, or absolutely nothing. Counting the possible combinations, the weak hands and air are far more numerous than the strong ones.

If the turn were a blank, you would probably have to check and give up the pot. But now you have two overcards and the nut flush draw. The pot is $113, and you have $144 left.

Stick it in.

Your opponent will fold most hands in his range. He's a good player, and your line represents too much strength for him to call with a weak hand. He will often fold 8♦8♣ and even T♠9♠. You could have a bigger pair and a heart draw, and his equity with weak hands is not good against your range. About the only bluff hand in your range is the one you have, so take advantage of it.

If you happen to get called, you have outs no matter what your opponent has. If he has an overpair, you could have as many as 17 outs (9 hearts, 3 aces, 2 non-heart kings, and 3 non-heart threes). And even if he already has a flush, you have seven outs.

Good fold equity combined with modest pot equity makes pushing all-in the right play.

A Commitment Bluff

Putting an opponent to a stack decision with a bluff is a great play. (See our sidebar below on the commitment threshold.) In fact, sometimes a bluff may be effective precisely because your opponent thinks you're committed. Here's an example:

Stacks are $200. A weak 21/6 player limps under the gun. The next two players fold, and you make it $9 on the button with Q♣T♣. The small blind folds, the 18/15 big blind calls, and the limper folds. The big blind is a fairly solid player, though a little on the tight side and not terribly tricky.

The flop comes 6♣2♦2♠. The big blind checks, and you c-bet $21 into the $21 pot. You usually c-bet about two-thirds of the pot, but this time you bet the full pot to discourage your tight opponent from calling with hands like ace-king or pocket threes. A big bet also discourages a checkraise bluff on this dry low board. He thinks for a few seconds and calls.

The turn is the A♥. Your opponent checks, and the action is on you. The pot is $63, and you have $170 left.

This is a good spot to continue bluffing. Your opponent's range is mainly medium pocket pairs, and the ace is a great scare card. He isn't quite good enough to know that many of your bets on turned aces are bluffs. Also, any big bet here puts him to a stack decision. He can plainly see that you have $170 left. If you bet $60 on the turn, he will likely assume you hit the ace and are committed. After all, why would you bet $60 with only $110 more remaining if you aren't willing to risk your entire stack?

A $60 turn bet carries significant fold equity. Your opponent will almost certainly fold everything but strong hands. If he checkraises, you are likely drawing dead.

If you had bet, say, $15 on the flop and $32 on the turn, your opponent would be much more likely to take a stand and call your turn bet with JJ-77 or a six. But by building the pot and putting him to a commitment decision, you increase the likelihood of your bluff succeeding.

Don't routinely bet a large percentage of your stack on a bluff. But when done judiciously against the right opponent, these big bluffs can be a potent weapon.

Commitment And The Commitment Threshold

In our book *Professional No-Limit Hold'em: Volume 1*, we argued that you should plan your play around commitment, and we introduced the concept of the commitment threshold.

Commitment is a simple but powerful concept. The idea is that the larger the pot becomes relative to the remaining stacks, the more committed you should become to seeing a showdown. Say there's $20 in the pot and you and your opponent each have $400 remaining. If your opponent does something to convince you that he likely has you beaten, then you should fold rather than risk $400 to win the $20 pot. But if there's $600 in the pot, and you and your opponent each have $400 remaining, then you will often be committed for the rest of your stack even if you suspect you might be beaten. Since you'll be risking $400 to win $1,000 (the $600 pot plus your opponent's $400 stack), you can win only 30 percent of the time and still be right to put the money in.

You should plan your play around commitment. Before you make the plays that build that $600 pot, think about whether you want all your money in. This way you avoid some nasty surprises.

As the hand proceeds and you gather additional information, reassess your commitment decision.

We discussed the commitment threshold in detail in *Professional No-Limit Hold'em: Volume 1*. The executive bullet points are:

- ♦ Don't put in a third of your stack (or any big chunk of it) and then fold…
- ♦ Unless you are bluffing…
- ♦ Or you thought you would have the best of it in a big pot but new information changed your mind.

Conceding a third of your stack is a disaster. Of course, some disasters are unavoidable. For example, say you flop two pair on a board with a flush draw. A third or so of the stacks go in, leaving one big bet behind. The flush hits on the turn. Your opponent pushes. If you think he has the flush, fold. You accept the small disaster to avoid a bigger one.

That said, because conceding a third or so of your stack is so expensive, we avoid it when possible. This requires thinking one big bet ahead. The rule of thumb is once 10 percent of the smaller stack goes in, think hard about commitment. Will getting all-in be profitable? If so, what is the most profitable betting line, and what cards or opponent betting actions would change your mind? If not, what will you do if faced with a big bet?

The commitment threshold is crossed when roughly 10 percent of the smaller stack goes in. Nothing magic happens at that point save that the next big bet gets around a third of your stack in, and two big bets gets you all-in or close to it. So it's time to decide whether playing a big pot is a good idea. Make a commitment plan.

Commitment plans are fluid. If you are committed but something happens to change your mind—like that flush draw getting there—fine. The point is to think about big pots before you create them. If you don't want a big pot, avoid big bets. Check or make a small bet instead.

Bluffing is the main exception to these recommendations. Bluffs are far more effective when they force opponents to stack decisions. Once 10 percent of the smaller stack goes in, there are two big bets between you and being all-in (or close to all-in). If you make that big bet bluff on the flop or turn, it will be obvious to an astute opponent that you might go all-in on a subsequent betting round. A big bet at the commitment threshold threatens your opponent with an all-in, putting him to a stack decision. But don't overdo it or he'll wise up.

A Suited Connector Out Of Position

Suited connectors usually depend on fold equity to be profitable. They are much more valuable with position, and you should often fold them out of position. But you can occasionally mix it up.

Say stacks are $200. The player under the gun limps, the button limps, and everyone else folds. You look down at 9♥8♥ in the big blind. You just sat down and don't have stats on anyone yet. But it occurs to you that limping is fairly rare at these stakes. Therefore, your opponents are probably both passive and holding weak hands, unless the player under the gun is planning a limp-reraise.

While you'd normally check in this spot, this time you decide to raise. You have a fair shot of winning the pot outright. And if called, you expect to have good control of your passive opponents, and you'll often steal the pot postflop. Plus, your raise balances your range so that you don't always have a big pair when you raise out of the blinds.

You raise to $12 and both opponents call. Their ranges are weighted toward medium and small pairs, but could also include suited connectors, suited aces, and some big card hands.

The flop comes K♥7♦2♦. You have nine-high but decide that this is a good flop to c-bet on because your opponents will fold often. You bet $28 into the $37 pot. The player under the gun folds, and the button calls. The turn is the 6♥. What should you do?

On just about any other turn card, you would check and give up your bluff. However, the 6♥ was the best possible card for you. You now have an open-ended straight draw and a flush draw. Your weak hand on the flop has turned into a strong draw on the turn. Still, with only one card to come, you are likely at best a 2–to–1 underdog against a made hand.

If you check and your opponent bets, you may not have sufficient implied odds to call. He could overbet the pot. Or even if he bets a reasonable amount, you may find yourself in a sticky spot on the river. You'll have to act first, and if you miss your draw, a bluff might be hopeless. If you hit your draw, you might not get paid, or you might discover that your opponent made a better hand such as a bigger flush.

Betting is the right play here. Your opponent's range rates to be weak. He limped on the button and flat-called on a flush-draw flop. He may occasionally be trapping with two-pair or a set, but more likely he has a king with a weak kicker, a middle pocket pair, or a flush draw. He won't often be able to call a big bet.

The pot is $93, and you have $160 left. An all-in is an overbet of about two times the pot, but it maximizes fold equity against your opponent's weak hands, and it also leaves you with no decision on the river. If you bet less and he has a strong hand, he will raise all-in and you'll have to call. If he has a weaker hand, the oversized bet will ensure that he folds hands like K♠8♠ or J♦T♦. You should bet it all unless you think an all-in will look weak, in which case you might bet smaller.

Delayed Bluff

The first two players fold, and you make it $7 in the cutoff with Q♠9♠. The button and both blinds are weak-tight. If instead the button were a tough player or the blinds were aggressive, folding might be a better play.

The button folds and both blinds call. The 16/11 small blind has $194 behind, and the 13/9 big blind has $128. You cover both with $945. (It's been a good day.)

The flop comes **8♥4♦2♠**. Both players check. Low dry flops like this are good to bet in $1–$2, because they are unlikely to hit your opponents, and weaker opponents are relatively unlikely to try a resteal. Plus, here you have some pot equity with your overcards and backdoor flush draw.

You bet $13 into the $21 pot. The small blind folds. The big blind thinks for a few seconds and calls. His range is weighted toward one-pair hands, including pocket pairs. He would probably have reraised preflop with a premium pair, and he would typically fold overcards to your bet. His checkcall suggests a set, a small pair, or gutshot.

The turn is the **A♣**. He checks again. This is usually an excellent spot for a second barrel. The ace is a scare card, and a bet will often chase out his middling one-pair hands.

However, you have another option. You can delay your bluff until the river. The advantage is that you mix up your play and gain one more street's worth of information. If he happens to have a set or be suspicious of your turn bet, you take advantage of the fact that he has to act first on the river.

You check behind on the turn. The river is the **4♥**, and your opponent checks one more time. The river card and check are good for you because they make a set less likely for him. The third check in particular makes this a good spot to bluff.

Your opponent most likely has one small pair. The pot is $47, and he has $108 left. Bet it all. He's not the type of player to make a hero call, so put the maximum pressure on him.[10]

If you think he'll fold nearly the same range of hands to a pot-sized bet that he will to an all-in, you can consider betting $40 or $50. That way you save some money in case he has a monster. But on the other hand, if he's not likely to try a sophisticated river trap, you might as well push. Sometimes players will fold to an all-in but talk themselves into a call for less, even if they're putting in three-quarters of their stack.[11]

A Three Barrel Bluff

The 31/13 opponent in this hand has the short stack at $140 and plays straightforwardly after the flop. He limps, and you raise to $8 on the button with 4♦4♥. Only the limper calls. The pot is $19.

The flop comes 9♥8♥3♥, giving you a small pair and a very weak one-card flush draw. The limper checks. You bet $12, just under two-thirds the pot. The limper calls.

The turn is the J♣. The limper checks, and you fire a $32 second barrel, about two-thirds of the $43 pot. The limper calls. After the call, the pot is $107 and the limper has $88 remaining.

The river is the Q♦. The limper checks, and you move all-in for $88. The limper folds.

---

[10] A *hero call* is a call of a large bet with a relatively weak hand in hopes of snapping off a bluff.

[11] The math here is counterintuitive. Say your opponent folds 60 percent of the time to a pot-sized bet of $47. So how can betting $108 be better if you can't win twice as often? The answer is you don't have to win twice as often. The pot-sized bet that wins 60 percent of the time shows a $9.40 profit. To show a $9.40 profit, the $108 bet has to win only 75.7 percent of the time. If it instead wins 78 percent of the time, the $108 all-in bet is superior to the $47 pot-sized bet.

Preflop, the choice to make an isolation raise with position and a small pocket pair was standard. You will likely have all the advantages in the hand: a stronger hand, position, and more postflop skill.

This flop is a decent one for a continuation bet. If the limper lacks a heart, it will be difficult for him to continue far in the hand. Also, since this player is straightforward after the flop, he isn't likely to try a rebluff checkraise.

The call could represent wide range of hands. It could be anything from a made flush, a set, or two pair to just a single pair, a straight draw, or a large heart like the naked **A♥**, **K♥**, or **Q♥**.

The turn **J♣** is a good card to fire a second barrel on. Since it's an offsuit overcard, it could scare off a flopped nine, eight, or three as long as he doesn't have a ten or big heart to go with it. The $32 turn bet is large enough perhaps to get the limper to fold the naked **K♥** or **Q♥**.

The river is another great bluffing card. It puts an overcard and a four-straight on board. If the limper was calling with a single pair, he'll likely fold to an all-in push. Notice also that the stack sizes are perfect for a bluff, as an all-in bet is just a bit less than the size of the pot. That makes the bluff profitable if it will elicit a fold from a better hand about half the time.

In reality, the player will likely fold more often than that. After the turn call, the most likely hands are two pair, one pair, or a draw of some sort. If the limper held a stronger hand like a made flush or a set, he might well have checkraised by now, or might at least have bet the river, particularly with a made flush.

Most of the time when you get called, the limper will have made a straight with a ten such as JT, T9, T8, or perhaps AT with the ace of hearts. These straight hands were relatively unlikely in the ranges we put the limper on for the flop and turn.

Sometimes the limper will call with two pair, and sometimes he'll fold two pair. If he has weaker hands than that, you can generally expect a fold. The turn and river cards are both good ones for bluffing, which is what makes this three barrel bluff worth trying.

Don't get too bent out of shape when a three-barrel bluff like this one fails. While it's tough to lose your stack bluffing, each bluff makes sense, and the overall line is profitable and helps you to get paid off when you flop a big hand and fire all the way.

Lessons for this hand:

♦ Non-ace overcards are often good cards to continue bluffs on the turn and river.
♦ River bluffs are often smart when the hands that can call the river are, generally speaking, not the same hands that called on the flop.
♦ River bluffs tend to be more effective when they are all-in, so you're in a prime bluffing situation when the remaining stacks are roughly pot-sized.

Three Barrel Bluff Against An Ace

Effective stacks are $200. The 16/13 under the gun player opens for $7 with **K♦Q♥**, and only the TAG big blind calls. The big blind plays a 21/17 game preflop and hasn't yet seen a showdown at the table.

The flop comes **A♠8♠4♣**. The big blind checks, the under the gun player bets $11, and the big blind calls.

The turn is the **9♦**. The big blind checks, and the under the gun player fires a second barrel of $28. The big blind calls.

The river is the **7♣**. The big blind checks, and the under the gun player bets $92. The big blind calls for time and folds after about 30 seconds.

Opening from under the gun with king-queen in a 6-max game is a fairly standard play. The big blind is tight, so his calling range won't be too wide given that he'll have to play the hand out of position against a raise from up front.

The ace-high flop is a good target for a continuation bet, so the under the gun player bets about three-quarters of the pot. The big blind calls. He could be calling with an ace, a flush draw, a pocket pair, or even a gutshot. He could also have a set or aces-up. Hands like 98s or 87s are possible as well.

The turn is an offsuit nine, which is a roughly neutral card for the player with king-queen. If the big blind has a flush draw or a pocket pair other than nines, the nine didn't improve him, but it makes two pair for ace-nine and nine-eight, both hands in the big blind's range. Given that the big blind is tight and unlikely to have improved on the turn, under the gun decides to fire a second barrel—$28 into the $37 pot.

After the big blind calls this bigger bet, we can put him on a stronger hand. Most likely he has an ace, probably with a weaker kicker than a queen since he's been 3-betting frequently preflop and probably would have done so with ace-king or ace-queen. He could also have a flush draw or possibly a stronger hand such as aces up or a set.

The river is the **7♣**. This card is good for under the gun because it doesn't complete the big blind's possible flush draw.

Also, it puts a possible straight on board which might spook the big blind a bit.

When the big blind checks again, we can discount sets and two pair from his range. With strong hands like that, most players would have bet or raised at some point by now. They aren't impossible, but at this point they're unlikely. So the most likely hands for the big blind are an ace with a non-premium kicker and a missed flush draw. Since the big blind is tight and doesn't get to showdown often, the under the gun player tries to push his opponent off a weak ace with a pot-sized third barrel. Since the big blind called for time before folding, a non-premium ace is likely exactly what he had.

Trying to push someone off top pair with a big river bet isn't wise against all opponents. Some opponents are simply too loose. When you make the bet, they may think to themselves, "I must be beat again," but eventually they'll call because they "have to see it." Against these players, consider making a small-sized river bluff like $20 or $30 into the $93 pot. It may be enough to push your opponent off a hand such as a small pair plus a flush draw that didn't improve. Bluffing is not a binary "to bluff or not to bluff" decision. You can make big bluffs, medium bluffs, and small bluffs, and they will fold out different ranges of hands. One bluff size can be unprofitable while another is profitable. Consider all possibilities before acting.

A full-bore 3-barrel bluff like the one executed in this hand can work well to push tight players off of top pair. If you put your opponent on a likely top pair due to the action, and you think your opponent really won't stack off with just top pair, consider launching a big river bluff.

We have given many examples of firing multiple barrels in this section. Before we move on, it's time to ground these plays in reality. We do *not* recommend firing two or three barrels at every "good" barreling opportunity. If you bluff too much, it becomes obvious, and opponents will start checking big hands to you and calling down with weak hands. But if you rarely fire a second or third barrel, your game has a serious flaw. Multiple barrel bluffs are mandatory in modern online 6-max $1–$2. Use them wisely, but don't be afraid to fire away when the situation is right for it. Also, be prepared to lose a few extra big pots. That is just part of the game.

Going For Value With Good Hands

Until now we've focused mainly on using position and an aggressive barreling strategy to steal pots. But going for value is just as important to no-limit success, and most people do it quite poorly. Learning to value bet correctly will help you in two major ways. First, you will extract value from hands you might have checked down before. Second, it will make you harder to read, and therefore your opponents will be more prone to making mistakes against you on all hands.

The classic value betting error most players make comes on the river. They check down far too many decent hands. For instance, a typical player will flop top pair with a strong kicker, bet it on the flop, bet it on the turn, and then check it down on the river. One major problem with systematically playing your decent hands this way is that it severely polarizes your river betting range. We're not saying you should avoid the bet-bet-check line entirely. It's often a solid line. But you lose value when you overuse it.

A *polarized range* is one that includes mainly very strong hands and very weak hands, but relatively few middle-strength hands. If a typical player shoves all-in for a pot-sized bet on the river on a K♦9♠8♦5♣3♦ board, for example, you can usually assume that the player holds either a flush or a bluff. Very few players would shove this river with a hand like KQ or 98, and many players would check down even KK or 76.

To some extent, everyone bets the river with a polarized range. It would not often make sense to bet a hand such as A9 on the above board unless you were trying to force out a better pair, as better hands will tend to call while worse hands will tend to fold. But the trick to betting with a polarized range is to keep your frequency of betting good hands roughly balanced with your bluffing frequency. If these two frequencies get out of whack, you become exploitable.

Balancing your value betting and bluffing frequencies doesn't mean you split them 50–50. According to game theory, if you play against a near-perfect opponent, the best balance is one such that your opponent is damned if he calls and damned if he doesn't. If he calls, he pays off your good hands, and if he folds, you win your bluffs. Game theoretically speaking, the optimally balanced frequencies against such an awesome opponent would depend on the pot odds your opponent is getting to call. If you make a pot-sized bet, for instance, your opponent is getting 2–to–1 on a call. (Betting $100 into a $100 pot offers your opponent a chance to win $200 at a risk of $100.) The optimal frequency (for game theorists) with this bet size when holding the nuts or nothing is therefore 2 value bets for every 1 bluff, or 67 percent value bets and 33 percent bluffs.

If you bet half-pot, you offer your opponent 3–to–1, and your optimal balance would be close to 3 value bets for every bluff.

In practice, you can't possibly hone your strategy to hit these frequencies every time. Nor do you want to! Your opponents aren't near-perfect. They are flawed, and you should exploit their flaws. For example, they will in general overestimate your bluffing frequencies, so you don't have to bluff as often. Just make sure that your river betting ranges include significantly more value bets than bluffs. Likewise, ensure that you do indeed make enough river bluffs.

For instance, say you bet only the nuts for good hands, but you bet all of your busted draws for bluffs. You would be making a lot of big river bets. Any opponent who watched you play for a while would realize that when you bet the river, you're almost always bluffing, since catching the nuts is uncommon. Rarely bluffing is similarly bad since an opponent can safely assume you have a huge hand when you bet.

Because you should keep your polarized range balanced, the fewer hands you value bet, the fewer bluffs you get to make. If you don't value bet aggressively enough, not only will you miss bets that you could have won from weaker hands, but you'll also have to skip profitable bluffs down the road to avoid unbalancing your range. Compulsively checking down rivers is a bankroll-killing double whammy.

The reason most players check so many rivers is that they fear a raise or checkraise. For the most part, that fear is unwarranted. Yes, if you start betting more rivers, you will get bluff-raised off your hand somewhat more often. But it won't be a frequent occurrence. Meanwhile, you'll be extracting more value from good hands and winning more pots by launching successful bluffs. The extra money your aggressive river strategy makes you will, over the long haul, dwarf the amount you lose to the occasional well-timed bluff-raise.

Bet the river. This may be the single most important thing you will do better than your $1–$2 opponents after reading this book. River bets are large and lucrative. Don't be shy. Bet your hand. Your opponents will call you with weaker hands. When you bet top pair on the river, you'll find yourself getting called by second pair, third pair, unimproved pocket pairs, even ace-high. Why are they calling? Because you could be bluffing.

Now you might say, "I'm not about to start betting top pair on all three streets every time. That's a recipe to get myself stacked every time someone makes two pair or better!" You definitely don't want to shovel money into the pot blindly every time you flop a pair. Going for value is more complex than betting like a robot. Nevertheless, betting the river with medium-strength hands has an undeniably positive effect on your strategy. What's the solution to the problem?

Plan your betting from the start. Think about your total hand range, not just the hand you happen to have. In this case, you have top pair, but from your opponent's perspective you could also have a flush draw or a straight draw or overcards. Plan your betting on all three streets so your top pair will, given favorable turn and river cards, look like a busted flush draw by the river. That could mean checking the flop or turn. Or it could mean making a small, weak-looking bet at some point. Then bet the river with gusto and watch your opponent call to snap off your "bluff." If you play this way, you'll extract value more consistently from weaker hands, and you'll offset your occasional losses when your opponent happens to hold a monster.

Also, don't worry too much about the hands your opponent *could* have. Consider mainly the hands he's *likely* to have. For instance, if you have KQ on a K8467 board, and you bet the K84 flop and your opponent called, he probably doesn't have a five. Few hands that contain a five would bother calling the flop. He's much more likely to hold a hand like TT or KT. Don't fear a hand just because it's possible.

Plan your betting with good hands. You'll extract more value and balance your bluffing. Use the following examples to spark your imagination. Getting value for good hands requires just as much inventiveness and planning as choosing the right situations to bluff.

But always remember that the river is the money round. If you adopt a more aggressive river strategy, you will be much harder to play against, and you'll gain a huge leg up on your competition.

Planning Betting Lines Around The Commitment Threshold

You are in a 6-handed $1–$2 game with $200 effective stacks. The first two players fold, and the 27/25 cutoff opens for $7. The button and small blind fold. You are in the big blind with **K♥Q♥**.

The cutoff is an aggressive player capable of opening a wide range in late position. He is smart, and his range narrows to a 3-bet. You are comfortable playing against him postflop, so you opt to flat call the preflop raise.

The flop comes **8♥4♣2♥**, giving you two overcards and a flush draw. You are first to act. What should you do?

In a situation like this, it's very helpful to sketch different postflop lines. Let's outline the pertinent information.

Stack-to-pot ratios. (See Sidebar.) SPR is very useful in postflop planning, even if it's not your primary preflop concern. Here the pot is $15 and the remaining stacks are $193, so your SPR is about 13. In other words, there are three pot-sized bets left before you are all-in. That's an important thing to know.

Your opponent's hand range and tendencies. The cutoff's range is wide here and usually weak. His strong hands include sets and big overpairs. His medium hands include small overpairs and top pair. His weak hands include underpairs and no pairs. He tends to be aggressive. He will definitely commit with his strong hands, but he will also bluff if you choose the right postflop line.

Your equity and your opponent's perception of you. You have two big overcards and a flush draw. You are a favorite over most of the cutoff's hand combinations, and your equity is favorable against his range. One thing to note, though, is that your equity drops considerably on a blank turn. That's pertinent because you're out of position. As for perceptions, you think he views you as solid. He would consider laying down medium strength hands depending on how the action unfolded.

From the above outline, you glean that committing to your hand is fine since your equity is solid even against your opponent's all-in range. Ideally, you prefer to be the one making the final all-in bet. That way you maximize fold equity. Also, while you prefer to get all-in on the flop, you don't mind getting it in on a blank turn so long as you are the one making the final bet. Calling an all-in on a blank turn is the least favorable option.

So, you have a few choices with regard to postflop lines. You can check the flop. Your opponent will c-bet a large percentage of the time. When he does, you can make a big checkraise. However, you should probably overbet if you choose this line. If you make a standard sized checkraise, your opponent will have the option of making the final commitment bet. Also, your opponent might view a standard sized checkraise as a bluff some percentage of the time, and he might decide to commit with some of his medium strength hands. Either of these lines loses fold equity. Checkraising all-in solves that problem, but it's a big overbet. Unless you balance your range by overbetting with other types of hands, your opponent might pinpoint your holding as a semibluff with a flush draw.

Another—and perhaps better—option is to lead into your opponent on the flop. Leading into the preflop raiser on an 8-high board may appear weak to him. Since he's aggressive, he may bluff raise a fair percentage of the time. He may also raise with some of his medium strength hands to take control and gain information. If he does raise, then you can reraise all-in. That way you take advantage of fold equity, and you have two streets to hit your hand if he does call.

Stack-To-Pot Ratios

A *stack-to-pot ratio*, or SPR, is a number that measures the size of the pot relative to the remaining stacks. You calculate it in a heads-up pot by dividing the size of the smaller of the remaining stacks by the pot size *on the flop before any flop betting*. For example:

You raise to $5 and the big blind calls. The pot is $11. You have $400 behind, and the big blind has $150. Your SPR is $150 (the smaller of the two stacks) divided by $11 (the pot size), or about 14.

SPRs help measure the risk versus reward of getting all-in. Suppose you raise with A♥Q♣ and the flop comes A♦6♠6♣. With an SPR of 2 (e.g., $40 stacks and a $20 pot), you would likely commit to the hand no matter the action. The pot would be far too large to consider getting away from top pair/good kicker. But with an SPR of 10 (e.g., $200 stacks and a $20 pot), you would often be taking the worst of it were all the money to go in.

Calculating the SPR is a useful exercise because it gives you an instant, concrete figure to use to decide whether to commit to a hand or not. It helps you plan your postflop play. You don't use it in isolation, but it supplements your hand reading. For instance, you might commit to a hand against a crazy player with an SPR of 8, but consider folding the same hand under heavy pressure from a nit with an SPR of 4. And you might go ahead and commit against the nit with an SPR of 1.

We discussed SPRs in great detail in our previous book, *Professional No-limit Hold'em: Volume 1*. Here are a few critical concepts regarding their use:

♦ Don't waste time calculating SPRs to three decimal places. "It's about 4" or "It's around 10" is all the precision you need.

♦ Top pair hands like AQo generally profit more with low SPRs below 5. It is much easier to steal if you can make top pair fold.

♦ When postflop stealing is a big part of your strategy, you prefer high SPRs that leave room for forcing top pair to fold. Usually this requires an SPR of at least 8.

♦ Small pairs and small card hands like 86s do better with high SPRs of at least 10. High SPRs are required for you to have large implied odds, and they also allow for more opportunities to steal.

♦ On dry boards like A♦6♠6♣, generally low SPRs are required to commit to medium-strength hands. Similarly, bet sizes should usually be smaller.

♦ On coordinated boards like J♠9♣8♠, you can often commit to made hands with relatively high SPRs if your opponents will get all-in with draws.

Our discussion of SPR in *Professional No-Limit Hold'em* focused on live games, which generally feature weaker and less observant opponents. For $1–$2 6-max games, we stress the following differences:

♦ Do not vary your preflop raise sizes based on your hand strength, at least not regularly against smart opponents.

♦ Raise the same regardless of which hand in your range you hold.

♦ If the effective stacks are 70bb or more, do not make SPR your primary concern with regards to opening raise size. See our chapter on "Understanding Fixed Bet Sizes" in Part 4: Beyond $1–$2 for more details.

♦ Pay more attention to SPR when making or facing a 3-bet.

♦ Sometimes online it is profitable to get all-in with top pair good kicker even with SPRs well above 5. This is because online play tends to be far more aggressive than live play.

Like implied odds and hand reading, SPR is just a tool. But mastering its use will help you make more confident and more accurate commitment decisions.

If you lead into your opponent on the flop, he might sometimes flat call instead of raising. If he sees your lead as weak, he may decide to float you. He may also flat call with some of his medium strength hands to keep the pot small. If the turn blanks, you can checkraise all-in. This takes advantage of his bluff aggression. However, he may check behind with some of his hands that want to get to showdown. In general, the more likely you think your opponent is to bet the turn, the more you should lean toward checkraising all-in on the turn. The more likely you think he is to check behind, the more you should lean toward firing another barrel on the turn.

Outlining possible betting lines can be very helpful to smart postflop play. Consider the usual pertinent information such as SPR, hand ranges, equity, tendencies, and perceptions. In situations where you are out of position with a big draw, try to plan your line such that you take advantage of fold equity, often by making the last and biggest bet.

Ace-Ten Suited In The Cutoff

Effective stacks are $200. Everyone folds to you in the cutoff, and you raise to $7 with A♦T♦. The button calls, and the blinds fold. The flop comes T♠5♥2♣. The pot is $17, you both have $193 left, and you are first to act. What should you do?

Make a plan. As usual, your plan should depend on ranges, tendencies, and stack and pot sizes. Let's take a look at different options based on different opponents.

Your opponent is loose. He plays almost 50 percent of the hands he's dealt. His range on this flop is quite wide and includes many worse hands like any ten with a worse kicker, and smaller pairs. Even with a relatively high SPR (about 11), against this opponent you can commit profitably with top pair/ top kicker. Figure out the best way to get all the money in. If he's aggressive, check to him with the plan of checkraising. If he's passive, the best plan is to simply value bet him hard. Realize that the turn will sometimes bring a scare card (any jack, queen, or king), and you may have to reassess your commitment decision or change your value betting line. But if the turn is any card less than ten, keep the pedal to the metal.

Your opponent is fairly tight and plays reasonably postflop. He will almost never get all-in on this board with a hand worse than yours. Against him, you should not be committed. That doesn't mean, however, that you can't get value out of your hand. If he's passive and will call at least one bet with a hand like a medium pocket pair, bet two-thirds of the pot, or whatever amount you might normally c-bet. Then consider checking the turn and making a value bet on the river. Assuming your opponent isn't very likely to bluff, you should probably fold if he shows aggression. For example, if he calls you on the flop and then bets the turn hard when you check, consider checkfolding the turn. Or even if he raises you on the flop, consider folding if he'll rarely raise with a worse hand. Another option for you is to check the flop and try to eke out some value on the turn and river. The bottom line is that you want to play a small pot.

Notice that a tight opponent might call a flop bet with a hand like pocket eights, but will probably fold that same hand to a turn bet, particularly if the turn is an overcard. That means a turn bet is less profitable for you. However, it should also give you ideas for how to play other hands. For example, if you had 7♦6♦ instead of A♦T♦, you might bet a queen on the turn exactly *because* you know your opponent will fold so many of his marginal hands.

Your opponent is tricky and aggressive, but smart. You might be conditionally committed against this opponent. For example, if you think he'll bluff-raise you on the flop and then continue his bluff on the turn, consider betting the flop, calling his raise, and then checkraising all-in on the turn. Or, if he'll bet worse hands if you check, consider checking then doing something goofy to try to induce a bluff, such as minraising, or raising small. You might also consider checkcalling all the way if he's the type to fire three barrels on a stone cold bluff. But keep in mind, you really need to know your opponent well to make plays like this.

Be sure to pay close attention to the tendencies of tricky opponents. Because their ranges are tougher to narrow than standard opponents', you really need to hone in on specific patterns. For example, say you know that your opponent will bet the flop often with air, but will rarely fire a second barrel. You might checkcall the flop with the plan of checkfolding the turn if he bets. Or, say your opponent will happily fire two barrels on a bluff, but almost never fire a third. You might checkcall twice with the plan of checkfolding to a big river bet.

Getting Value In Medium And Small Pots

Playing big pots is often easier than playing medium and small ones. If you've been following our advice, when you create big pots you already know whether you're committed or not. But medium and small pots, almost by definition, require more decision making. With more money left in the stacks relative to the pot, you are likely to play more postflop streets and have more decisions to make.

Playing medium and small pots well is an integral part of winning in 6-max games. In these situations, ranges tend to be wider, and hand reading is paramount.

Your goals in medium and small pots should be to gain information early, extract value from weaker hands, and control the pot to your liking. Let's take a look at a few examples. All are from 6-handed $1–$2 games with $200 effective stacks unless otherwise specified.

Checking Behind On The Turn For Pot Control

You open for $7 in the cutoff with **K♥J♥**. The button folds and an aggressive opponent calls in the small blind. The big blind folds.

The flop comes **K♦T♣5♠**. The small blind checks, and you bet $11 into the $16 pot. He calls.

The turn is the **6♠**. The small blind checks. Your opponent is wily, and a turn checkraise would put you to a tough decision. You decide to check with the intention of calling a river bet. This is a classic pot control line with top pair/medium kicker.

If you instead had middle pair, you might bet the turn. Since you have less pot equity relative to your opponent's range, a turn checkraise doesn't bother you as much. Also, calling a river bet has less value. But with top pair, checking the turn to pick off a bluff (or weak value bet) on the river is a smart play.

Betting The Turn In A Multiway Pot

Everyone folds to you on the button with **K♠8♠**. You raise to $5. You are fine with winning the blinds outright, but if called you are comfortable playing a postflop pot with position. Both blinds call.

The flop comes **K♦T♣5♠**. The 29/17 small blind leads for $10, and the big blind calls. The small blind is fairly loose, so he could have a lot of possible hands on this board. You haven't played much with the big blind, so his range is more unknown to you. However, you have top pair in a three-handed "button versus blinds" pot. Ranges tend to be wider in these situations, and you could easily have the best hand. You decide to flat call the $10. This allows you to keep the pot small for now and gain more information on the turn.

The turn is the **Q♥**. Both players check to you. Here you should bet because your opponents are likely weak. On this board you will get called by weaker hands like a pair and a straight draw, and usually only very strong hands will checkraise. It makes no sense to give both players a free card. Checking the turn and calling a river bet doesn't have good value because your opponents aren't very likely to bluff. They'll usually either have hands that are better than yours, or they'll have hands that want to see a showdown. Also, opponents generally play more straightforwardly in multiway pots. Bet about two-thirds pot and fold to a checkraise.

Overriding Pot Control

You open for $5 on the button with **T♥9♥**, and only the big blind calls. He is a loose-passive player with stats of 38/4.

The flop comes **K♦T♣5♠**. The big blind checks, and you bet $8. This bet serves the purpose of gaining information as well as getting value from weaker hands. Your opponent's response to the bet will help you narrow his range. If he checkraises, he likely has you beat, and you can safely fold. If he calls, he could have one of any number of weaker hands like a straight draw, an ace, any pocket pair, or a five.

If the turn is a blank, consider betting again. If he checkraises you there, he probably has you crushed with a slowplayed monster. You don't mind that he's putting you to a commitment decision, because you have no intention of calling.

Controlling the pot to your liking sometimes means denying your opponent the opportunity to put you to a stack decision *unless* you are confident in that decision. Here you are confident that you will fold if checkraised, so denying a free card and extracting value from weaker hands takes precedence.

Checking The Flop

You open for $7 in the hijack with **A♣2♣**. Only the 22/20 small blind calls. He is a solid regular in this game.

The flop comes **A♦9♥3♣**. The small blind checks. This is a good spot to sometimes check the flop. A free card is unlikely to hurt you, and it may even help you because your opponent could catch a pair on the turn. Or he may simply decide to look you up on the turn and/or river with a hand he would have folded on the flop.

Checking the flop works better with top pair than with second pair. You should be more inclined to bet second pair because you don't mind a checkraise as much. Also, checking the flop works better the higher your top pair is. Top pair of aces is best for this play, whereas top pair of tens isn't so great since so many overcards can come. With top pair of kings you can also check the flop. Top pair of queens is a judgment call since there are eight potential overcards.

Saving Your Value For The River

The button opens for $7, and the small blind folds. You are in the big blind with **Q♦T♦**. Folding isn't an awful plan. The button is a solid regular who plays about 25 percent of his hands and raises about 20 percent of the time. However, his opening range on the button is wider. You think he'd open about a third of his hands on the button, so routinely folding your blinds to his late position steals is not ideal. You should be able to defend yourself, particularly when your hand has decent equity against his range, as **Q♦T♦** does. Reraising him is an acceptable option, and so is calling, particularly if you feel comfortable playing a postflop pot out of position against him. You decide to call.

The flop comes **Q♣J♥6♠**, giving you top pair. The pot is $15, and you have $193 left. You are not committed to getting all-in, so you opt to take a line that keeps the pot small. You check, and your opponent bets $11. You call.

The turn is a **5♦**. You check, and the button checks behind.

The river is a **9♣**. You lead for half the pot—in part because you think your opponent will raise only with better hands but will sometimes call with worse hands like a weaker queen, a jack, and sometimes less. Most importantly, you think that you will be ahead on average when he calls. You might bet more if he viewed you as bluffy or if you thought a smaller bet might induce a raise that you don't want to face. You might check if your opponent would rarely call with a worse hand but might bet worse hands or bluff if checked to. Against standard opponents, a half pot value bet works well.

Changing Your Commitment Plan, But Still Value Betting

You raise to $7 under the gun with black kings, and only the button calls. He is a solid player with stats of 19/17. He views you as being smart and aggressive.

The flop comes **Q♦6♦4♣**. Your opponent could easily raise and get all-in on this flop with a good queen or a flush draw. So, you bet $13 into the $17 pot and plan to commit. If he calls, you will reevaluate the situation on the turn. The button calls.

The turn is the **J♦**. This is not a good card for you. It completes the flush and may have given your opponent two pair. If you get all-in here for $180 into a $43 pot, you are usually in bad shape and possibly drawing dead. You decide you are no longer committed. However, if you check, your opponent may still bet some of his worse hands. So you opt to checkcall and then reevaluate on the river. You check, and he checks behind.

The river is a **7♥**. Just like in the previous hand, you lead for half the pot because you think your opponent will raise only with better hands but will sometimes call with worse hands. (The same caveats apply.) Even though you are not committed, you can still extract value.

Eking Out Value On The River

You open for $7 in the hijack with **A♥Q♥**, and only the big blind calls. He is a predictable regular who sometimes errs on the loose and passive side. His stats are 26/12.

The flop comes **K♥8♣5♣**. The big blind checks, and you c-bet $11 into the $15 pot. He calls.

The turn is the **A♣**. Since your opponent is predictable, you decide to bet for value against worse hands, such as a pair with a club, but plan to fold if checkraised. You bet $25 into the $37 pot. He calls.

The river is a **2♥**. Your opponent checks. Do you typically check here? If so, you are losing value. Your opponent has shown weakness and knows it. If you bet another $25, he will often look you up with anything that has showdown value. These small river value bets have a tremendous effect on your bottom line. Eke out value wherever you can.

A7s From The Cutoff

You remain in a 6-handed $1–$2 game with $200 effective stacks. The first two players fold. You have **A♠7♠** in the cutoff. The 28/24 button is a tough player, and both blinds are weak. You raise to $7. The button calls, and the blinds fold. The flop comes **A♥9♣5♠**. How should you proceed?

With top pair/weak kicker and an SPR of 11 on an uncoordinated flop against a good player, you are not committed. So, usually your goal is to keep the pot small.[12] Many players understand this but apply pot control in a suboptimal way.

---

[12] Sometimes you might risk creating a big pot in order to force a better hand to fold.

Namely, they bet the flop and check the turn. Betting the flop can backfire. This opponent is capable of raising with a wide range of hands, including complete air. If he does raise your flop bet, you won't know where you stand.

You should check the flop fairly often. You keep the pot smaller right from the get-go and deny your opponent stack leverage. You encourage him to bluff, but don't allow him to threaten you with a commitment decision. Weaker hands that check behind are drawing slim, so a free card seldom benefits your opponent. And those same weaker hands may call a value bet on the turn or river because you checked the flop.

If you check the flop and he bets say, $12, you should at least call. How you proceed on the turn and river depends on which cards come and your opponent's particular level of aggression. If he's not super aggressive, you might consider checkfolding the turn. If he's aggressive but won't often three-barrel bluff, you might consider checkcalling the turn but checkfolding to a big river bet. If he's hyper-aggressive, you might occasionally consider checkcalling him all the way down, but that line should be used only if you read the opponent well.

You can also consider checkraising the flop. A checkraise essentially turns your hand into a bluff because you will almost never get called by a worse hand. But it has a few benefits:

♦ You make it hard for your opponent to bluff again.
♦ The rest of the hand becomes trivial to play, because unless you improve you're essentially done with the hand, save for maybe calling a small bet.
♦ You penalize him for betting the flop when you check, which helps you defend those times you check with weak draws and weak made hands.

Also, if your opponent will rarely fire more than one barrel, denying him a free card has more value. The downside of checkraising is that you discourage him from bluffing again with worse hands, and you lose more money against better hands. You also leave yourself vulnerable to a rebluff or a delayed bluff if your opponent is tricky and aggressive enough to try those plays.

One last thing to consider is folding preflop. While you would have ideally liked to raise and play the hand heads up with position against one of the weak blinds, you sometimes need to adjust your opening strategy when a tough player is directly to your left. If he is very aggressive and will often play back at your preflop raises from a steal position, consider tightening up a little. You might also change seats.

The Freeze Play

Effective stacks are $250. A decent 23/19 player opens for $7 in the hijack seat. The cutoff folds, and you have **A♦Q♦** on the button. Both blinds are tight, unimaginative players. The hijack's opening range is fairly wide. You might call or reraise in this spot, but this time you call. Calling keeps him in the pot with some dominated hands that might fold to a reraise.

The blinds fold, and you are heads-up in a $17 pot. The flop comes **A♠K♥9♣**. Your opponent bets $12, and you call. You decide not to raise for a couple reasons, the biggest being you don't want to shut him out if he has an ace with a weak kicker. You also will, on average, tend to profit most in this hand if the final pot is medium-sized. You don't have quite enough hand to want to get all-in against this opponent.

The turn is the **8♠**. Your opponent bets $26 into the $41 pot.

This opponent would bet the turn with a fairly wide range. He could have a stronger made hand like two pair or a set, a weaker made hand like an ace with a lower kicker, or a drawing hand like J♠T♠. What should you do?

A good option is to freeze the action by minraising to $52. The small raise has several benefits. It gets value out of worse hands. Your opponent may get confused, but will often call with hands like ace-jack or ace-ten simply because the raise is small. That ensures some value if the river is a scare card.

The raise makes drawing hands pay. While it doesn't price certain draws out, it at least charges them something. It also often reveals the opponent's draw, which helps you make a good decision on the river. For example, say he calls your minraise, and then on a 7♠ river he goes all-in. You have an easy fold against most $1–$2 players.

Another benefit to the small raise is it lets you get away cheaply when your opponent has a strong hand. If you minraise on the turn and then he reraises big, you are almost always way behind, and often drawing dead. Whereas if you call the turn and then your opponent makes a large bet on a blank river, you end up losing more money to his strong hands.

Small turn raises work best when you have a decent made hand with little chance of improving and are not sure if you are behind a strong hand, ahead against a weaker made hand, or up against a draw. With a decent made hand with several outs, like top pair and a big flush draw, you should call more often. This is because you don't want to get blown off your draw if your opponent reraises with a strong hand.

Turn minraises also work much better in position. You might occasionally use it out of position, but the showdown benefits won't be as great. When you minraise in position in $1–$2, your opponent will usually reraise the turn with strong hands, and call with draws and modest hands. If he flat calls, he will usually check the river. Much of the value in the play lies in having your opponent check to you on the river. If you instead minraise out of position, your opponent gets the final betting decision knowing you checked the river and are probably weaker than your turn raise suggested. An out-of-position turn raise may freeze him into checking behind on the river anyway, but it's riskier. For example, say you are out of position and check-minraise the turn, and he calls. If the river is a blank and you check, he might launch a big bluff with a busted draw. Or he might value bet a better hand since you checked.

You might not want to use this play against players who are predictable on the river. For example, if your opponent will rarely call a raise on the turn or bet the river with a worse hand, you are better off flat calling the turn and then folding to a river bet.

Don't use this play against players who might reraise your freeze with a worse hand. For example, if a smart, tricky player figures out what you're up to, he may go all-in over your turn raise with a big draw, hoping you'll fold. Also, if your opponent is so aggressive that he will often bet the river with his busted draws, you are better off calling the turn and then calling a bet on the river.

Finally, the freeze play doesn't have to be a minraise. The point is just to make a turn raise that freezes up worse hands and doesn't pot commit you against better ones. Whatever raise size accomplishes that is fine.

Here's another example.

Effective stacks are $400. You open for $7 in the cutoff with Q♥Q♠. Only the big blind calls.

The flop comes J♣T♣6♥. Your opponent leads for $10 into the $15 pot. You call.

The turn is the 2♠. Your opponent bets $25 into the $35 pot. You make it $60, and your opponent calls.

The river is the 8♣. Your opponent checks. Freeze accomplished, you check behind. What do you expect him to have?

Sometimes he shows a jack or weaker pair and you win. Sometimes he shows a flush. Only rarely will he show a strong non-flush hand. Overall, on average you profit from the small turn raise. If he blows you off the turn by reraising big, so be it. The vast majority of the time he does that he'll be ahead, so you can safely fold. And you didn't have enough outs to worry about drawing.

If he instead would push the turn with draws or other weaker hands, the small turn raise loses value.

An Uncommon Line With Top Pair

Mixing up your play is critical. You should play similar hands in different ways sometimes, and you should play different hands in the same way sometimes. Following this simple principle will make it much more difficult for opponents to read your hands.

Often you should play a hand in a non-standard way even if you think the normal way might, for just this hand, be more profitable. Poker is always played in context, and in no-limit the context takes on an enormous role. You want opponents to misread your hands and generally be confused by your play. Confusion ultimately causes your opponents to make big mistakes against you. If you can sow a little confusion in exchange for a few theoretical cents in equity, go right ahead.

This hand occurred in a $1–$2 6-max game. The effective stacks are $230. The cutoff opens **7♥6♥** for $7, and only the aggressive big blind calls.

The flop comes **6♦3♣2♠**, overall a good flop for the hand. The big blind checks, and instead of making the standard play of betting about $11, the cutoff checks.

The turn is the **T♠**, putting a flush draw on board. The big blind bets $5, and the cutoff raises to $15.

The big blind thinks briefly, types, "Nice aces," and folds.

From the big blind's perspective, this betting pattern is consistent with pocket aces. Since the flop is small and ragged, a player with pocket aces hoping for action might be unconcerned about giving a free card and check behind. Nevertheless, the pocket aces read was obviously bad. You want your opponents to make bad reads like this one. Perhaps it didn't help the cutoff on this particular hand, but if you play overall in a way that's difficult to decode, eventually your opponent will trip himself up.

Going back to the hand, sometimes checking behind on the flop has two tactical advantages over the standard bet. First, the big blind is aggressive, so checking behind controls the pot and makes it more likely that the pair will reach showdown. Second, checking behind may induce a bluff. The obvious downside to checking is that a free card could beat you. It's a tradeoff.

The turn raise in this hand is designed to do three things:

1. It freezes the betting and helps get the pair to showdown. If the big blind puts in more action after this raise, the cutoff can put him on a stronger range and fold. If the big blind folds or calls and checks the river, then the cutoff can show the hand down.
2. It punishes the big blind if he's semibluffing a flush draw or gutshot.
3. It might induce a slightly better hand to fold. For instance, if the big blind has **9♣6♣**, he may lay it down to the raise.

You shouldn't play a weak top pair like this every time, but it has some advantages over a flop bet. It works particularly well against aggressive foes. Try it out.

An Overpair Value Bet

Effective stacks are $140. Our Hero opens the pot for $7 from the second seat with **K♥K♠**. Both blinds call, so it's three players to the flop and there's $21 in the pot.

The flop comes **8♣8♠3♥**, giving Hero an overpair with position on a dry, drawless board. The 25/9 small blind bets $12, a little over half the pot. The big blind folds. Hero calls.

The turn is the **8♥**, and the small blind bets $20, which is now less than half of the $45 pot. Hero calls again.

The river is the **Q♥**. The small blind checks, and Hero bets the pot, $85. The small blind thinks and then calls, showing **6♦6♠**. Pocket kings are good.

When you have an overpair on a paired dry flop with no straight or flush draws, you are in a classic way ahead or way behind situation. Either your opponent has trips or a full house and you are drawing to two outs, or you have him crushed and he's drawing to six outs or less.

In way ahead or way behind situations, you should often dial your aggression way down and make small bets or allow your opponent to control the betting. If you are way behind, then you'll be happy you didn't put in extra action. And if you are way ahead, then you don't want to give your opponent an easy fold.

For instance, if Hero had instead made a nice-sized raise on the flop, perhaps to $48, many players would immediately fold their sixes, assuming that only a bigger pocket pair or trips would make that raise. By flat calling the flop, Hero kept his range wide in his opponent's mind. The small blind can hope that his opponent had two big unpaired cards.

Furthermore, since if Hero is ahead, he is way ahead, his opponent will seldom draw out on him. There is no urgency to get the money in. There are two more betting rounds, and Hero has position so he always has an option to bet.

After the turn, Hero's way ahead or way behind status is cemented, and he's a big favorite to be way ahead. The **8♥** is a good card for pocket kings in two ways:

1. In the unlikely event the small blind has pocket threes, the kings have now drawn out.
2. The appearance of a third eight makes it less likely that the small blind holds one.

Hero flat calls the weak turn bet for the same reasons he called the flop. He has another round to get value for his hand, and he wants to keep his range as wide as possible in his opponent's mind. Don't give your opponents a cheap signal to fold weaker hands if you can avoid it.

After the small blind checks the river **Q♥**, it's time for Hero to spring to life. Given the two weak leads on the flop and turn, there's a good chance the small blind has a smaller pocket pair. Hero should bet an amount that is reasonably likely to get called by smaller pairs. Against very loose players, that could be an all-in push. Against tight players, a half-pot bet might be better.

Some players are less willing to call value bets, especially with a marginal hand like a pocket pair smaller than top pair, if the call will bust them. Sometimes leaving your opponent a little bit left after the call will increase your chances of getting the call.

The river value bet is the key decision in the hand. Checking these kings down would be terrible against most opponents. You are a big favorite to be ahead on the river, and weaker hands will often call, so don't be shy about betting for value.

Lessons for this hand:

- ♦ When you're way ahead or way behind, consider allowing your opponent to push the betting.
- ♦ The turn card making trips added value to the big overpair by increasing the chance it was ahead.
- ♦ Even though it's not a lock, a bold river value bet in this situation offers the highest long-term expectation.

A Top Pair Value Bet

You're playing a $1–$2 game with $200 stacks. You open on the button with **K♥9♥**, making it $6 to go. Only the big blind, a somewhat passive, unremarkable 24/14 player, calls. You think the table views you as a bit aggressive.

The flop comes **K♦8♠4♣**, giving you top pair on a ragged board. Your opponent checks, you bet $11, and he calls. The turn is the **3♥**. Your opponent checks, and you check. The river is the **6♥**. Your opponent again checks.

You should bet for value. Consider your opponent's range. Preflop, you opened on the button and he called out of the blind. His range is fairly wide calling from the big blind against a possible button steal.

On the flop your opponent checked, and you made a continuation bet. His call is somewhat more telling. The board is dry, so it's likely he has a made hand of some sort and not a draw. He probably knows you c-bet with made hands and air, so he might call with weak hands like an eight, a four, a small pocket pair, or even ace-high. Other possibilities are a king or better, though he may have checkraised with a strong hand.

On the turn a blank comes, and you check behind. Since the board is still relatively draw-free, if you're ahead, your opponent likely has at most five outs, so checking will rarely cost you the pot. This check keeps the pot small and gets your opponent to the river with his entire weak flop-calling range. Many of the hands in his flop-calling range are strong enough for him to call a modest river bet, but too weak to call a turn bet with the looming threat of another bet on the river.

After your opponent checks a blank river, you have the all-clear to bet for value. You have top pair with a decent kicker, and your opponent still has the wide range of hands he'd call with on the flop. Further, you can discount the stronger hands in that range due to his turn and river checks. If, for instance, he had flopped a set or top two, he may have checkcalled the flop and checked the turn. But after your turn check, most players would bet the river at least some of the time. His river check suggests that he has a weak made hand. Your hand is a favorite against his river bet calling range.

How much should you bet? The pot is $35. If you bet the pot, you'll find your opponent folding many hands you'd like him to call with. Try a bet of around half the pot, perhaps $20. You lose less those odd times you find yourself beaten, and you'll encourage a wider range of hands you beat to call.

Against a loose player, you might consider a different line. Instead of checking the turn, try betting around $20 and following up with a $20 to $40 bet on the river. To play for three bets, you would want him to be loose enough to call down with hands like **K♣5♣**, **9♠9♦**, and **A♦8♣**.

Out of Position On The River

When you're playing a big pot out of position, river scare cards can pose a major problem. They tempt you to check, but before you do, stop and consider your options. Sometimes you should bet anyway.

For instance, say your opponent has the smaller stack at $125. You open for $7 from two off the button with **A♥A♦**. Only the button calls. The flop comes **T♥6♥6♣**. You bet $15 and the button calls. The pot is now $47. The turn is the **9♣**.

You bet $40, and your opponent calls. Now the pot is $127. The river is the **8♦**, making the final board **T♥6♥6♣9♣8♦**. Your opponent has $63 remaining, just over half the pot.

The river card put a four-straight on board. On top of that, you could be behind to trip sixes or a full house. But before you check in fear, consider your opponent's tendencies. Depending on how your opponent plays, going all-in, checkcalling, and checkfolding can each be the best play.

If your opponent is aggressive and loves to bluff scare cards, then the natural inclination to check and call can be the right play. He could hold a busted heart draw or a small pocket pair and be unable to resist betting. Some bluffy players end up firing away in this situation with unusual holdings like **Q♦9♦**.

Checkcalling a bluffy player works best if he would bet many hands worse than yours after a check that he would otherwise fold to a bet. For instance, if you bet this river all-in, your betting pattern will look quite strong. You raised preflop and then bet big at every opportunity despite the scare card. Your opponent with a hand like **Q♦9♦** might grudgingly fold. Checking and calling works well against an opponent who will attack your show of weakness.

If your opponent is timid and passive, checking and folding can be the best play despite the fact that half the money is already in the middle. A timid player may fold to a bet on this scary board without trips or better. And a timid player might bet this river only with a straight or better. Since he'll rarely call you with a weaker hand and rarely bet a hand you can beat, you cannot profit by betting, and you cannot profit by calling. So, you should check and fold.

If your opponent is loose, suspicious of you, or generally bad, then pushing all-in can be your best play. Sure, he'll sometimes have a straight or a full house. But if he's the sort of player who will also call with hands like **K♦T♠**, **T♦9♦**, or possibly even **2♥2♣**, then going all-in captures these loose calls and becomes superior to checking.

Overall, the river scare card shifts value from you to your opponent, and position allows him to take advantage of this shift. He can fold his weak hands to your all-in, or check them behind if you check.

Loose or suspicious opponents fail to take advantage of this shift. They call your bets with too wide a range. Timid players also fail to take advantage by checking behind with too many hands. Against a strong player, often you just have to take your lumps. With $127 in the pot and $63 behind, you'll be getting 3–to–1 on a river call. If you check and your opponent bets weaker hands than yours a fourth of the time or more, you must call due to pot odds. He makes money on the bet, but your call is correct.[13]

Oddly, sometimes you should still push all-in against strong opponents. This is a defensive bet. It works when you expect calls from a fair number of second-best hands that your opponent would otherwise check behind. For example, say your opponent is savvy enough that if you check, he will value bet with trips, straights, and full houses and bluff about a fourth of the time with air, an eight, or a pocket underpair. He will check behind with a ten or nine, because he knows you must call with anything that beats those hands. If he will call with most of those tens and nines, and those calls outnumber his bluffing

---

[13] More specifically, he makes money if he bluffs less than half the time.

hands, pushing captures more value than checking.[14]

Here's another example of a river scare card in a big pot. Hero has $294. His adversary, an extremely loose and poor player with 65/35 stats, has him covered. He is playing haphazardly postflop. He's been lucky so far and run up a huge stack.

The poor player opens for $7 on the button. Hero reraises from the big blind to $22 with T♣T♠, and the button calls.

The flop comes 9♠6♣4♦. Hero bets $30, and the button calls.

The turn is the 6♥. Hero bets $70, and the button calls.

The river is the J♥. Hero shoves for $172, and the button calls with 8♣8♥.

After flopping an overpair and surviving the middle card pairing on the turn without getting raised, Hero can expect his overpair to be well ahead of this terrible player's range. The river jack is a scare card but only a minor one, as there is no

---

[14] This player's river betting strategy is excellent against skilled opponents. Use it when you have position in a big pot on the river and it is checked to you. Once the pot becomes bigger than the remaining stacks, the dead money forces smart opponents to call all-ins with a much wider range. You should bet all hands that expect to beat this widened calling range. Many $1–$2 players fail to bet enough hands for value against strong opposition in such circumstances.

You should also bluff with the right proportion of hands. Many $1–$2 players don't bluff enough in big pots with position against strong opponents. For example, here a river all-in offers about 3–to–1, so you should bluff about a fourth of the time or a little less. (People tend to overestimate how often opponents bluff, so it's usually better to bluff a bit less frequently than game theory suggests.) Bluff with your weakest hands, and check the medium strength ones. Again, we're talking about betting into skilled opposition in big pots here. If your opponent doesn't know enough to call more often when the pot is big, don't widen your range of betting hands. And if the pot is not big, sometimes medium hands like those tens deserve a pot-sized or larger bet, not for value but to force better hands to fold.

particular reason to believe the button has a jack. Since this opponent is wild and erratic, he could easily call a large river bet with a worse hand.

Bad players like this make some terrible river calls. Don't give them more credit than they deserve. When out of position and on the fence about value betting such an opponent, just stick the money in. And don't forget to mark the name so you can find him later.

When a Bad River Card Should Not Affect Your Commitment Plan

Stacks are $200 in this 6-handed $1–$2 game. You raise to $7 under the gun with K♠K♣. A loose player calls on the button, and everyone else folds. This opponent has been at the table for an hour and has played 70 percent of his hands. He has made several weak calls postflop.

The flop comes J♥T♦5♣. The pot is $17, and the remaining stacks are $193. You are first to act. What is your plan?

Commit. Your opponent's range is extremely wide, and he is likely to pay you off with a weak hand. Your plan should be to value bet hard and try to get all-in.

You bet $15, and your opponent calls.

The turn is the 4♥. You bet $45, and your opponent calls.

The river is the 9♥, which makes a straight and flush possible. Should the bad river card affect your commitment plan?

No. You have less than a pot-sized bet left, and your

opponent's range still includes many weak hands. Furthermore, if you checked, you would probably call his all-in. Since you don't plan on folding, you should bet the rest of the money yourself. That way you don't allow your loose opponent to check behind with weak calling hands.

The river was not a pleasant card. Your opponent may have outdrawn you by making a straight, flush, or two pair. Nevertheless, the situation calls for you to stay committed and bet the rest of your chips.

When a Bad River Card Should Affect Your Commitment Plan

Stacks remain $200. You raise to $7 under the gun with **K♠K♣**. A decent and moderately aggressive regular calls on the button, and everyone else folds. Your opponent plays about 25 percent of his starting hands, and he plays well postflop. He views you as being capable and aggressive.

The flop comes **J♥T♦5♣**. The pot is $17, and the remaining stacks are $193. You are first to act. What is your plan?

You likely have the best hand, so betting for value makes sense. Further, if you get raised, you don't mind getting all-in against this opponent. He knows your preflop range is wider than just premium hands, and he knows you'd often c-bet the flop. If he flopped top pair, he probably feels confident about his hand. He could also call or raise with overcards, straight draws, underpairs, or air. Your plan is to bet with the intention of being committed.

You bet $15, and your opponent calls.

The turn is the **8♥**. This adds flush and straights draws and may have completed a straight. Nevertheless, you remain committed. You bet $45, and your opponent calls.

The river is the **9♥**, which completes a possible flush and puts a one-card straight on the board. Should this bad river card affect your commitment plan?

Yes, here it should. Even though you only have about a pot-sized bet left, your opponent will probably fold any worse hand, including a jack, to an all-in. Betting yields no value. And betting as a bluff doesn't make sense because your opponent will only rarely fold a better hand. Checking to pick off a bluff isn't wise because your opponent's range doesn't include many hands that would call a turn bet and then need to bluff on this river. Every draw made it. If you check and your opponent shoves, you are very likely behind. Your plan should be to check and fold to any decent-sized bet.

You don't fold the river because the board got scary. You fold because it is the best play given your opponent's likely range. A bad river card should not necessarily change your commitment decision. When one falls, reconsider your opponent's range and your equity against that range. Sometimes you should still bet for value, and sometimes you should checkfold.

Value Betting The River

Stacks are $200. You open for $7 on the button with **A♥4♥**. The small blind folds, and the big blind calls. He is a loose-passive player who plays about 35 percent of his hands.

The flop comes **Q♦6♦5♠**. The big blind checks, and you c-bet $9 into the $15 pot. He calls.

The turn is the **8♠**. Your opponent checks. While he may be weak, a turn bet will get called too often to be profitable. You check behind.

The river is the **7♠**. Your opponent checks. Even though there is a flush out and you only have the bottom end of the straight, it's a clear value bet. Your opponent may have called your flop bet with a queen. He may have been planning a turn checkraise with a set. He might have a busted straight draw that backed into a pair or two pair. He is loose, he can have many worse hands, and he will call a value bet with a lot of them. Checking behind here leaves money on the table. Since the pot is still a fairly small $48, you can probably bet around $40 and expect to get called by many worse hands.

When you have position, your opponent's actions on the turn and river will often tell you whether to value bet.

For example, say you open for $7 on the button with **A♥4♥** in the same game as above. Only the big blind calls, but this time he is a solid 21/18 regular. He views you as solid and tricky.

The flop comes **7♥3♥3♦**. The big blind checks, and you c-bet $11 into the $15 pot. He calls.

The turn is the **2♠**. Your opponent checks. This time you think a turn bet is profitable because he will fold several hands and is unlikely to have you crushed. Also, if he checkraises, you aren't too concerned because it usually means he has a big hand. Your draw isn't worth as much with the pair on board. You bet $40, a slight overbet, into the $37 pot. He calls.

The river is the **A♠**, and your opponent checks again. You missed your flush, but you paired the ace, albeit with a weak kicker. Many players check behind here. But this is a profitable spot to value bet.

Your opponent is more likely to call with a hand weaker than your aces than he is to have a strong hand. His checkcall on the turn often indicates an attempt to take a stand with a seven or medium pair. The ace on the river is a scare card, but your opponent knows that *you know* it's a scare card, and he may take a stand again.

The pot is $117, and you both have $142 left. This is a good spot to balance your overbet river bluffs by occasionally overbetting as a thin value bet. Stick it in. Keep him guessing.

River Value Bet On A Double-Paired Board

Effective stacks are $200. Everyone folds to the button who makes it $8 to go with **J♥9♥**. Only the big blind calls.

The flop is **A♥Q♦J♣**. The big blind checks, and the button bets $12 into the $17 pot. The blind calls.

The turn is the **Q♣**. The big blind checks, and the button checks.

The river is the **J♦**. The big blind checks again, and the button bets $24 into the $41 pot. Is this a good play?

Once the big blind calls the flop continuation bet, he is unlikely to have small cards. He probably caught a piece of the flop. The board gets worse for the button on the turn when the queen pairs, so he checks behind.

On the river the button catches another jack, and the big blind checks again. This is a terrific situation for a value bet. If the big blind held a queen, he usually wouldn't check the turn and river. It's much more likely that the big blind holds an ace than a queen, and many players would call a modest bet on the river here with any ace. So the button has a solid value bet for half the pot or a little more. Checking is a significant mistake.

Minraising The River

This time effective stacks are $400. The big blind is a very loose, passive player with stats of 65/4.

You open from the cutoff for $7 with **6♣6♦**. The big blind calls.

The flop comes **A♥9♣6♠**, giving you bottom set. The big blind checks, and you bet $11 into the $15 pot. He calls.

The turn is the **2♣**. Your opponent checks, and you bet $35 into the $37 pot. He calls.

The river is the **J♣**, putting a possible flush on the board. The pot is $107, and you have $347 left. Your opponent leads out for $35. What should you do?

This is a great spot for a small raise. While your opponent could have a backdoor flush, he is more likely to have an ace or two pair. His small river bet appears weak.

The beauty of minraising here is that your opponent will likely reraise only with the flush but will call with most of the hands in his range. In addition, there is plenty of money left behind such that a minraise doesn't pot stick you into calling an all-in. This makes the small raise far superior to a call.

Minraising the river is a great play when:

♦ You don't have the nuts.
♦ You have a hand that you think is best.
♦ You think your opponent will call a minraise but fold to a bigger raise.
♦ You don't think your opponent will bluff reraise you.
♦ The stack sizes are such that a minraise doesn't commit you.

River Overbet For Value

Stacks are $200. Everyone folds to you on the button. The blinds both are regulars. They each play about 20 percent of their hands and 3-bet about 5 percent of the time. Neither is overly aggressive or tricky.

You should be stealing their blinds often and laying as small a price as you can get away with to do it. You open for $5 with **Q♥8♥**. The small blind calls, and the big blind folds.

The flop comes **A♥T♣4♥**, giving you the second nut flush draw. The small blind checks, and you bet $9 into the $12 pot. He calls.

The turn is the **9♥**, completing your flush. Your opponent checks, and you bet $30 into the $30 pot. He calls.

The river is a **J♠**, and the small blind checks. He has $156 left, and the pot is $90. How much should you bet?

Many players make a standard two-thirds pot value bet. However, an all-in overbet is usually better.

Your opponent checkcalled twice, including on the turn when a flush was completed. He probably has a fairly strong hand. Also, the river was a good card for you because it could have improved his hand. Your opponent's range includes hands like AxJ♥, K♥Qx, AT, A9, A4, TT, and 44. He might have been planning a checkraise somewhere and then decided against it, or he might have been planning to checkcall all the way. It doesn't matter. Shove it in and let him decide what to do.

In order for a bet of, say, $75 to be as profitable as a $156 all-in, your opponent has to call $75 about *twice* as often as he would $156.[15] Needless to say, that will hardly ever be the case.

Remember to occasionally shove as a bluff in river situations like this. That way, your opponent will either fold winning hands or look you up more often than he'd like.

---

[15] We're assuming a smaller bet wouldn't entice a bluff-raise. You will get all-in anyway if he has the nut flush, so that situation does not matter.

3-Betting Light and the 3-Bet, 4-Bet, 5-Bet Game

You can play for hours in some live no-limit games and never once see someone 3-bet preflop. Online 6-max games couldn't be more different—3-betting plays a large role in many players' strategies.

In general, you 3-bet preflop for three reasons:

1. To get value for excellent hands.
2. To resteal preflop from players who are opening with wide ranges of hands.
3. To take the momentum so you can steal postflop.

In other words, sometimes you 3-bet for value, and sometimes you 3-bet as a bluff or semibluff. The more often your opponents open with weak hands, the more often you should 3-bet. When you increase your 3-betting frequency, you should do so both with strong hands and weak ones.

For example, say against a tight open raiser you 3-bet with JJ+ and AK and occasionally with weak hands as a bluff. Against a looser open raiser, you should bluff more often to resteal, but you should also widen your value 3-betting range to perhaps 99+ and AQ+. Increasing your bluffing frequency without also increasing your value raising frequency unbalances your range and leaves you vulnerable to a rebluff. Don't let your ranges get unbalanced.

When you increase your bluffing range, you should also increase your value betting range to keep your overall range balanced.

You should 4-bet over a 3-bet for the same two reasons: for value and as a bluff. The wider your opponent's 3-betting range, the more hands you should 4-bet. Again, when you increase your bluffing frequency you should also add more hands that you 4-bet for value.

The same logic applies to 5-betting over an opponent's 4-bet.

This, in a nutshell, is the 3-bet, 4-bet, 5-bet game. The wider your opponent's raising range, the wider you should 3-bet. The wider your opponent's 3-betting range, the wider you should 4-bet. And the wider your opponent's 4-betting range, the wider you should 5-bet. The game typically concludes with a 5-bet because that bet will usually put a 100bb stack all-in.

A Typical 5-Bet Situation

This is how a typical 5-bet pot plays out.

It's a $1–$2 6-max game. Everyone has a $200 stack. The first two players fold, and the cutoff opens for $7. The button folds, and the small blind 3-bets to $24. The cutoff then 4-bets to $56. Finally, the small blind pushes all-in for $200.

Notice the somewhat small size of the 4-bet. The open raise and the 3-bet are both roughly pot-sized. But the 4-bet is just a bit more than a minraise—a $32 raise into a $50 pot. This 4-bet size stems from a simple no-limit bet sizing rule: If making a bet or raise would commit you to calling a shove because of the pot odds, generally you should either make a smaller bet that doesn't commit you or shove all-in yourself.

If your 4-bet is pot-sized or more, often you are committed to calling a shove even with your bluffing hands. For instance, if you were to make a pot-sized 4-bet to $74, and your opponent shoved, you would be calling $126 to win $274, offering pot odds of over 2–to–1. These pot odds are enough to justify (or at least come close to justifying) a call with a hand as weak as 97s.

In general, there's no need to raise so much on a 4-bet. Raising to $56 or so forces your opponent either to commit or to fold, so it is nearly as effective as a larger 4-bet, and it risks significantly less money.

The 5-bet should typically be a shove. There's no way to 5-bet without committing yourself to calling a shove, so whenever you 5-bet you should just move all-in yourself.

These are the basics of playing the 3-bet, 4-bet, 5-bet game. Now let's talk about why you might engage in this game.

Why 3-Bet?

With premium hands, 3-betting preflop typically increases profitability. If you 3-bet with pocket aces, for instance, you tend to get more value. You significantly increase the chances that you'll stack an opponent holding top pair or a draw. You also ensure that you win at least a medium-sized pot when your opponent misses the flop.

The benefits of 3-betting premium hands can easily be explained. These hands have more showdown equity than a typical calling hand, so they profit from every dollar that enters the pot preflop. Furthermore, after a 3-bet the pot will be relatively large compared to the remaining stacks, typically creating an SPR of 4 or less. Premium hands tend to make top pairs and overpairs, and these hands play well with low SPRs.

So you'd like to 3-bet your premium hands to make them more profitable, but there's a potential pitfall. If you 3-bet *only* your premium hands and nothing else, you telegraph your hand and allow your opponents (the ones who aren't living under rocks at least) to avoid your strength. This is where the light 3-bet comes in.

The Light 3-Bet

A light 3-bet is any 3-bet made with a hand that normally wouldn't be strong enough. It's a type of semibluff. You raise with the hope of stealing the pot immediately, but you retain a chance, if called, to win after the flop. Any strategy that includes 3-betting for value should also include some light 3-betting.

Potentially, any time the pot is raised and the action is on you, you could 3-bet light. Obviously you want to pick your spots, as 3-betting every time would unbalance your strategy.

When choosing your spots, follow these principles:

Attack Players With A High Fold To 3-Bet Percentage

Modern poker tracking software maintains a stat called "Fold To 3-Bet Percentage." This stat measures how frequently a player folds when confronted with a 3-bet.

If your opponent's Fold To 3-Bet Percentage (FT3B) is sufficiently high, 3-betting them with any two cards when they open raise can show an automatic profit. Even if they don't fold quite often enough to show an automatic profit by 3-betting, you can still frequently attack their raises with light 3-bets. Players with FT3B stats of 75 or higher are particularly vulnerable to attack.

Attack Players Raising From A Steal Position

A light 3-bet will succeed more often against a player opening from a steal position than one opening from up front. This tends to be particularly true against raisers with a high Attempt To Steal (ATS) Percentage. ATS measures how frequently a player opens the pot from the cutoff, button, or small blind when everyone in front folds. For example, everyone folds to the button who opens for $7. He has an ATS of 45, a relatively high number for this stat. You can 3-bet this player liberally from either the small or the big blind.

An ATS above 35 indicates a loose raising range, while an ATS below 25 indicates a tighter player.

Attack Players Who Tend To Call Rather Than 4-Bet

Most players will try to defend themselves if they think one of their opponents is 3-betting light against them. Some players defend mainly by calling the 3-bet and seeing a flop, while others use a light 4-betting strategy. Both of these options are exploitable if executed poorly, but the players who tend to call and see a flop are typically more exploitable.

Callers are weaker because their opponent always gets to see a flop, and most players who call adhere too closely to a fit-or-fold strategy postflop. For instance, such a player might open from the hijack seat with pocket threes and get 3-bet on the button. They'll call, planning to commit if they flop a set but fold if they don't.

This strategy is a mathematical disaster. The player with the threes will flop a set or better roughly 12 percent of the time. The other 88 percent of the time, they will lose their $17 preflop call of the 3-bet. To make this strategy break even, the player with the threes would have to *average* a win of at least $125 each time they make a set.

Unfortunately, the player with the threes won't come close to averaging $125. Most of the time that he shoves on the flop, the 3-bettor will fold. After all, he 3-bets light, and therefore he often won't have a strong enough hand postflop to commit. So most of the time the set doesn't get paid off. Overall, you expect to lose several dollars every time you call that $17 3-bet with a pocket pair then play fit-or-fold postflop. Indeed, even if you improve the strategy by throwing in a few postflop bluffs, playing fit-or-fold in 3-bet pots is so bad to begin with that you can't really make it profitable.

Calling light 3-bets with big cards and suited connectors can work better, but fit-or-fold still doesn't work. You have to bluff aggressively postflop to call a 3-bet profitably with any non-premium hand. Since most players who call to defend against your light 3-bets won't play nearly aggressively enough postflop, you can exploit them by pouring on the raw aggression. Against these fit-or-folders, bet the flop frequently and, if called, follow it up with a generous number of turn barrels. They'll fold too often to make their strategy profitable.

If you identify a player who calls 3-bets frequently and plays fit-or-fold postflop, you should 3-bet them light over and over again. The more you 3-bet them, the more money you make, at least until they adjust.

Attack More Frequently When Callers Have Entered The Pot

Light 3-betting is often more attractive when one or more players have called the original raise. These callers rarely end up calling your 3-bet. After all, if they held a hand strong enough to play a 3-bet pot, they would frequently have 3-bet themselves. Launching a 3-bet in a pot with one or more callers is called a squeeze play or squeezing.

The benefits of squeezing are obvious—you win a significantly bigger pot when successful. The pitfall is that you will succeed less often. Also, good players are naturally suspicious of 3-bets made in squeezing situations, and that suspicion may encourage them to play back at you.

But overall, squeezing tends to be quite profitable. You should be squeezing a significant minority of the time you're presented the opportunity to do so.

Examples Of Light 3-Bets

All examples take place in a $1–$2 6-max game with $200 stacks.

Example 1. Everyone folds to the player in the cutoff who raises to $7. This player is playing a 22/19 game over several thousand hands. His Fold To 3-Bet stat is 88 percent. His Attempt To Steal is 33 percent.

The button and small blind both fold. You're in the big blind.

You should 3-bet very liberally in this situation. With a Fold To 3-Bet stat of 88 percent after thousands of hands, your opponent will fold often enough for you to show an automatic profit with any two cards. Feel free to 3-bet here with 72 offsuit.

Just try not to be too obvious about it lest he catch on and adjust. Even then, most players like this one who adjust do so poorly because they aren't used to playing 3-bet pots. So, for instance, he might start calling your 3-bets with weak hands and playing fit-or-fold postflop. If he does that, you can keep on 3-betting light.

Example 2. The under the gun player opens for $7. He plays a 17/13 game. His FT3B is 77 percent, and his ATS is 28.

Everyone folds to you in the small blind. You have **8♣6♣**.

Typically you should fold in this situation. Your opponent frequently folds to a 3-bet, but overall he's a tight player, and he's opening here from under the gun. So you can expect him to fold far less often than 77 percent of the time in this situation. In general, don't 3-bet very often against tight players opening from under the gun, even if their Fold To 3-Bet stat looks attackable.

But go ahead and try it occasionally. You would 3-bet premium hands for value in this situation, and therefore, in order to keep your range properly balanced, you should also 3-bet light every once in a while. Still, fold most of the time.

Example 3. The cutoff opens for $7. He plays a 27/11 style with an Aggression Factor of 0.5. His FT3B is 35 percent, and his ATS is 24.

You're on the button with **K♦7♦**.

You can 3-bet frequently in this situation. Why? Because a wet noodle like this opponent, while he rarely folds to 3-bets, is very likely to call and then play fit-or-fold postflop. His passive preflop and postflop stats indicate he rarely 4-bets and does not often bluff postflop. If he's not folding to 3-bets, and he's also not 4-betting or bluffing postflop, then he's probably calling and then playing fit-or-fold. (The other alternative is that he takes weak hands to showdown often. This tendency is just as exploitable, so 3-betting preflop is still a strong play.)

A light 3-bet against this player is an isolation play. You're trying to get heads-up with position against a player who will make significant mistakes after the flop. As a result, choose situations where you have position and where your hand has some value. If you're out of position in the blinds, you won't have as much postflop edge. And if your hand is trash, you'll typically be forced to abandon too many pots. So against this opponent, K7s from the button is a 3-bet, but T6o from the small blind is a straightforward fold. (As an aside, you don't want to make this play if stacks are significantly shorter than 100bb. You won't have enough maneuvering room to gain from your postflop edge.)

Example 4. A 39/26 player opens for $7 from under the gun. His FT3B is 72 percent, and his ATS is 46. A 21/12 player calls in the cutoff. His FT3B is 77 percent, and his ATS is 28.

You're on the button with **A♣4♠**.

This squeezing situation is fairly juicy, and you should strongly consider 3-betting to about $28 or so. The opening player is under the gun, but he's very loose, and he also likes to fold frequently when 3-bet. The caller is weak and will often have a small pair or a marginal suited hand.

If the blinds and the original raiser all fold, you're likely to be in an excellent situation no matter what the caller does. If the caller folds, great. If he calls, he probably has a hand like a small pair that will play poorly in this 3-bet pot as long as you keep betting. He's quite unlikely to 4-bet.

Defending Against 3-Bets

You aren't the only player who will be 3-betting. All of your decent-playing opponents will 3-bet at least sometimes, and some of them will try it quite often. Here's how you can defend yourself.

For the sake of the following discussion, let's assume that you're playing $1–$2 6-max with $200 stacks, and you have just opened from the cutoff for $7. The button and small blind both have folded, and the big blind has 3-bet to $22.

No Fit-Or-Fold

You cannot profitably call for implied odds alone. Fit-or-fold doesn't work against a 3-bet. If you call with a small pocket pair or suited connector with the plan of folding unless you hit a big hand (two pair or better or a good draw), you have no chance. You are putting in too much stack, and the SPR is too low. So, before you call, consider how likely you are to win the hand with less than two pair. If the answer is "rarely," then you should fold regardless of what you have.

We're beating this point to death because it's probably the most important 3-bet pot concept. Playing fit-or-fold against a 3-bet is both a common and an extremely expensive mistake. Don't do it.

So fit-or-fold is out. Let's take a look at what strategies are profitable depending on your opponent and cards.

Against A Tight Opponent

Say your opponent has a very tight 3-betting range. Even against a possible button steal, he reraises only with AA-TT, AK, and sometimes AQ. The solution to combating this type of opponent is simple. Fold.

Don't try to set mine. Don't talk yourself into a call with AJs. Just fold everything except premium hands.

The only exception is *maybe* if you have a dead read on a specific tendency he has that would enable you to steal the pot. For example, if he'll almost always checkfold to a flop bet with less than top pair or an overpair, it can be profitable to occasionally call and steal on the flop. But his range is so tight that any plan to steal can only be marginally profitable.

For the most part, just fold all but the best hands when this opponent 3-bets.

Against A Loose Opponent

Say your opponent is an aggressive player who 3-bets a wide range against a possible steal. If you open from the button or cutoff, he reraises with

22+, A2s+, KTs+, QTs+
JTs-54s
ATo+, KQo

This is about 18 percent of his starting hands. If called, he c-bets two-thirds of the pot on any flop.

Once again, you cannot profitably call his 3-bet for implied odds alone. Most of the time you hit a big hand, he won't have anything. If you lose the pot every time you have less than two pair, he will rob you blind.

However, your opponent's strategy is highly exploitable. By putting in 11bb out of 100bb preflop with almost 18 percent of his hands, he is too frequently creating big pots with a weak range. In addition, he is often putting in another 16bb on the flop for a total of 27bb with that same weak range. You can combat him in several ways.

The All-In 4-Bet

One way to exploit your opponent's loose 3-bet range is to 4-bet him more frequently. The important consideration here is how he adjusts his range to a 4-bet.

For example, if he 3-bets with about 18 percent of his hands, but calls a subsequent all-in with only AA-TT and AK, you can profitably 4-bet push with a wide range of hands.

Say you have ace-queen with $200 stacks and raise to $7 on the button. Your opponent 3-bets to $22. If you simply push all-in, your line yields about $5.20 in average equity for you and –$4.20 for your opponent.[16]

The weaker your hand, the less equity you have with a 4-bet push. A push with pocket fives yields about $3 for you and –$2 for your opponent. Six-five suited yields about $0.60 for you and $0.40 for your opponent. However, even with the lowly 32o, a push yields about –$5.40 in equity for you. That's better than folding to his 3-bet, which is worth –$7.

The conclusion is that if your opponent 3-bets really loosely but tightens up a lot to a push, you can profitably 4-bet all-

---

[16] We derived these numbers by running simulations on the program Pokerazor.

in with a wide range of hands. But before you start liberally opening with 32o and pushing all-in, keep one thing in mind. Your opponent can (and probably will) adjust to your constant pushing. He may start calling you lighter, or he may tighten up his 3-bet range. As he adjusts, you should also.

The Small 4-Bet

You can also 4-bet an amount less than all-in. If your opponent will fold the same range of hands to a smaller 4-bet that he will to a push, you have great incentive to 4-bet smaller.

For example, you open for $7 with **6♥5♥**, and your opponent makes it $22, which he does with about 18 percent of his hands. If you 4-bet to $56, he will call or push with TT+ and AK and fold everything else. Now your best play is to make it $56 with the plan of folding to a push. Taking that line with **6♥5♥** yields about $5.40 in equity for you and –$3.40 for your opponent. That's much better than the $0.60 you'd yield from 4-bet pushing with **6♥5♥**.

When you 4-bet with the plan of folding to an all-in, your cards are meaningless. You are purely bluffing. And with 100bb stacks, as in the example above, you are often bluffing for a third of the effective stack. Therefore, you should not make this play unless you have a solid read on your opponent's 3- and 4-bet tendencies, and you are confident you won't make a mistake. Incorrectly folding in a pot of that size is a significant mistake.

One suggestion when 4-betting small is to do it with excellent hands and suspect hands, but not with pretty good hands. If you 4-bet small with **A♥A♦** or **7♠4♠**, you have a pretty clear decision if your opponent pushes. But if you do it with **A♣Q♥**, you run the risk of making a big mistake. For example, if your opponent pushes with **A♠J♠**, you might incorrectly fold.

The Flat Call

Another way to exploit your loose-aggressive opponent is to flat call preflop with strong hands. This takes advantage of his loose 3-betting by keeping him in the pot with a weak range. It also takes advantage of his flop aggression. When he c-bets the flop with hands he'd otherwise fold to a preflop 4-bet, you not only gain the money from his bet, but you also may pot commit him. Remember, once he 3-bets preflop and c-bets the flop, he's already put in about a third of his stack.

For example, say you open for $7 on the button with pocket aces, and your opponent 3-bets to $22. His 3-betting range is the same 18 percent from above, and he folds to a 4-bet unless he has TT+ and AK. If you call the 3-bet, he c-bets every flop and plays fit-or-fold after that, meaning if you raise the flop or fire on the turn, he only continues on with top pair or better, a decent flush draw, or an 8-out straight draw. In this scenario, calling the 3-bet then pushing all-in on the flop over his c-bet is better than 4-betting preflop.

4-betting all-in with aces preflop yields you about $43 in equity (we've made some simple assumptions to get that number). Now suppose instead that you call his preflop 3-bet, let him c-bet the flop, then push all-in. This yields about $58.40. The extra profit comes from his c-bet.

You may be surprised how effective a strategy it can be to flat call and push any flop against a loose-aggressive 3-bettor and c-bettor.

Say you have ace-queen in our same example. If you 4-bet all-in preflop, your equity is about $5.20. If you push any flop on which you have top pair or better, or an 8-out straight draw or a flush draw, but otherwise fold to his c-bet, your equity is about –$1.60. Remember, calling 3-bets purely to make a big hand is rarely profitable with 100bb stacks. Add gutshot straight draws to your flop pushing range, and your equity goes up to $1.40. Add overcards and you're up to $10.80. But flat call preflop and push *any flop* and your equity is $14.40.

Flat-calling with strong hands is a great way to exploit a loose-aggressive 3-bettor. The usual caveats apply. Know your opponent well before making a sophisticated play, and remember to adjust as the opponent adjusts. If your opponent tightens up his 3-bet range while you get fancy with ATo, you will end up trapping yourself.

Final Thoughts About Defending Against 3-Bets

Playing against a 3-bet is not much different than any other no-limit situation. Correctly utilizing hand ranges, equity, and commitment is key. And as is often the case, your success will ultimately be determined by hand reading.

Some Points About 4-Betting

Small 4-bet bluffing, if overused, is extremely vulnerable to 5-bet rebluffing. Small 4-bets have to work most of the time to be profitable. For instance, if you open for $7, your opponent 3-bets to $24, and you 4-bet to $56, you are risking $49 (the amount beyond your original $7) to win somewhere between $32 and $34 depending on whether the 3-bettor is in the blinds or not. That leaves you laying significant odds ($49–to–$34), and since you don't get to see a flop if your opponent shoves over top of you, your bluff has to succeed often to be profitable.

The math of the 5-bet shove is more forgiving. In the above example, a shove for $200 risks an extra $176 to win about $83.

At first glance it might seem like you're laying heavy odds, but remember that you will always get to see a showdown when you shove, so you will always have showdown equity as well as steal equity. Your light 3-betting hand matched up against a typical hand that might call your 5-bet will usually offer you about 25 percent showdown equity. So you will, on average, recover about $100 from a $400 all-in pot. Thus, the 5-bet shove risks effectively $76 ($176–$100=$76), and you're not really laying odds since you are risking effectively $76 to win $83.

The chance to win when called allows your 5-bet shoves to work less than half the time and still remain profitable. Thus, don't be shy about trying out a 5-bet shove bluff on a player whom you suspect is 4-betting light frequently. If you catch your opponent bluffing too often, you stand to gain a lot. And if you happen to be wrong about your opponent's bluffing strategy, your equity when called will cushion the blow.

Thus, most of your small 4-bets should be made with hands you intend to get all-in with if 5-bet. As a good rule of thumb, don't allow more than 1 out of every 3 of your small 4-bets to be a bluff that you intend to fold to a 5-bet. You do not have to have the best hand or likely best hand to get all-in. Rather, you should expect to have enough showdown equity that calling the 5-bet shove makes sense.

Four-bet bluffing gets expensive if overused. To protect yourself, make sure that at least two-thirds of your 4-bets are made with hands you intend to call a shove with.

When you're against a player who 3-bets light very frequently, and you're tempted to 4-bet bluff more often than the rule of thumb allows, start calling the 3-bets with hands like suited connectors and big cards that play decently postflop. Save your 4-bet bluffs for when your hand has little to no postflop value. Remember to play an attacking style postflop, frequently semibluffing with draws as weak as two overcards or a gutshot. And balance your calling range by also calling sometimes with premium pairs.

Basic Outline For An Open/3-Bet/4-Bet/5-Bet Strategy

Let's put all these ideas together to outline a basic strategy for playing 3-bet/4-bet/5-bet pots. This topic is complex enough to fill a book in its own, so we can't possibly explore every possibility here. But we can give you the knowledge necessary to take control of a typical $1–$2 online 6-max game.

We'll start the outline from the perspective of the player who opened the pot, and then we'll take the perspective of the player defending against the opening raise.

When Making The Opening Raise

If your opponent tends to call your opening raise and play fit-or-fold postflop:

- ♦ Continuation bet most flops and follow up frequently with second and sometimes third barrels.

- ♦ Raise as a steal frequently, and choose a large raise size so the pots you win will be bigger.

If your opponent tends to call your opening raise and call bets frequently with weak hands all the way to showdown:

♦ Focus on betting for value. Continuation bet fairly frequently still, but be more willing to give up on the turn and river without a decent hand.

♦ Forgo stealing with your worst hands. Since you'll see showdowns so often against this player, don't bother opening offsuit junk and weak suited hands.

♦ Lower your threshold for value betting. When your opponents like to call to showdown with second pair and worse, top pair regardless of kicker tends to be worth three solid value bets.

If your opponent tends to call your opening raise and then play back at you frequently postflop:

♦ Players like this are somewhat uncommon. Verify that this is really the strategy your opponent is using. It's possible he's playing fit-or-fold and just caught a few good hands in a row.

♦ Forgo stealing with your worst hands. You won't be seeing showdown that often, but you will be forced to make large semibluffs. The more equity you have when bluffing, the more profitable the bluffs will be.

♦ Be prepared to rebluff. For instance, say you open on the button and this player calls from the big blind. The flop comes T44 rainbow. He checks, you bet half the pot, and he makes a small checkraise. Sometimes reraise even with nothing. Also sometimes call the raise with the intention of bluffing the turn or river. You can and should also fold sometimes to the suspected bluff, but you have to sometimes rebluff opponents who play like this.

If your opponent 3-bets only strong hands:

♦ Fold most hands to a 3-bet whether you're in or out of position.

♦ Do not try to play back often against players with strong 3-betting ranges. For the most part, you'll just be ceding them the advantage. Once in a blue moon you can try 4-betting or calling the 3-bet to make a play postflop in order to keep your range somewhat balanced. But when your opponent has strength and you are weak, folding is usually the right play.

If your opponent 3-bets mostly strong hands with the occasional light 3-bet:

♦ Same as above. Fold. Your opponent is entitled to work some light 3-betting into his strategy, and there's little you can do about it. As long as the overall range is still strong, mostly you just have to fold.

If your opponent 3-bets strong hands, but also 3-bets light frequently:

♦ Fold most stealing hands to the 3-bet.

♦ Look to play back sometimes to attack your opponent's weak range. How best to play back depends on your opponent's tendencies.

If your opponent 3-bets light frequently, and if called nearly always follows up with a flop continuation bet:

♦ When your opponent continuation bets nearly every flop with a weak 3-betting range, he's just hanging money out to dry. You know he has a weak range, and betting the flop doesn't imply that his range is any stronger than it was before the flop. Therefore, tend to *flat call the 3-bet* with the intention of *shoving the flop* any time you catch any piece of it. You're calling the 3-bet rather than 4-betting because you want your opponent to put more money at risk before you drop the hammer.

♦ Remember that you have to play very aggressively postflop. If you flop a gutshot or anything stronger, generally you should shove the flop. If you fail to challenge many pots aggressively, you'll be playing too close to a fit-or-fold strategy, and your preflop calls will be unprofitable.

♦ Because you're calling the 3-bet, choose hands that have value. Suited connectors are good hands for making this play. Lower offsuit two-gappers are no good.

♦ You can call from out of position almost as easily as you can call with position. Since you can count on your opponent to bet the flop for you, you can count on being able to check-shove the flop.

If your opponent 3-bets light frequently, but is selective with flop continuation bets:

♦ When small 4-betting against a savvy opponent, make sure that at least 2/3 of the time you hold a hand that you plan to go all the way with. If you 4-bet and fold to a shove more often than about 1/3 of the time, you become exploitable. A savvy player will begin to 5-bet you nearly every time you 4-bet. You do not necessarily need a strong hand to 4-bet, however, just one that has some showdown equity.

◆ Use a mixed strategy of small 4-betting and calling the 3-bet. Tend to 4-bet with strong hands and sometimes with weak hands. Since 4-bets usually elicit either folds or shoves from your opponent, hand strength when bluff 4-betting doesn't much matter. Hands with aces in them, such as A3o, are particularly good weak hands to 4-bet. Weak aces have a surprising amount of equity against narrow ranges, typically over 30 percent. They are also poor for calling 3-bets with the intent to push any draw or pair on the flop, because they rarely flop draws.

◆ Call sometimes with very strong hands and also with hands that have some postflop value.

◆ When calling with weak hands, remember to challenge many pots aggressively. Fit-or-fold is not profitable.

◆ With AA and KK, you should call sometimes and 4-bet sometimes to balance your strategy with both lines. Your 4-betting range should be stronger on average than your calling range, but you should still mix in some calls with premium hands.

◆ You can 4-bet small more often as a bluff against players who rarely 5-bet. Call more frequently with marginal hands against players who 5-bet often.

◆ Tend to 4-bet or fold more frequently when out of position, and tend to call more frequently when in position.

If your opponent 3-bets light very frequently, approximately 18 percent of hands or more:

◆ Consider 4-bet shoving as an alternative to a small 4-bet. This play locks in profit, but it can be less profitable overall than small 4-betting or calling. Nevertheless, if you are unsure of how to proceed against a tricky opponent because he 5-bets often over your small 4-bets and because he plays well postflop in 3-bet pots, you can always fall back on 4-bet shoving as a bluff.

In all cases, when you get 3-bet, if you don't feel like you will be able to challenge for a significant percentage of pots after the flop, *just fold to the 3-bet.*

When Defending Against A Possible Steal Raise

If your opponent's stealing range is relatively tight:

♦ Usually fold. Don't try to defend against openers with tight ranges. Being out of position with a weaker hand usually makes the hand not worth getting involved with.

♦ Consider calling with some "implied odds" hands, particularly small pairs. Small pairs don't play well against loose ranges, but they perform better when your opponent is likely to have a strong hand.. Be careful not to call too big a raise with a pocket pair when playing for set equity. In general, set mining with pocket pairs becomes profitable when you expect to win at least 12 times the amount of your call when you flop a set or better and win the hand. Your opponent won't always get all-in with you, so don't overestimate your implied odds.

If the steal raise is 3.5 times the big blind or more, and this size is typical for your opponent:

♦ Tend to 3-bet when defending. You are looking to resteal. When your opponent has made a large steal raise, it hurts your immediate pot odds, but at the same time it sweetens the pot, increasing the reward for restealing it. Thus, calling becomes less attractive, and 3-betting light becomes more attractive. However, if you are unlikely to take it down preflop or postflop, 3-betting is a mistake.

♦ Watch out for opponents who sometimes raise small and sometimes raise large. Often they will be raising more with their stronger hands and less with their weaker ones. If your opponent plays that way, 3-bet the small raises and generally fold to the large ones. You can call with small pairs to try to stack them with a set. Calling single raises to try to flop a set is usually fine.

If the steal raise is small, 3 times the big blind or less, and this size is typical for your opponent:

♦ Be more willing to flat call the steal raise and less inclined to 3-bet light. The raise is small, so it doesn't cost much to enter the pot. Since the pot is smaller it is less attractive for an immediate resteal.

♦ If you flat call the raise, don't play for implied odds. Instead, plan a way to attack the pot postflop. If your opponent is raising a wide range, often he'll be vulnerable to a flop checkraise or some other play at the pot.

♦ Delaying your steal by flat-calling preflop allows your opponent to put more money in the pot via a flop continuation bet before you drop the hammer. This extra bet will sweeten the pot and make your steal more profitable than a preflop 3-bet would be.

If your opponent has a high Attempt To Steal percentage or a high Fold To 3-Bet percentage or both:

♦ Don't be shy about 3-betting light. Many players will fold their steal raises to a 3-bet 75 percent of the time or more. With that success rate, 3-betting light becomes profitable no matter what cards you hold.

♦ If you 3-bet the same player a few times, try to anticipate any adjustments your opponent might make to combat your thievery. Don't assume that your opponents' play will always be consistent with their stats. Just because a player's Fold To 3-Bet percentage is 80 doesn't mean that he will fold 80 percent of his hands to *your* 3-bets.

♦ When 3-betting light, try to choose hands that have some postflop value. Suited hands, connected hands, and small pocket pairs are all better choices than offsuit trash. If your 3-bet gets called, the more postflop value your hand has, and the more frequently you can continue your aggression profitably postflop.

♦ Having said that, don't pass on juicy opportunities just because your hand isn't so great. For instance, if a loose player opens in the cutoff and two weak players call on the button and in the small blind, you have an excellent squeezing situation. Don't be afraid to put in the light 3-bet even if you have offsuit trash. But be more selective in the less attractive, more common scenarios.

If your opponent likes to make small bluff 4-bets over your 3-bets:

♦ Try 5-bet shoving liberally. If your opponent will fold his small 4-bet to your shove *half the time or more*, 5-bet shoving shows an automatic profit with nearly any hand you might have 3-bet. Most players at the $1–$2 level who bluff 4-bet do it too often and are quite vulnerable to 5-bet shove bluffs.

♦ If your opponent balances his small 4-bets well between bluffs and strong hands, try a mixed defense strategy of light 3-betting and flat calling the initial steal raise. If your opponent's 4-betting strategy is balanced, he won't 4-bet you too often since a balanced strategy requires many premium hands in his 4-bet range. So you can 3-bet light and usually expect not to get 4-bet. But you still want to mix calls into your defense strategy to avoid leaving your 3-betting range unbalanced and weak.

If your opponent has a loose stealing range, and you choose to defend your blind by flat calling:

♦ Remember that to defend your blind you should attack your opponent. You are defending because your opponent's stealing range is weak, and that will tend to leave him with weak hands after the flop.

♦ Your postflop strategy should revolve around stealing pots when your opponent is likely to have missed the flop. As a backup if your opponent seems to have hit a pair and refuses to fold, value bet aggressively with weak top pairs and better.

Above all, remember that when you're defending your blinds, you're at a major disadvantage when an opponent open-raises. You're out of position, and you will often have a marginal or weak hand. Many times you should just fold your blind to a steal raise, even when you know the stealer opens with a wide range. But to better defend your blinds, add some judicious light 3-betting, and use an attacking mindset postflop.

A Series Of 3-Bet Situations Against A Solid Opponent

You are in a 6-handed $1–$2 game with $200 stacks. In the following examples, you are heads up against the same opponent. He is a solid regular capable of being aggressive at times. He plays a 25/20 style. You don't know much else about him.

Example 1. You open for $7 in the cutoff with 6♥6♦. The button and small blind fold, and your opponent reraises to $22 from the big blind.

You don't have implied odds to call for a set, and you aren't comfortable playing a big pot with one small pair or making a big bluff, at least not yet. You're not quite sure of your opponent's tendencies. Calling 3-bets from solid players with small pocket pairs is typically a leak. Just let this one go.

Example 2. You open for $7 in the cutoff with K♣T♥. The button and small blind fold, and your opponent reraises to $22 from the big blind.

Once again, he's caught you with a marginal hand. This is the second occasion in a short period of time that he's 3-bet you. He may just be picking up good hands. You aren't sure yet. But at this point you don't want to play for stacks with a fairly weak big card hand. You fold.

Example 3. You open for $7 in the cutoff with 6♦4♦. The button and small blind fold, and your opponent reraises to $22 from the big blind.

This is the third time in a few rounds that he's 3-bet you. That combined with his aggressive raise percentage leads you to think he might be reraising light. You decide to play back at him a little and see how he responds. You 4-bet to $56 with the intention of folding to a push. He folds.

Example 4. You open for $7 in the cutoff with **A♦K♥**. The button and small blind fold, and your opponent reraises to $22 from the big blind.

This time you have a hand you're comfortable getting all-in with before the flop. You might make another small 4-bet in hopes of inducing a bluff push. The problem is that not many opponents, even aggressive ones, will push all-in as a bluff, particularly if they don't know your tendencies well. The other problem is that a lot of his bluff hands have decent equity against yours. For example, you are only about a 58-to-42 favorite over **8♠7♠**, and you are a slight underdog to small pairs. Your best play is probably to push all-in over his 3-bet. That way you give *him* the opportunity to fold a lot of hands that have decent equity against you.

While your equity with ace-king is good against your opponent's range, you don't dominate his range like you would with pocket aces. If you instead had pocket aces, you would seriously consider making a small 4-bet, because then you'd welcome a push. You might also flat call a 3-bet with aces against opponents who are reluctant to go all-in preflop, so you can trap them postflop.

Example 5. You open for $7 in the cutoff with **J♠J♣**. The button and small blind fold, and your opponent reraises to $22 from the big blind.

Your hand is too good to fold. Four-betting small with plan of folding to a push is absurd because you essentially turn your hand into a pure bluff. Save your bluffs for hands like **6♦4♦**, not pocket jacks. Four-betting small with the plan of calling a push is okay if your opponent will push with a wide range. But many will not.

The best plan is often to call the 3-bet. You keep him in the hand with the weak portion of his 3-betting range. Further, the SPR is low enough that you have a fair chance of getting him all-in postflop with hands he would have folded preflop had you 4-bet. If you 4-bet shove you're going to go broke against his better preflop hands anyway, so you might as well call to gain maximum value from his worse hands.

For instance, say you call the $22 and the flop comes T♣5♠2♥. If you get all-in and he has pocket queens, you are no worse off than if you had gotten all-in preflop. But if you get all-in on the flop, he will sometimes have ace-ten, king-ten suited, ten-nine suited, or even pocket nines. He would have folded many of these hands preflop had you 4-bet. In addition, you do have position. So, by flat calling preflop, you'll occasionally be able to steal. For example, if the board comes ace-high you might be able to force pocket queens to fold.

Another Situation: 44 On The Button

You open on the button for $7 with 4♥4♦. The small blind folds, and the big blind reraises to $22. What should you do?

Consider the big blind's range. Say he's a tight player who'd reraise only with AA-TT, AK, and AQs. You do not have implied odds to call against that range. Further, he'll often have strong hands on the flop, so you don't have good steal equity. You should fold.

Now say your opponent is a loose, tricky player who'd reraise with a wider range than just premium hands. You still do not have implied odds to hunt for a set, as he won't often have a strong hand on the flop. But your steal equity might be decent. If you call preflop, your primary plan should be to steal the pot, *not* to make a hand and get paid off.

Even when you are stealing, you prefer to have as much pot equity as possible. One problem with flat calling preflop with the intention of stealing the pot postflop is that your hand doesn't have great pot equity against even a wide range. The more pot equity you add to your folding equity, the more overall equity you have.

Another option is to 4-bet to $56. If your opponent will 3-bet fairly light, but fold most of his hands to a 4-bet, you can make it $56 with the intention of folding to a push. Doing this turns your hand into a bluff, but that's not necessarily a bad thing. Your showdown equity isn't worth much to begin with.

The profitability of 4-bet bluffing depends on how wide your opponent's 3-bet range is. You may be surprised at how wide it needs to be for you to show a decent profit. Even against an opponent who 3-bets 11 percent of his hands, 4-bet bluffing is only slightly more profitable than folding to his 3-bet. 10 percent is about the break-even point, and many opponents don't 3-bet that widely. For reference, 10 percent of hands would be a range like

88+, ATs+, KJs+, QTs+
No suited connectors
AJo+, KJo+

Note that this assumes your opponent will get all-in preflop with only AA-TT or AK. If he'll get all-in with a wider range than that, your equity is worse. If he'll get all-in with a tighter range, your equity is slightly better.

When you open on the button with pocket fours and an opponent makes a pot-sized 3-bet, your default should be to fold.

Squeezing From The Small Blind

Stacks are $140. The cutoff opens for $7, and the button calls. Both players are straightforward and predictable. You are in the small blind with 7♠5♠. What should you do?

This is a standard squeeze situation. The opening player is in late position, which means that his raise includes many non-premium hands. The button's flat-call also indicates a fairly weak hand because he would likely have reraised with something big. He probably figures the cutoff is stealing, and he's calling to keep him honest.[17]

If you make a solid reraise, say to $28, you'll win the pot often. This move gets its value from forcing opponents to fold. If you knew either opponent to be a calling station, you might not make this play. But even if one of them calls you preflop, you'll often win on the flop with a continuation bet. And as a backup for when your steal fails, occasionally you'll actually make a big hand.

Suited connectors and one-gappers are great for preflop squeezing and stealing because they often flop at least something to semibluff with.

---

[17] If the button were a sophisticated player, you'd need to keep in mind that he could be flat-calling the cutoff's raise with a big hand to try to induce a squeeze from you.

Isolating Bad Players

If you start to play a lot of online $1–$2 6-max, you will soon come to an unhappy conclusion. The games are somewhat tough. On a site with 50 games going at a time, you might find two to four with two bad players. And these good games will often have waiting lists a mile long. The bulk of the games will feature solid players or only one bad player. You will often sit in games where four or all five of your opponents are either nits, TAGs, or decent LAGs.

Work hard and you'll gain edges over these regulars. You'll make good bluffs and value bets that your opponents miss. But these edges alone will produce only a modest winrate. To really crush the game, you have to find and dominate the bad players.

The first step is to put the bad player on your right. Your goal is to play as many pots with this player as possible, and you want to have position when you play those pots. Say a table has an open seat with a weak player to the left of it and four decent regulars in the others. This game is not great. The regulars have a better shot at the weak spot's money than you will. If the player looks atrociously bad and has a $400 stack, by all means sit. But if he's just a run-of-the-mill wet noodle with a standard stack, you can find a better opportunity elsewhere.

Put that same player to the right of the open seat, and you should sit in the game. If the weak spot is in one of the three seats across from the open seat, generally speaking, the table will be marginal but playable. Just keep the lobby open looking for better games.

When you have a bad player on your right, you want to play as many pots as you can with them, and you want those pots to be larger than an average pot. The more and bigger pots you play with position, the more money you'll make on average from the bad player.

When your target enters the pot in front of you, loosen up your preflop requirements and raise to try to get the hand heads-up. From that point, you leverage position and your hand reading skills to exploit the mistakes your target makes.

Most decent players know that you can isolate bad players to make more money. But relatively few understand how far you should go to make the most off of bad players. If we've done our job in this section, you'll read some of these examples and say, "Wow, that's crazy." And they would be crazy if your opponents were equipped to take advantage of your play. But that's the point—if you've chosen the right targets, your opponents won't know how to protect themselves, and you'll end up with the money.

Isolation In Practice

A weak 64/30 player is sitting directly to your right. Your goal is to play as many pots as you can within reason against him. Heads-up pots where you have position are ideal. This type of opponent is easy to manipulate, so you want to take full advantage.

Here are examples from one orbit in a 6-handed $1–$2 game with $200 effective stacks. Your other four opponents are standard regulars ranging from TAG to nit.

Example 1. The first two players fold, and the weak player limps in the cutoff. You have A♥7♠ on the button.

This is an easy raise. Ace-seven offsuit is not a great hand, and if a solid 20/18 opponent open-raised from the cutoff, you might fold it. But here is what a 64 percent preflop range looks like:

22+, A2s+, K2s+, Q2s+, J2s+, T2s+
98s-54s, 97s-64s, 96s-74s, 95s-84s
A2o+, K2o+, Q7o+, J7o+, T7o+, 98o-54o, 97o-75o

You have plenty of pot equity, plus you have position. A solid raise will usually fold out the blinds and sometimes even win the pot outright. At the least, you will usually get the pot heads-up with the weak player. Go ahead and raise the pot to isolate.

You raise to $9, and only the cutoff calls. The flop comes K♠3♥2♦. Your opponent checks.

Once again, you should stay on the attack. A two-thirds-pot or full-pot-sized bet will often take it down.

You bet $20, and your opponent folds.

Example 2. The player under the gun folds, and the weak player minraises to $4 in the hijack. You are next to act with K♣8♣.

Your hand is plenty good enough to play against the loose player, particularly in position. Be aggressive! Three-bet to $10–$14. That will take control of the hand, often isolate the weak player, and sometimes win the pot outright. It also forces your other opponents to narrow their ranges. For example, if a 17/14 player in the big blind reraises your 3-bet, he rarely has anything but a premium hand. And if he flat calls your 3-bet, he probably has a strong hand.

You reraise to $12, and only the weak player calls. The flop comes **Q♦8♦4♣**. He checks.

You only have middle pair with a backdoor flush draw, but you likely have the best hand. Bet for value. Your opponent will often call with all kinds of garbage.

You bet $15 into the $27 pot. That's a little over half the pot, which is fine here. Your hand is not great, and you don't mind keeping the pot on the small side for now. Consistently varying your bet sizes based on hand strength is bad against smart opponents, but it's a useful weapon against weak players. Weak opponents often do not consider your hand, much less your range of hands, before making a decision.

Your opponent calls the $15. The turn is the **6♥**, and he checks.

Bet again. You still probably have the best hand. Sure, your opponent could have a timidly played queen, pocket nines, or some other hand that beats you. But more likely he has some low pair, ace-high, flush draw, gutshot, or other weak hand. And if he has you beat, you still often have five outs.

You bet $32, and your opponent folds.

Example 3. The weak player again opens for a $4 minraise, this time under the gun. You are next to act with **J♠7♠**.

Like last hand, this is a situation where a lot of players in your position would fold. But this is a fine spot for another small isolation 3-bet. You make it $12, and only the weak player calls.

The flop comes **A♥9♣5♦**. Your opponent checks, and you c-bet $18 into the $27 pot. He check-minraises to $36.

Here you should fold. Your passive opponent is showing aggression, and he's showing it on an ace-high flop. This is the type of player who plays any ace. Attempting a rebluff would be a bad idea. Part of playing a loose-aggressive style requires folding well in spots where you get played back at. Continuing on in this hand would be spewing.

You fold.

Example 4. You are under the gun with **Q♥8♥**.

Your general plan is to aggressively isolate the weak player and play as many pots as you can against him. But here you should fold. Your hand is weak, you are first to act, you are opening for the first raise, you have the whole field behind you, and you have shown aggression in the last three hands you've played. Low fold equity combined with low showdown equity equals fold.

You fold.

Example 5. Everyone folds to the weak player in the small blind who completes. You have **K♦6♠** in the big blind.

At this point you are guaranteed position in a heads-up pot against the weak player. King-six offsuit is plenty of hand in this situation. Stick with your usual strategy of raising preflop and c-betting the flop. A pot-sized preflop raise here would be to $6. You can make it a little more than that.

You raise to $8, and the weak player calls. The flop comes **5♥5♣3♦**. He checks, and you bet $11. He folds.

Example 6. The first three players fold, and the weak player limps on the button. You are next to act with **5♦5♥** in the small blind. The big blind is a 15/12 regular.

A lot of players just complete here, hoping to see a cheap flop. But raising is far superior. You can still win by making the best hand, but you greatly increase your steal potential. The big blind will likely fold, and you will be heads-up with the weak player. While you don't have position, you will still often win the pot. Plus, while the bigger preflop pot cuts your implied odds for making a hand, it does make it easier for you to win your opponent's stack when you flop a set.

You raise to $8. The big blind surprisingly calls, and the button calls. The flop is **J♣9♦5♣**, giving you bottom set.

You should play this hand very aggressively. You have recently shown a lot of aggression, so there's no reason to slow down now that you actually have a big hand. One of the most common mistakes that weak opponents make is over-adjusting. If they see you bluff or even just see you play aggressively, they think you are always bluffing, and they will not hesitate to call you down very lightly. Take advantage of that tendency by value betting mercilessly. A flop like this connects in some way with a wide range of hands.

You bet $25 into the $24 pot. The big blind folds, and the button calls. The turn is the **4♣**. Do not be deterred by the possible flush. There are plenty of non-flush hands in your opponent's range. And even if he has a flush, you have ten outs to beat him.

You bet $75 into the $74 pot. Your opponent calls. The river is the **J♠**. You shove for the remaining $92. The weak player calls, and you beat his **Q♣9♠**.

Most players, even winning regulars, do not take sufficient advantage of high-equity situations against weak opponents. We recommend beating up on them whenever you can. To profit from weak opponents, loosen up your range, isolate, aim for heads-up pots with position, steal when possible, usually give up when played back at, and value bet aggressively. This relentless strategy will frustrate your targets, encouraging them to play even worse. And it shuts out the other players at the table, hoarding most of the spoils for yourself.

Here are a few more examples against bad players.

Hand Against A Maniac

In a 6-handed $1–$2 game, the player under the gun opens for $7. He is a loose cannon with stats of 76/52 and a 3-bet percentage of 20. The next three players fold, and you are in the small blind with Q♣J♦. The big blind is a 26/7 with a 3-bet percentage of 3. The under the gun player has $106. The big blind and you each have $200. What should you do?

Queen-jack is too good a hand to fold against the opening raiser's range. Reraising is an option. You will likely get the pot heads up, and that is good for an offsuit big card hand. On the other hand, 3-betting will rarely win the preflop pot outright against a player so loose. It also reopens the betting, which is not ideal here. Your opponent is so aggressive that he could 4-bet you with a pretty wide range. And his 50bb stack size makes it just tricky enough so that you don't love folding to a 4-bet, and you don't love calling either. Getting all-in preflop here is not terrible by any means. If you reraise and he 4-bets, at that point you likely have enough equity to get all-in. But you are essentially flipping coins. You can probably find a better way to play this hand.

Flat calling the preflop raise is a good option. The big blind is a bit of a wet noodle—on the loose side, and not very aggressive. Since you don't have much steal equity anyway, you might as well let him in. He will probably call the extra $5 with a fairly wide range. Playing solely to make the best hand in a multiway pot with queen-jack offsuit is usually not a great idea, but here it is fine. You have only two opponents, and one is loose and passive while the other is very loose and has a half stack. You will generally have no trouble playing after the flop.

You call the $7, and the big blind calls. The flop comes K♣J♥5♦. You check, both to see what develops and to let the aggressive preflop raiser make a likely c-bet. The big blind checks, and the loose cannon bets $18 into the $21 pot. With only another $81 remaining in his stack, you should be committed against him. Even though you only have second pair, you crush his range for raising preflop and c-betting the flop.

However, raising the flop does not make much sense. Getting the money in quickly typically has more upside against drawing hands than against made hands. People don't call large river bets with busted draws, but they do call them with made hands. Put another way, charging made hands is less urgent than charging draws. Since this board is fairly dry, you won't often be up against a draw, so there's no rush to get the money in.

Calling also allows you to see what the big blind does. If he checkraises, you should probably fold. And you want to give the aggressive player rope to hang himself. Calling the flop then checking the turn makes more money than raising the flop.

You call the $18, and the big blind folds. The turn is the 3♣. You check again, and your opponent goes all-in for $81 into the $57 pot. It's an overbet, and you still have just second pair. Nevertheless, you should call. You committed on the previous street, and you have no reason to change that decision here. One of the worst mistakes you can make against hyper-aggressive players is building big pots on early streets only to fold later. While your opponent will occasionally have a king or some other hand that beats you, he'll also show up with all kinds of random stuff, including pocket eights, ace-ten, six-five, ten-nine, or any flush draw.

Value Betting Against A Weak Player

A loose and bad player in the cutoff open limps. The button and small blind both fold, and you make it $10 in the big blind with **J♥J♠**. The cutoff calls.

The flop comes **A♦A♠7♣**. You check. Giving a free card cannot hurt you much if you are ahead. Also, you think this player is far more likely to give you action with a worse hand if you check the flop. He will bluff the flop sometimes, and if he checks the flop, he'll sometimes get tied to his hand if he picks up a weak pair or draw on the turn.

The cutoff checks behind. The turn is the **A♣**. You bet $20. You expect him to call with any pocket pair or 7, any flush draw, or possibly even king-high. With the case ace he could call or raise. He calls.

The river is the **Q♠**. You bet $50 into the $60 pot. Your opponent raises all-in, and you fold.

The river bet is the critical play in this hand. Many players would check, figuring that an overcard hit the river, so they're likely behind or won't get called by a weaker hand. But you should bet against a loose and bad player.

After the turn call, his range is roughly the case ace, any pocket pair, any seven, and many king-high hands. You're well ahead of his turn calling range. He'll call the river with most of the hands he called with on the turn. The only hands in his range that improved to beat you are king-queen and queen-seven and any random queen-high hands he may have peeled the turn with. Since you were well ahead of his turn calling range, you're also well ahead of his river calling range, and therefore betting is the best play. (Checking is better if he would bet more losing hands than he would call with, but that's unlikely to be the case here.)

Once he raises all-in, you have a fairly easy fold. The way you've played the hand, you could hold the case ace, so a bluff here is unlikely enough that you don't have the necessary odds to call.

Opening Light With A Bad Player In The Blinds

You're first to act. Stacks are 100bb. The worst player at the table is in the small blind. He's playing 80 percent of his hands and playing them badly.

You hold **Q♦T♠**. Under normal circumstances, this hand is too weak to open under the gun. But you should make a routine open-raise here. Against a loose and bad player, every hand becomes more profitable. Marginal hands like QT that are losers under normal conditions become worth playing. If the bad player calls with 80 percent of his hands, QT will play favorably against his range.

If the bad player has position on you, then there is less incentive to play marginal hands. But when the bad player is in the blinds, opening a little lighter than usual is a no-brainer.

T7s Flop Semibluff

Stacks are $200. The 39/13 player to your right is loose, weak, and easy to read.

The first two players fold, and the weak player minraises to $4 in the cutoff. You are on the button with **T♦7♦**. You reraise to $15 to isolate the bad player, take control of the hand, and possibly win the pot outright. The blinds fold, and your opponent thinks for a few seconds and calls.

The flop comes **A♦J♦7♠**. The cutoff bets $22 into the $33 pot. What should you do?

Raise big. You have a pair, a flush draw, and a backdoor straight draw. Your equity is excellent against your opponent's range. He is a loose and weak player, so he could have a number of mediocre hands like an ace with a weak kicker, a jack, a middle pocket pair, a straight draw, or a flush draw. He's unlikely to have a strong hand. With pocket aces or pocket jacks he would probably have opened for more than a minraise or reraised your 3-bet. With two pair or three sevens he would probably have gone for a checkraise.

This is the type of opponent whose bets can normally be taken at face value. A weak bet usually means weakness, and a strong bet means strength. He flat called your 3-bet preflop, and now he's leading for two-thirds the pot into you. He probably has a modest hand and wants you out.

With $55 in the pot and $185 left, you cannot let your opponent see another card without putting more money into the pot. Your combined showdown and steal equity are excellent right now. Calling would create a $77 pot with $163 behind. But on the turn if your hand doesn't improve, your overall equity decreases significantly. If your opponent improves on the turn, your steal equity vanishes. And if you make your flush on the turn, your opponent might get scared off.

Put him to a stack decision. Push all-in. Your opponent will fold a ton of hands better than yours. And if he calls with one of those, you'll usually have plenty of outs.

Handling Opponent Aggression

When you're up against weak players, tight players, nitty players, and just generally bad players, aggressive strategies work. Aggression maximizes value for your medium-strength and strong hands, and it also helps you win most pots where no one makes a hand.

But not all of your opponents will lay down, pay off, or generally allow you to control the game when you come out betting. Some will play back at you. And some are plain crazy. Here's how to adapt to opponent aggression.

Your first instinct might be to fight fire with fire. If your opponents seem to be bluffing a lot, you may be tempted to bluff-raise them back. While this tactic certainly has its place, trying to run over hyper-aggressive players with big bluffs and rebluffs is often counter-productive. The game devolves into one where you and your opponent are both gambling lots of money, but neither of you holds a strong edge. And if you are careless, you and your adversary could offer up bloated pots to another player who wakes up with a hand.

Against an aggressive opponent, you often should back off a bit. Check in some situations where you would normally bet. Call in some situations where you would normally raise. Allow your opponent to think he can launch a profitable bluff or thin value bet, and then snap him off.

This adjustment sounds simple, but watch out for these two pitfalls:

Don't pay off big bets against an opponent who is aggressive only for small bets. There are aggressive players, and then there are *aggressive* players. Don't assume that just because one particular opponent likes to c-bet every flop that he also will make huge bluff-raises on the river. You'll come across a lot of players who like to 3-bet preflop and c-bet a lot of flops. Players who love to make huge turn and river bluffs are much rarer. Don't pay a guy off for $200 with middle pair just because you saw him 3-bet to $24 a few times.

Don't fold just because the going gets a little rough. When you are up against a truly hyper-aggressive player who bets big on every street, and you decide to adopt a calling rather than betting strategy, hold on tight! Say you have pocket aces and call a turn bet rather than shove because you think calling the turn will induce a river bluff. Inevitably, a scary river card will come and your opponent will test you with a huge bet. Often you should call anyway. Follow through with your plan. Sometimes you'll find out that you did indeed get rivered. That's just bad luck. But abandoning your plan is worse, because it plays into an aggressive player's hands. There's no worse strategy against a hyper-aggressive player than building many big pots only to fold the river. This is not to say that you should never fold when a scare card hits. Rather, it should be quite an unlucky card.

Let's look at some examples of adjusting to opponent aggression.

Aces In The Hijack

Stacks are $200. The player under the gun folds, and you make it $7 with red aces. Only the button calls. He is a solid, aggressive player, and is a regular in this game. You think he views you as solid.

The flop comes **J♦6♣2♦**. You bet $11 into the $17 pot. The button immediately raises to $25. What should you do?

Even though his raise is smallish, the pot will be $67 and the remaining stacks $168 if you call. A turn bet would put you to a stack decision. You think he could have anything from a set, a jack, a medium pocket pair, or flush draw, to a total bluff. You have good equity against that range.

You decide folding is out of the question, so how should you proceed? If you reraise, you believe he'll fold everything except a set and sometimes a flush draw or ace-jack. If you call, you think he'll bet the turn a high percentage of the time when checked to. It's true that if he has a flush draw, by calling you let him see the turn cheaply. However, a flush draw is only a small part of his range, and if a diamond comes on the turn, you have a redraw to the nut flush.

You call, and the turn is the **2♠**. That's an excellent card for you because it makes a set even less likely for him, and it also negates any two-pair outs he might have had. You check as planned. Unfortunately, he checks behind.

The river is the **7♦**. What should you do?

This is a spot where many players check with the intention of calling a reasonable bet. However, given both your opponent's range and the river card, betting is better. Heads-up and out of position on the river, when you plan on calling a bet, you should often bet yourself unless your opponent is likely to bluff. Here he is not likely to bluff if checked to. Why? He checked the turn, and subsequently the pot is not all that big on the river. He probably expects you to call with any decent hand as long as he doesn't make a big overbet. Also, the flush card just came in, and he knows you could have one. If he were going to continue bluffing with air after the flop action, he probably would have just bet the turn (as opposed to checking the turn and then betting the river when checked to).

A flush, a jack, and a medium pocket pair are your opponent's main non-air hands. So if you check, you give him too much flexibility. He can check behind when he wants to see a showdown and bet when he wants to extract more value. If you bet, you force him to pay with those hands he would have checked if he wants a showdown. And when he has a better hand, you lose about the same amount as checkcalling, because you aren't planning to call a raise. Betting is the best play here.

How much should you bet? That depends on how likely he is to bluff-raise you if he senses weakness. If he is unlikely to bluff, you can make a half-pot or smaller blocking bet, because worse hands are more likely to call a smaller bet. However, if he might pounce on a blocking bet with a big bluff-raise, you should make a larger bet of about two-thirds the pot. He'll be a little less likely to call the larger bet with worse hands, but you want to be reasonably sure you're beat if he raises. Note that if the river were a blank instead of a diamond, you might decide to induce a bluff by checking or leading weakly.

Bluff Raising The Flop After Raising Preflop

When you are the last raiser preflop, you will usually have the option to put in the first bet on the flop. But sometimes an opponent will lead into you. Often you should treat this bet like you would any other. But sometimes the bet signals weakness, and you should consider bluffing.

Example 1. Stacks are $200. One player limps, and you make it $10 in the cutoff with A♥K♣. The button calls, and the limper calls. The limper is a weak 26/7 player. The button is a solid 19/17. The flop comes **T♠5♥3♥**. The limper leads for $15 into the $33 pot. You make it $60 straight.

There are several great things about this bluff. Your large raise in a three-way pot looks strong. The button, being a decent player, might well think you are committed. He will almost always fold hands weaker than top pair, probably fold hands like JT, and may fold hands as strong as JJ. The weak early position player will probably fold too. After limping and then overcalling preflop, then leading weakly into you, he most likely has a marginal hand. Your strong flop raise will probably scare him into folding anything less than an overpair.

You always prefer to have a little pot equity when you bluff. Here you have two overcards plus a backdoor straight draw and backdoor nut flush draw. If your raise is called, you might hit one of your overcards and win a showdown. Or, you might pick up a better draw on the turn and fire again or take the free card if you think your opponent won't fold to a second barrel.

Example 2. It's folded to you in the cutoff, and you make it $7 with **6♦5♦**. Only the 17/12 big blind calls. He is a predictable player. The flop comes **9♠8♥2♣**. Your opponent bets $7 into the $15 pot. You are quite confident he is making a feeler bet with a weak pair hand, and he will not play for big money. You raise the pot to $36.

The bluff works because your steal equity is good, and you do have a little showdown equity. Here you raise the flop because you read the opponent as weak and feel a raise will take the pot down often. However, you also have four outs to a straight, which does add to your overall expectation. On the rare occasion that he calls your bluff, you'll sometimes hit your straight on the turn. Or, sometimes you'll both check the turn and you'll hit on the river.

To be clear, the flop raise is a bluff. If your opponent comes back over the top, you will fold. Your showdown equity is not good enough to do anything else. The little bit of showdown equity you have helps only when he calls your raise.

Note that this is completely different than if you raised on a **8♦7♦2♣** flop. In the latter case your showdown equity is so good that you'd be raising with the intent of being committed. Technically in both hands you are semibluffing, yet your hand strengths and plans are quite different.

Example 3. You raise to $7 under the gun with **9♥7♥**. You often fold this hand first to act, but a weak player is in the big blind, and you hope to isolate him. Only the small blind calls. He is a 14/11 regular, and you've played with him several times. The flop comes **J♠3♠2♣**. He bets $11 into the $16 pot. You make it $36.

While you prefer to have pot equity when bluffing, it's not a requirement. If your fold equity alone is favorable, fire away.

Your opponent is tight, and he's a decent player. He knows that you generally play tightly under the gun. Your under the gun open, followed by a big flop raise, shows considerable strength. He will probably fold often on this board, because he is tight and your range is narrow and strong.

Now suppose the board were **K♠J♠T♦** and the same action occurred. Should you bluff-raise the flop? No, because you are far more likely to be called on a heavily coordinated board. You do not have enough fold equity.

Bluff raising the flop can be a good play. Remember:

- Don't overdo it.
- Do it only when you expect your opponent is weak.
- Consider your opponent's range, as well as what he thinks of your range.
- Prefer to have some outs.
- Avoid bluff raising the flop on highly coordinated boards.

Dealing With A Floater

Position allows you to get more value from your good hands and to steal a few pots with your bad ones. But some players go overboard with position and try to steal far more than their share by floating pot after pot.

In a "float," a player with position calls a bet or two with nothing or a marginal hand, waiting until the out of position player blinks by checking. When that happens, the position player springs to life with a hard-to-call bluff.

Unfortunately, it can be difficult to defend yourself even if you know your opponent is overreaching. Most of the time you won't make a great hand, so against someone who pounds position on you, you won't have many weapons. One of your best defenses is the occasional checkraise resteal.

For example, say the cutoff opens to $7 with **A♥T♥**, and the button, a player who likes to float, calls. Both blinds fold.

The flop comes **K♣5♦5♥**. The cutoff bets $13, and the button calls. Since the button floats so often, he will have a wide range of hands. The flop is dry, so he won't have a draw and chances are he missed it completely. He's likely calling solely to take the pot away later if you check.

The turn is the 2♠, leaving the board dry as a bone. The cutoff checks, and the button dutifully bets $24 into the $43 pot. Then the cutoff checkraises to $84.

On this board against this player, you should play many hands this way—bet the flop, checkraise the turn. Since your opponent likes to float, he will call your flop c-bet often with weak hands. A well-timed turn check can maximize value for your good hands and punish him for floating.

For instance, say you had pocket aces instead of just ace-high. After you bet the flop and get called, your opponent will still be a big favorite to have nothing. If you follow through with a big bet on the turn, chances are he'll give you credit for a hand and give up. Checking is better because it mimics how you play when you give up. Then, when he bets, you can checkraise for value and hope he caught a king. But even if he has nothing, you make more than if you lead again on the turn.

Since this line is a good one to take with a strong hand, your bluff has credibility. You are representing a hand like pocket aces or ace-king. The dry nature of this board means that it's likely your opponent is weak, and therefore your bluff has an excellent chance to succeed.

If someone is floating you continually and stealing many pots, turn checkraise bluffs are a great way to fight back. You don't want to try it every time, but if you sneak in a few here and there, you're likely to make back most of what he's stealing from you, and your aggressive play may set you up to win a big pot if you catch a big hand against him.

Blind Versus Blind Flop Float

If you have position in a blind versus blind battle, often all you have to do to win the pot is call until your opponent gives up.

This hand occurred in a $1–$2 6-max game. Everyone folds to the small blind who makes it $6 to go. The big blind, holding **K♥8♥**, calls. The flop comes **J♥5♣2♠**. The small blind bets $8 into the $12 pot, and the big blind calls. The turn is the **7♦**. The small blind checks, the big blind bets $24 into the $28 pot. The small blind seems to give up on the turn by checking, so the big blind bets and takes it.

Against a small blind who could be opening many hands, **K♥8♥** is easily good enough to call with. In some cases you might reraise it.

The **J♥5♣2♠** flop is dry. It's unlikely to have hit the small blind's hand, and if it did, most likely he won't have anything better than a pair of fives. This makes it easier to steal, so the big blind calls with the intention to reevaluate on the turn.

The big blind could have raised the flop instead. This raise also works because the small blind is so unlikely to have a hand. You should mix your play up, sometimes calling in situations like this one, and sometimes raising. Raising the flop denies the small blind an extra chance to hit his hand. Calling allows the big blind to gather more information before committing a significant chunk of his stack. Both options have upsides, and both should be a regular part of your game.

Adjusting Commitment Based On Postflop Betting Line

When you play against solid opponents, you often have to rely on conditional commitment. Solid opponents are generally more aware of your range than the average player, so a robotic strategy of waiting for premium starting hands, jamming the preflop pot, and then auto-committing postflop doesn't work well against them. You have to mix up your play to disguise your ranges. You also should keep commitment decisions fluid. Here's an example.

Effective stacks are $200. A solid player opens for $7 on the button, and the small blind folds. You are in the big blind with **A♥Q♣**. The button plays 20/17 overall, but his range is probably wider when opening in late position. He views you as semi-tricky.

Reraising is a fine option, but you should also flat call a fair percentage of the time. Calling keeps the preflop pot smaller, allows you to gain more information postflop, and balances your range for calling out of the blinds. You are comfortable playing against this player postflop, so this time you opt to flat call.

The flop comes **Q♥6♠5♦**, giving you top pair/top kicker. The pot is $15, and the remaining stacks are $193. What's your plan?

Right now you are probably committed. Your opponent's all-in range is wide enough for you to commit profitably on this flop. Checkraising is your first choice of action because this opponent c-bets frequently. Also, if you checkraise, your range in his eyes is wide enough to include many worse hands, including pure bluffs. He may continue on with any queen, or possibly even JJ or TT.

You check, and surprisingly, he checks behind. That could mean he is trying to keep the pot small with a marginal hand, or he has nothing and is giving up on the pot, or he flopped a monster and has decided to slowplay.

The turn is the **7♦**. You bet $11, both for value against worse hands and to deny a free card on what has become a coordinated board. Your opponent raises to $44. Now what should you do?

The raise could mean several things. Your opponent could hold a strong hand like a slowplayed set, two-pair, or a straight. Or, he could be trying to freeze the action with a worse made hand. Or, he could be pure bluffing or semibluffing. You think the latter is unlikely because this opponent isn't very bluffy and isn't the type to semibluff the turn with a draw. You also don't think this opponent would try a big river bluff. In this scenario, river bluffing frequency is a key factor.

Against a tricky player who bluffs rivers, your best play can be to call the turn raise and then checkcall any river. But against this opponent who does not bluff many rivers, calling the turn raise and then checkfolding to a big bet on the river works. Since he doesn't make many big river bluffs, you can safely fold to a big river bet. You might also bet certain river cards, planning to fold to a raise.

You call the raise. The river is the **K♦**, completing the flush. You check, and your opponent bets the pot, $103. Should you call, fold, or raise?

You already determined that this opponent would rarely bluff the river. What's more, the river completes the flush, so an aggressive value bet from even middle two pair is unlikely, particularly since you called a sizable turn raise. Your opponent's range for betting the pot on this river is pretty much flushes, straights, and sets. Your best play is to fold.

Note that you were committed on the flop but ultimately decided to fold. The turn and river cards combined with your opponent's betting line and your analysis of his range tipped the scales. Keep your commitment decisions fluid, especially against solid, thinking opponents.

Flop Checkraise Bluff Against An Aggressive Player

This hand occurred in a $1–$2 6-max game. Both players started with around $200.

Everyone folded to the player in the small blind who raised to $7 with **A♣5♦**. Weak offsuit aces are generally bad hands in no-limit, but in a blind-versus-blind battle they will usually be worth playing. Pitted against one random hand, the showdown value of the ace makes it a decent starter, even out of position. However, if you feel the big blind is a tougher and trickier player than you are, you can just fold. Ace-rag is still a marginal hand, and you'll be playing out of position.

The big blind reraised the minimum to $12. In a blind-versus-blind battle, this min-reraise doesn't necessarily signify a strong hand. In the actual hand, the small blind thought that after the flop, he would have the advantage of being the better hand reader, so he called.

The flop came **Q♠7♣5♠**. The small blind checked, and the big blind bet $20 into this $24 pot. The small blind bluff checkraised to $68, and the big blind folded.

The flop bluff checkraise is an invaluable defensive play when you're out of position against an aggressive positional player. Many of your opponents will raise preflop with position and then continuation bet nearly every flop. To defend against this strategy, checkraise those c-bets sometimes, both with good hands and with bluffs or semibluffs.

This flop presents a good opportunity to bluff. The checkraise size puts about 40 percent of the total stacks in the middle, putting the big blind to a commitment decision. Relatively few hands are strong enough to commit reasonably on this flop. Without at least a decent queen, an overpair, or a strong spade, most opponents will give up.

This play only works if the big blind could have a wide range of hands after min-reraising preflop and c-betting the flop. But as long as the big blind is aggressive, this is usually a good spot for a checkraise bluff.

A Turn Semibluff

Stacks are $200. Everyone folds to the 29/26 small blind who raises to $8. He is an aggressive regular who likes to bluff, but he's also a smart player and a good hand reader. You are in the big blind with **A♥T♣**.

Reraising is almost always a decent option when this opponent opens from the small blind, as his range is so wide. However, you don't mind calling in this spot. You have a good but not great hand, and you have position in a heads-up pot. Calling keeps the preflop pot smaller and allows for more flexibility postflop. Reraising increases the preflop pot, chases out the weaker hands in his range, and leaves you susceptible to a bluff 4-bet.

This time, you call. The flop comes **Q♥T♥3♣**. The small blind c-bets $16 into the $16 pot. You call.

The turn is the **K♥**. Your opponent bets $48 into the $48 pot. Action is on you.

This is a good spot for a big semibluff. Your opponent is very aggressive, and he isn't afraid to fire two barrels with a wide range of hands. You have third pair, a straight draw, and the nut flush draw. Your pot equity is good, but your implied odds aren't, as both of your draws are obvious one-card draws.

You have $172 left. Push it all in. Your fold equity is good due to your opponent's wide range. Your move is strong, and he'll have a hard time calling without a strong hand. And if he does call, you have outs no matter what he has.

You must occasionally make moves like this against good hand readers in order to balance your lines. If you always have strong made hands when you push the turn, your stronger opponents can correctly get away from hands like top pair, two pair, and in extreme cases even a straight or set.

A Flop Sandwich Bluff

Players generally play more straightforwardly in multiway pots. Checks mean weakness more often, and bets are more likely to mean strength. Aggressive opponents often won't be shy to shove good draws in multiway pots, but they are generally less likely to try a stone bluff on a coordinated **T♥9♠7♠** board than a dry **J♣2♦2♠** board.

In this hand, one player uses both of these principles to steal the pot on the flop. Effective stacks are $220. An aggressive player opens from under the gun for $7. Our hero for the hand calls next to act with **K♣Q♣**. A loose player calls on the button, and it's 3-handed in a $24 pot.

The flop comes **T♠7♥6♥**. The first player checks. Our hero bets $17, and both players fold.

The under the gun player raised preflop, a strong move. But then he checked this coordinated flop into two players. In multiway pots and on coordinated boards, checks more often mean weakness. This player is likely to have a good preflop hand that missed this board, such as ace-queen or pocket fours. If the stacks were shorter, the check could be setting up a checkraise all-in with a strong hand. But that play is unlikely with these stacks.

What about the button? Even with a wide starting range, he misses this flop more often than he hits it. When he does connect, his hand is usually marginal. So bluffing into the button is reasonable.

In addition, bluffing here has two more things going for it:

The button may not notice how weak the under the gun player's check is, and he may feel sandwiched between the bettor and the preflop raiser. This may induce him to fold marginal hands such as **6♦4♦**.

The hero has two overcards to the board, so even if the button calls with a flopped pair, hero might get a chance or two to catch top pair and win at showdown.

Finally, this bluff is more credible coming from the middle player than it would be coming from the button. It would be a good bluff on the button also, since two checks would imply a lot of weakness. But creative players who initially check a weak hand might decide to try a resteal against the button's obvious position bet. That will happen less often when the middle player bluffs, because his bet represents more strength.

Attacking A Weak Pair Of Bets

Weak small bets of one-third the pot or less are a common and exploitable vice among bad players. Such small bets aren't inherently flawed, but when bad players make them, they typically indicate a weak hand. These weak bets practically beg good players to take the pot away.

In many cases, exploiting a small bet that likely means a weak hand is as easy as raising. This hand was more involved.

Effective stacks are short at $80. The weak player limps in from the cutoff seat. The button folds, and you call the in the small blind with **J♠7♠**. The big blind checks.

The flop comes **K♣Q♠T♦**, giving you a one-card open-ended straight draw and a backdoor flush draw. You check, the big blind checks, and the cutoff bets $4. You call, and the big blind folds.

The turn is the **2♠**, giving you a flush draw to go with your straight draw. You check, and the cutoff bets $2.

Coming from a poor player, this betting sequence, first $4 into a $6 pot and then $2 into a $14 pot, usually means a weak hand. In this hand, it could represent a jack such as **J♥5♥**, an ace such as **A♣3♠**, a pair of queens or tens, or even an underpair.

Using the straight and flush draws as backup, you decide to exploit the weak bet by putting in a roughly pot-sized semibluff checkraise to $20. Sometimes this bet will win immediately, folding out the weak pairs. Sometimes the opponent will call, most likely when he has a jack, but possibly also with a pair, an ace, or some other hand we didn't account for. In this hand, the opponent calls.

The river is the **6♦**. You go all-in for $54 into the $54 pot. This final bet should fold out lingering hands like jack-eight, ace-rag, and possibly some weak pairs. Overall it should show a profit because it will fold out more hands that beat you (all the naked aces and many weak pairs) than the few hands that may still call like queen-jack.

If you were to check, however, you should absolutely not fold if your opponent makes another tiny bet at you. He'll have a jack or other hand you beat too often to fold getting $54 to $2. You can call or checkraise.

The point of this hand is that you can often exploit bad players who make tiny bets by raising them. When you don't win immediately, as in this hand, you may be able to narrow down your opponent's range. That knowledge may allow you to bluff profitably on the following round.

Beware strong players making small bets. They may be trying to lure you into attacking them with bluff-raises. Some players are overwhelmingly weak when they bet like this, and some aren't. Before you attack, verify that you're against the weak player.

Hand Against A Tough Opponent

In a 6-handed $1–$2 game with $240 effective stacks, the player in middle position opens for $7. You have played with this opponent quite a bit. He is a tough, loose-aggressive player, and he views you as the same. His stats are 28/26 with a 3-bet percentage of 10. The cutoff folds, and the button calls. The button is a tight 16/14 player who is straightforward postflop. The small blind folds. You are in the big blind with **K♠9♠**.

All three options are viable here. Folding is okay because you are out of position with a fairly marginal hand against decent opponents. 3-bet squeezing is decent, but the problem is that you have a history of getting into 3-bet/4-bet wars with the player in middle position. You think a squeeze here would look transparent and there's a good chance he'd 4-bet you. You decide to call because you are closing the action, you feel comfortable holding your own postflop, and, to some extent, the tight button's presence in the hand will keep the middle position player in line.

The flop comes **K♥Q♣3♠**, giving you top pair and a backdoor flush draw. The pot is $22, you have $233 behind, and you are first to act. You decide to check to keep the pot small for now, let the original raiser c-bet, and see what develops. Surprisingly, both opponents check.

The turn is the **7♣**, putting two clubs on board. What should you do?

The action on the flop should give you a good clue as to what your opponents have. After raising preflop, the aggressive middle position player would almost never check a big hand in a multiway pot on this flop with just one player behind him who is tight. He probably checked because he was concerned about what the tight button had. He most likely has nothing or a modest hand like a queen or a middle pocket pair. But he almost never has a big hand unless he hit a set of sevens on the turn. And the button also likely doesn't have a big hand. We know he plays straightforwardly, and he checked behind on the flop to close the action.

You almost always have the best hand on the turn. The only better hands that your opponents are likely to be playing so carefully are king-jack and king-ten. However, those hands are unlikely given that you are holding a king and that they would have bet the flop a good percentage of the time.

You should be willing to back your hand with your whole stack against the middle position player, and you should be willing to call at least one bet against the button.

If you lead out with a bet, both opponents will often fold. And if they call, you may be in a tricky spot on the river, given that the board now has multiple draws.

If you check the turn, you will often see a bet from either a hand that picked up a draw, or a medium strength made hand that was keeping the pot small on the flop. The middle position player may simply bet because he cannot resist it after seeing you check twice.

You check, the middle position player bets $18, and the button folds. You checkraise to $68, and your opponent makes it $118. The reraise surprises you, and you start to think that maybe you misread his hand, or that maybe he picked up a miracle set on the turn. However, you played the hand very suspiciously, and there's an excellent chance your opponent thinks you have absolutely nothing, particularly given your history with him. Most importantly, you anticipated this and made your commitment decision before making the checkraise. Stick the rest of your chips in.

This is an out-leveling play. You are checking a solid hand twice in an unlikely situation in order to confuse the strong player and induce a mistake from him. Out-leveling plays are lethal when used sparingly, but very vulnerable when overused. If your opponent knows to frequently expect such trickery from you, he may learn to check pocket aces on the flop to induce bonus turn action. That would be him out-leveling you. Before you try to out-level your opponent, be fairly certain you will usually come out on top.

Against tough, aggressive opponents, you need to mix up your play with occasional unorthodox lines. With wider opponent ranges come looser and more aggressive commitment decisions. As always, let good hand reading and knowledge of what your opponent thinks of your hand guide when and how you make those decisions.

Specific Preflop Decisions

We haven't given you cookie-cutter preflop guidelines yet—no exhortations like play this hand but not that hand from the hijack seat. And we aren't going to. You don't play a hand in no-limit because you're in the right seat for it or because it's on a chart. You play a hand because there's something you can gain from it. Following this principle correctly will have you making many plays that are hard to capture in a simple rule or on a chart. Sometimes you will be folding 55 to a single raise. And other times you will be 3-betting with Q4s.

We've already talked about many of the common preflop situations. We've talked about stealing and defending the blinds. We've talked about playing the 3-bet/4-bet/5-bet game.

There are some situations we haven't talked much about, but that we hope you can figure out for yourself. If you get a good hand in early position, go ahead and open it. If someone raises and you have J5o in the small blind, usually fold.

In this section we talk about some interesting preflop situations that come up frequently. For instance, how should you play hands like 87s when you have the button, but someone has raised in front of you? What should you do if you open from under the gun with a good hand, but someone 3-bets you? We can't cover every preflop situation. What we have done instead is illustrate the thinking we use to make these decisions.

Pocket Sevens Under The Gun

It's a fairly tough 6-handed $1–$2 game with $200 stacks. You have pocket sevens under the gun and raise to $7. Pocket pairs are good for balancing narrow ranges because they can flop monsters and are easy to play out of position.

The next two players fold, and the tricky, aggressive 25/23 button reraises to $22. Both blinds fold. What should you do?

Players often call here, thinking that the button's range is fairly wide. They think their hand is too good to fold, and that they should at least call for set value. This is terrible thinking.

If the button's range is fairly wide, and he plays well postflop, you don't have good implied odds. You won't flop many sets, and when you do he'll often have a weak hand that won't pay you off. The rest of the time, when you don't flop a set, he will put you to a tough decision. You will quickly find yourself in a big pot playing for stacks with a marginal hand. Calling for set value is not profitable here.

Don't call unless you plan to sometimes win the pot without a set. The problem with trying to outplay your opponent postflop in this spot is that you're out of position. Even if you are just as good a player as your opponent, his position and initiative give him a big edge. Also, while the button is aggressive, he's not stupid. He saw that you raised under the gun, so his 3-bet is more likely to be a real hand.

Folding is the best play. Don't try and take a stand every time an opponent plays back at you. It might turn out that you're overestimating your opponent's bluffing frequency. All you have is a pair of sevens, and it's common for him to have a range that does well against you. You're playing a strong range under the gun, so if your opponent truly is getting out of control with his 3-betting, you'll easily trap him in the future.

Pocket Fives On The Button

Stacks are $200. The first two players fold, and the 24/21 cutoff opens for $7. He is a solid player capable of opening a wide range here. However, he isn't too tough postflop, and you feel comfortable playing against him. The blinds both are weak-tight players. You are on the button with **5♠5♣**. What should you do?

Calling and 3-betting are both decent options. Your opponent likely has a weak hand since he is opening in late position, suggesting a reraise. And mixing in a 3-bet now and again with a small pair is good for range balance. However, you have position, and the blinds are unlikely to enter the pot or squeeze, suggesting a call.

All in all, you opt to call because you think it is the most profitable. When you play as well or better than your opponents postflop, look to play hands where you have position in a small or medium sized preflop pot.

You call the $7, and the blinds fold. The flop comes **A♠Q♦7♠**. The cutoff bets $11. You plan to implement the classic float play. You call the $11.

The turn is the **6♠**. Your opponent checks. You bet $30, and he folds.

Deuces In The Big Blind

Stacks remain $200. Everyone folds to the 20/18 button, who opens for $7. He is a solid player who opens looser in late position than in early position. The small blind folds, and you have 2♣2♠ in the big blind. What should you do?

Your default should be to fold. You don't have implied odds to play for set value alone. The button has a fairly wide opening range, and he won't have a strong hand on most flops. If and when you flop a set, you won't often get paid off.

Since you can't profitably play for set value alone, for these deuces to be profitable you'd need to win many times that you don't flop a set. You might do that by introducing a randomized bluffing strategy like checkraising him on certain flops, or by trying to win a showdown by checkcalling him down on certain boards. However, 2♣2♠ is a poor hand for implementing either of these strategies. It's hard to make a stand with deuces unimproved, and you will rarely have more than two outs postflop, leaving you few semibluff opportunities.

You can also sometimes reraise preflop. This works best against opponents who tighten up to a 3-bet. Against an aggressive raiser who does not fold to 3-bets, it's better to fold the deuces.

If you must call heads-up out of the blinds to keep a loose button raiser in check, do it with a hand that plays better postflop than pocket deuces.

Pocket Tens In The Small Blind

In a $1–$2 game with $200 effective stacks, the cutoff opens for $7, and the button folds. You are in the small blind with pocket tens. What should you do?

The short answer is "it depends." But let's elaborate.

When To 3-Bet

Three-betting should be your default play in this situation. Your hand does well against a typical cutoff opening range, and a 3-bet here will usually isolate the opening raiser. Often the raiser will just fold, and you'll win the pot outright. That's a good result. When he doesn't fold, he'll frequently play suboptimally against your 3-bet. That's also a good result.

Many opponents make the typical mistake of calling your 3-bet to play fit-or-fold. They'll call your 3-bet with big cards and small pairs. Then they'll fold on the flop unless they flop top pair or a set. They won't steal enough, and they won't put you to tough postflop decisions. When they 4-bet, they'll always have a premium hand. Against these opponents, you should 3-bet just about every time with pocket tens and play a standard aggressive postflop strategy. Be careful when you face aggression. You should usually fold to a preflop 4-bet.

Against aggressive opponents who 4-bet more liberally or who call to try and take pots away postflop, adjust your strategy. Be more willing to get all-in preflop, and check more often postflop to induce bluffs.

When To Flat Call

Under the following circumstances, flat calling the original bet can be superior to 3-betting.

♦ The big blind likes to squeeze.

♦ If you know the big blind to be aggressive and squeeze-happy, call the original raise with the intention of 4-betting (or pushing all-in) over the big blind's 3-bet.

♦ The opening raiser has a tight range and plays it well.

♦ Say the cutoff is a 12/10 and plays well against a 3-bet by flat-call trapping and 4-betting with a balanced range. You are better off calling the original raise and playing carefully after the flop.

♦ The big blind is an exceptionally weak player and will often call $5.

If the big blind is, for example, a 52/3, you prefer to play many hands with him. Flat calling keeps him in the pot. Postflop, you need to adjust to the fact that you're in a multiway pot with a bad player. Play fairly straightforwardly and don't get too tricky.

This situation confuses many players. They don't know which factors are most important when they decide between calling and 3-betting. Further, no matter whether you call or 3-bet, if the stacks aren't short then playing pocket tens from out of position sets up tricky postflop decisions. Often people will remember the last time they got stacked with the hand, blame the bad result on their preflop play, and vow to do the opposite next time.

We suggest you approach the decision consistently. Pocket tens is a strong hand, and reraising it for value is generally a safe play. It's not safe in the "you can avoid tough postflop decisions" sense, but it's safe in the sense that if you were to reraise the hand every time, over the long haul, even if you messed up some of the tricky hands here and there, you would almost certainly show a solid profit. So, unless you can think of a good reason to call like the ones we listed above, reraise for value.

Flat Calling With Position

Stacks are $200. The first two players fold, and the cutoff opens for $7. You are on the button with A♥J♠. The blinds both are weak-tight. Should you fold, call, or reraise?

If the cutoff is a super tight player, folding is a decent option. Your hand doesn't have much pot equity against a tight range. Position makes it easier to steal, but probably not easy enough. Your opponent's strong range means that he will often have a decent hand on the flop. If he is at all aggressive, he's not a good target to try and push around postflop.

But let's say he's not very tight. He opens about a quarter of his hands in the cutoff. A♥J♠ is strong against that range, and you'll have position. So you aren't folding. Should you reraise or call?

Pros to reraising are that you can win the pot outright, you discourage the blinds from entering the pot, and you have initiative on the flop if called. Cons are that you put more money at risk, you create a big preflop pot with a somewhat marginal hand, you give yourself less wiggle room postflop due to the smaller SPR, and you eliminate a lot of the weak hands in your opponent's range.

Pros to calling are that you keep the preflop pot smaller, you give yourself more stack room postflop to take advantage of position, you keep your opponent in the pot with dominated hands, and you don't need to worry much about the blinds since they're weak-tight. Cons are that you cannot win the pot outright, you let your opponent keep initiative, and you don't put pressure on the blinds to fold.

All in all, calling is a good option in this spot. The pot is likely to be heads-up due to the tendencies of the players in the blinds. You may as well take advantage of your position by keeping the preflop pot smaller. Higher SPRs benefit position and good postflop play.

Calling works well for big card hands. With a marginal big card hand, you may not always want to commit with top pair, particularly against a decent opponent. But if you reraise preflop and create a big pot, it will be difficult to get away from top pair. To boot, your odds of running into a better hand postflop increase in a 3-bet pot, since your opponent will fold many of his weaker hands to your 3-bet.

Calling gives you more options. If you hit top pair, you can obtain more information before having to make a commitment decision. And you can still steal as well. In fact, even if you bluff raise the flop and get thwarted, you don't lose much more than if you 3-bet preflop.If you had a different type of hand, you might not want to call preflop. Say you had 6♣4♣. You won't flop a good hand often, so the value of winning the pot outright increases. This encourages you to 3-bet or fold instead of call. Although you'll occasionally flop a strong hand with 6♣4♣, the implied value of making these strong hands is usually less than the value of winning the pot preflop.

Calling a preflop raise with position can be a good option. It works particularly well when the raiser is not very tight, you expect the pot to be heads up, you prefer the preflop pot to be smaller, and you are comfortable playing against your opponent postflop.

Calling When Out Of Position

Many of the same principles apply when you are out of position. If you have a hand that prefers a smaller preflop pot, and you are comfortable playing against your opponent postflop, calling can be a better option than 3-betting. That might be the case when you have a hand like AJo.

If you 3-bet with AJ, you may find yourself in a quandary if you hit top pair. The pot will be big, so you will immediately be put to a commitment decision. If you are comfortable committing because your opponent has a very loose range, then 3-betting is fine. If you are uncomfortable with that, consider calling preflop.

Keeping the pot small is more difficult out of position. You have to act first on each of the remaining streets, and your checks may encourage your opponent to bet. It's easier to keep the pot small when you call preflop rather than 3-bet. And calling preflop gives you the benefit of being up against a weaker range.

Calling A Preflop 3-Bet With Pocket Aces

A weak player with $80 limps from up front. Everyone else has $200. The next player to act makes a pot-sized raise to $9. The cutoff reraises to $26. Hero is in the small blind with A♠A♥ and flat calls. The big blind folds, the limper calls, and the original raiser folds. The pot is 3-handed and contains $89.

The flop comes **9♦4♥3♦**. Everyone checks to the preflop reraiser who bets $56, a little less than two-thirds of the pot. Hero checkraises all-in for $118 more. Both players call. The limper shows **8♥8♦** and the reraiser shows **Q♠Q♦**. Two threes come on the turn and river, and the aces hold up.

When you hold pocket aces, flat calling a preflop 3-bet can greatly increase your chance to stack your opponent. Think about what hands you would 4-bet from the small blind after a raise and a roughly pot-sized 3-bet. Presumably that range is narrow. For many $1–$2 players, it is only pocket aces and kings.

Your opponents know this, and any 3-bettor will be alerted if one of the blinds makes a big 4-bet. Even some otherwise loose players will fold hands like pocket jacks, ace-king, and occasionally pocket queens in this situation.

With pocket aces, your goal is to stack opponents who flop top pair or an overpair. If you simply shove preflop, usually you'll get called by kings, but queens or jacks may fold. You may also fold out players with ace-king and ace-queen. If you wait for the flop to make your move, your targets will often make one more bet, which is great for you if they miss the flop and may be enough to pot commit them if they hit top pair or an overpair.

For instance, if Hero had 4-bet all-in preflop, there's a good chance everyone would have folded, and Hero would have won the $40 in the pot. By calling and checking the flop, Hero induced an extra $56 bet from the player with pocket queens—a bet that also pot committed him to playing for stacks.

Naturally, waiting for the flop can hurt you too. Most obviously, your opponent could outflop you by hitting a set or better. That will happen about 11 percent of the time.[18] An overcard could also come that would deter your opponent from getting all-in. If your opponent has queens, an overcard will flop about a third of the time, and if he has jacks, an overcard will flop about half the time.

But the rest of the time, you stand a good chance to stack him. Big pairs will flop an overpair far more often than they'll flop a set. So, as long as he will get all-in with either hand, you're a big favorite when all the money goes in. And if he has ace-king or ace-queen, waiting for the flop gives him little chance to outflop you, but gives you a good chance to stack him the roughly 22 percent of the time that he flops a pair.

You shouldn't automatically reject a 4-bet preflop every time you have aces. But sometimes waiting for the flop to pull the trigger can significantly increase your earn.

Lessons for this hand:

◆ Mix up your preflop play with pocket aces. In particular, consider flat calling a 3-bet if 4-betting would essentially turn your hand face up.

◆ Calling 3-bets with aces is especially worthwhile if the stack sizes are such that the preflop betting isn't enough to commit your opponents to their hands, but one more flop bet will do the trick.

---

[18] Anyone with a pocket pair has a 1 in 7.5 chance of flopping a set or better. If he flops a set, your aces will also flop a set just under 9 percent of the time. So overall the smaller pair outflops the aces about 11 percent of the time.

Pocket Aces With Deep Stacks

You are in the small blind with a $450 stack. The 25/22 button opens for $7, and he has you covered. The 27/25 big blind has $200. Both opponents are smart, aggressive players capable of making tricky moves. You have A♦A♥. What should you do?

A pot-sized reraise to $23 would likely push the big blind out of the hand and get it heads-up with the button. The problem is, unless you habitually 3-bet out of the blinds, the button may peg you for having a big hand. And with an SPR of about 9, he could make life difficult for you postflop. He can call for implied odds, plus he has position and plenty of steal equity.

You could make a big overbet reraise, as that would kill the button's implied odds and steal equity, thereby negating the cost of giving your hand away. The problem is that he will fold a very high percentage of the time.

If you don't 3-bet much out of the blinds, this is a decent spot for a flat call. Calling encourages the big blind to squeeze, and because no one will put you on aces, you may get a lot of preflop action. For example, if the big blind squeezes, the button may suspect him for just that and re-squeeze (4-bet). Or, if either player has a hand like JJ, TT, or AQs, they may overvalue it due to your flat call. They'll think they have more equity than they do and may stack off where they would not had you 3-bet.

If the big blind doesn't squeeze, you are still in good shape because your hand is disguised and the pot is small. For example:

You call the $7, and the big blind folds. You are heads up out of position against the button, but your range is wide in his eyes, and the SPR is about 28. The flop comes Q♠J♥7♣. You check, and he bets $11 into the $16 pot. You call.

The turn is the **3♣**. With a $38 pot, $432 behind, and only one more street to come, you have a few good options. You can lead big on the turn and fold to a raise. You can checkcall the turn and then either lead the river or checkcall the river. Or you can use the freeze play and check-minraise the turn. Which option you choose depends on how likely you think the button is to bluff missed draws, bet worse made hands, or call with worse made hands. But all the options can work because it is hard for the button to put you on aces.

Leveraging Stack Sizes To Get Action With Pocket Aces

The hijack player limps in. He started the hand with only $36. The cutoff raises to $12. He has $232 total. Everyone folds to the big blind who has **A♥A♦** and has the table covered. He merely calls.

The hijack player now goes all-in for his $36. The cutoff reraises to $90 total. The big blind springs to life and moves all-in, and the cutoff calls.

The hijack shows pocket fives, and the cutoff shows pocket jacks.

In this hand, the player with pocket aces leveraged the short stack to try to escalate the preflop betting far beyond what he could normally expect. The short stack limps in, and then a fairly big raise comes behind him. When the action gets back to the short stack, he'll usually either fold or push all-in.

The big blind takes advantage of this fact by just calling the preflop raise. If the limper pushes, then the cutoff will be squeezed between the all-in player and the big blind.

Indeed, from the big blind's perspective, since the cutoff made a larger-than-average-sized preflop raise, he may have a better-than-average hand and he might make a big reraise. Little does he know that the big blind holds pocket aces.

Consider what might have happened if the big blind had reraised instead.

The hijack player limps, and the cutoff raises to $12. The big blind now makes a pot-sized raise to $39. The hijack either calls or folds (if he's smart he'll fold), and the cutoff calls. In this scenario, only $39 enters the pot from each player preflop.

Another option is to try a small reraise that allows the short stack to reopen the betting by pushing all-in. The hijack limps, and the cutoff raises to $12. The big blind min-reraises to $22. Now perhaps the hijack pushes all-in, and the cutoff calls. That allows the big blind to reraise again, since the raise from $22 to $36 was bigger than the one from $12 to $22. So the big blind makes a pot-sized reraise to $144. Or the big blind pushes all-in. Or the big blind makes a slightly smaller reraise, hoping to get the rest in on the flop.

This last option has merits, but it has two downsides compared to the initial flat-call betting line. First, the short stack will be less inclined to push all-in facing a raise and a reraise versus facing a raise and a call. Second, after 3-betting preflop and getting 4-bet by the short stack, the big blind shows a whole lot of strength by 5-betting. That may allow the cutoff to get away from a hand he would otherwise go broke with.

Nevertheless, the minraising option has merit, and it may work out better than the original line if the short stack would have folded rather than move all-in.

The main lesson is that when a short stack has entered the pot, you can often play the hand in several ways. Some will allow the short stack player to reopen the betting by going all-in, and some won't. With aces or kings, you may want to allow the short stack to push all-in and reopen the betting for you.

Ace-King Out Of Position

Effective stacks are $200. The button open raises to $7. You are in the small blind with A♥K♦. What should you do?

The key to playing ace-king preflop is planning what you'll do postflop, both when you hit your hand and when you miss. As usual, let hand ranges and stack-to-pot considerations guide you.

Start with the button's range. Assume you have previously played with this player and know him to be solid. You think he'd open about a third of his hands here, and therefore you have excellent equity against his range. Folding is obviously out.

Calling keeps him in the pot with dominated hands that might fold to a reraise. Also, if he plays predictably postflop, you don't have to worry much about being bluffed off the best hand. Risking less money preflop could outweigh the advantage of taking initiative.

Reraising is good if the button will call with hands like A♠T♥. If so, you can reraise for value.

Next take into account stack-to-pot considerations. If you call, will the stack-to-pot ratio be low enough for you to be comfortable committing with top pair on most flops? Also think about what you'll do if you miss the flop. Will you bet?

All things considered, if your opponent is solid and also views you as solid, reraising to about $21 is probably the best play. You'll often win 4.5bb uncontested. If called by only the button, you'll have a $44 pot with $179 behind, for an SPR of 4. That's a good stack-to-pot ratio for committing with top pair, semibluffing, or sometimes firing a continuation bet if you miss completely.

Reraising also balances your range so that you have more than just big pocket pairs when you 3-bet. It's also a good play if your opponent will call with hands like 4♥4♦ looking to flop a set, and then fold on a flop like J♥8♦6♠.

What if your opponent 4-bets when you reraise? You are facing a commitment decision, so you should think carefully about your opponent's 4-betting range. You are getting an overlay of 1.25–to–1 to get all-in, so it becomes a math problem. If your opponent will make this move with only aces or kings, you have about 18 percent equity, not nearly enough. Even if his range is aces, kings, queens, jacks, tens, and ace-king, your equity (about 40 percent) is still not enough. For you to want to get all-in, his range must include unpaired hands other than ace-king. If that's not the case, you should fold to a big 4-bet.

In a typical button-versus-blinds scenario, 3- and 4-bet ranges tend to be wide. You can typically expect your opponents to 4-bet with unpaired hands weaker than ace-king. Therefore, getting all-in preflop with ace-king is the standard play.

Consider the tendencies of the player in the big blind. If he's an aggressive player who likes to squeeze, you might call the button's opening raise with the plan of letting the big blind 3-bet, and then reraising or pushing. If the big blind is a loose calling-station, you have more incentive to 3-bet for value.

One final point. Suppose the button open-raised two-thirds of his hands rather than one-third. In this case you should 3-bet far more often out of the blinds. Reraising is the easiest way to punish loose button raises.

Ace-Queen Under The Gun

Stacks are $200. You raise to $7 under the gun with **A♥Q♥**. Everyone folds to the small blind, who reraises to $23. He is a tight regular who plays 14 percent of his hands and raises about 7 percent. You aren't sure how often he 3-bets. What should you do?

Here a player who raises only 7 percent of his hands is 3-betting you, despite the fact that you opened under the gun. His range is extremely narrow and likely is AA-QQ.

You have weak showdown equity and weak steal equity in this situation. Fold.

Adjusting To A Short Stack

You are dealt **6♦5♦** in the small blind. The player on the button is a solid 22/20 regular, and both of you have $200 stacks. He opens light in late position, and he generally tightens up to a reraise. Your plan in this hand is to 3-bet if he opens.

The first two players fold, and the cutoff makes it $7 to go. He is a tight player with a $75 stack. He plays about 13 percent of his hands, and raises about 7 percent of his hands. The button folds, and the action is on you. What should you do?

You should change your plan, and fold.

You are up against a completely different range and a completely different stack size than originally anticipated. You need to adjust accordingly.

The button would open a wide range and then fold a significant part of it to a 3-bet. Reraising him with 65s would be profitable because you'd often win the pot outright. And if called, you'd usually still have some fold equity on the flop.

The cutoff, on the other hand, is opening a much tighter range. Your odds of winning the pot with a 3-bet are significantly less than they would be against the button. Plus, now your opponent has less than 35bb left in his stack. You don't have implied odds to call. And if you reraise and he calls, he would only have about a pot sized bet left, so he is probably not folding at any point.

When your opponent has a short stack, so do you.

Putting It Together

You've now read about all the main skills necessary to beat an online $1–$2 6-max game. You can steal the blinds and play position. You can profile your opponents and target their weaknesses. You can deploy an aggressive, but smart, barreling strategy to steal pots and balance your value betting. You can plan your betting lines to extract the most value from your good hands. You can hold your own in the preflop 3-bet/4-bet/5-bet game. You can make unorthodox plays designed to isolate and exploit bad players. You can adjust your strategy correctly to handle aggressive opponents. And you can balance competing factors to make sharp preflop decisions.

Let's put everything together and play some $1–$2 6-max. To work through each of these examples you'll have to use several of the skills you've learned. If you can choose the right concepts to use in the right situations, you'll be well on your way to becoming a small stakes no-limit hold'em master.

Hand 1

You are in a mostly tight 6-handed $200 max buy-in $1–$2 game. One loose, bad player is at the table. He has run up a big stack by getting very lucky. He is passive, a classic calling station with stats of 55/4. The player to your right is a solid 27/23 pro, and the other three players are tight and unimaginative. You believe a perceptive opponent would view you as solid.

Here is the lineup:

SB: Very tight ($95)
BB: Loose and bad ($900)
UTG: Tight and unimaginative ($200)
MP: Very tight ($150)
CO: Solid pro ($300)
BTN: You ($390)

The under the gun and middle position players fold, and the solid pro opens in the cutoff for $7. You look down at 9♥7♥. What should you do?

Many options are viable here. Folding is okay because your opponent plays well and your implied odds for making a hand are poor. Your implied odds are poor because your solid opponent is opening with a wide range. If you hit a big hand, you won't often get a big payoff.

Reraising is a decent option. Your opponent often won't have a hand that can call a 3-bet. His range is wide, and he would be out of position. You're also both fairly deep, so he's unlikely to play a marginal hand in a reraised pot. If you 3-bet, your main goal is to win immediately. If you get called, you are happy to have position, but you can't be thrilled about the lower stack-to-pot ratio that comes with the 3-bet and call. In general, the lower SPR makes it harder to steal postflop.

Calling has its advantages as well. You can't win immediately, but by keeping the preflop pot smaller, you can apply more stack leverage postflop. Your opponent will have a tougher time committing, which makes it easier to steal postflop.

Before you call, however, consider the players in the blinds. If you just call, you'll be vulnerable to a squeeze reraise from one of them. Fortunately, in this case both blind players are unimaginative, and you can expect them to play fit-or-fold postflop. Also, you want the loose, bad player with the big stack in the hand with you.

Folding, calling, and raising can all be right in various situations. Here with a strong raising opponent and weak blind players, calling often maximizes your positional advantage. Against tougher blinds, you would be more inclined to reraise or fold.

You call the $7, the small blind folds, and the big blind calls. The flop comes **Q♥8♦5♠**. The solid player bets $18 into the $22 pot. What should you do?

All you have is a gutshot straight draw and a backdoor flush draw. Your chances to make a hand aren't good. Your implied odds are only fair if the bad player has hit the flop hard enough to go with his hand but won't checkraise the flop. However, if the bad player folds, your steal possibilities are promising. You know that the solid player continuation bets a very high percentage of the time after raising preflop. His range is still wide, and he has likely missed this flop. You have a good chance of stealing.

The combined possibility of making a big hand and stealing the pot make this a profitable situation. Should you raise or call? To steal, you must risk a bet on the flop or the turn. Raising the flop takes that risk without knowing what the big blind will do, and without knowing whether the cutoff will check the turn. Calling allows you to defer that risk until you have more information. You call. The bad player folds. The turn is the **K♦**. The solid player checks. What should you do?

Don't check. First, a free card does not help you much. Your opponent is not likely to have a big hand, so your implied odds are poor for hitting your longshot card. Second, checking keeps the pot small, which benefits your opponent if he has a marginal hand that wants to get to showdown. Betting the turn puts him to a decision. If he happens to have a big hand he will checkraise you off the pot. But your opponent is unlikely to have a big hand, and since your draw is weak, you don't lose much if you are forced to fold. Your fold equity outweighs your implied odds here. Bet enough to put your opponent to a stack decision.

You bet $60 into the $58 pot. Surprisingly, your opponent doesn't fold or checkraise, but calls. The river is the **3♣** and he checks. What should you do? You should fire a huge river barrel. Why? There's almost no way your opponent can have a big hand. He checkcalled the turn on a draw-heavy board and then checked the river when no draws were completed. He either picked up a draw on the turn and missed (but can likely beat nine-high), or he has a one-pair hand that desperately wants a cheap showdown. The pot is $178 and your opponent has $215 left. You should bet it all. (You might bet a little less if you think that will look more powerful.) Your stack leverage is perfect. Your opponent didn't raise you on the turn, so he likely can't call an all-in here.

It might seem crazy to risk so much on a bluff, but good hand reading can lead you to make aggressive plays like this occasionally. Do not do it often. But being a tough, aggressive player who plays position well and is willing to make big bluffs when you know the opponent can't call will make you a nightmare to play against. If your opponent calls you on the river with one pair, you can adjust to that in the future. If he checkcalls this turn and is willing to put that much money in with one pair, he is essentially playing guessing games, and therefore, in future hands, he will be at your mercy.

Hand 2

You are in a 6-handed $1–$2 game. Most of the players at the table have $200 stacks, but you have $500, and the cutoff has you covered. The first two players fold, and the 28/24 cutoff opens for $7. He is a tough player and a regular winner in this game. The button folds, and the small blind folds. You have A♦K♣ in the big blind. What should you do?

With 100bb stacks, you would play this hand very aggressively. You'd reraise and even be willing to get all-in preflop. But with stacks this deep, you should reconsider that plan.

The cutoff is capable of 4-bet bluffing, but this deep he will not get all-in preflop with less than AA or *maybe* KK. So, if you 3-bet and get reraised, you are in a tough spot because he could be bluffing, but he will not put any more money into the pot unless he has you badly beaten.

When ace-king connects with the flop, it usually makes top pair. You'd prefer that your opponent make a weaker top pair. If you 3-bet, he will fold many weak aces and kings, hands you would like to play against. Further, heads-up out of position against a tough player and with a top-pair type of hand, you prefer to have only a small amount left behind in the stacks postflop. If the stacks are too deep to allow for that, you may prefer to keep the preflop pot small. Top pair hands work best with low stack-to-pot ratios. If a low SPR cannot be achieved, high SPRs over 20 are easier to play than medium ones. What you often don't want is to reraise and build the pot, but still have enough stack left such that your aggressive opponent can put heavy pressure on you postflop. If you make a standard pot-sized reraise to $22 and get called, the pot will be $45 with $478 left in the stacks. That's a stack-to-pot ratio of 11, ugly for a top-pair hand out of position.

Consider calling. A call keeps your opponent in with weak aces and kings and creates a $15 pot with $493 behind, for an SPR of 33. An SPR that high leaves tons of room to maneuver postflop. You can play against more second-best hands, control the pot, acquire more information, get value out of your hand, and never let your opponent put you to a tough stack decision.

You call the $7. The flop comes **K♥9♦2♣**.

You are obviously not committed. If 33 times the pot goes in on this flop against this opponent, you can expect to be way behind. Your goal is to keep the pot small, gain information, get to showdown, and gain value out of your hand.

With that in mind, you check. Your opponent bets $11 into the $15 pot. You call.

The turn is the **J♠**. Your opponent's range is still wide. He could have been betting the flop with a weaker king, a smaller pair, a straight draw, a set, two pair, or nothing at all. The jack on the turn makes him a pair if he has jack-ten, two pair if he has king-jack or jack-nine, a set if he has pocket jacks, or a straight if he has queen-ten. He can also still have a different set, a weaker one-pair hand, or absolutely nothing.

You check, and your opponent bets $25 into the $37 pot. You call.

The river is the **3♣**. The pot is $87, and you have $457 left.

You have a couple different options here. You are not committed, but you want to choose the action that maximizes your expectation, given your opponent's range.

You can checkcall a reasonable bet. The upside of this is that you let your opponent bluff at the pot if he has a weaker pair or nothing and thinks he can get you off your hand. Also, he may occasionally value bet if he has king-queen or king-ten and puts you on something weaker.

You can make a value bet yourself. The upside of this is that you make weaker hands pay to see a showdown. If your opponent is not likely to bluff if you check, you may as well make a bet and at least give him the opportunity to make a bad call with a weaker hand. Since you lose a bet either way if he has a better hand, betting and folding to a raise is superior to checkcalling. Sometimes he may just call with a better hand like middle two pair, and that allows you to dictate the price of showdown. But be careful about betting too small an amount. If your opponent is capable of making a big bluff raise, you don't want to encourage him by betting a weak amount. Since you plan to fold to a raise, you want to bet enough that he will raise only with stronger hands.

Ace-king is a strong preflop hand, but it can lose value as stacks get deeper. Off-suit and heads-up out of position against a tough player, big card hands can get you in trouble postflop. If reraising will create a difficult situation due to a bad SPR or folding out too many second-best hands, consider flat calling and keeping the preflop pot small.

Hand 3

Three players limp to the small blind who calls with Q♥T♠. The big blind checks. The pot is five ways for $10.

The flop comes 8♠4♠2♣. The small blind checks, and so does everyone else.

The turn is the **8♥**. The small blind bets three-fourths of the pot, $7.50, and everyone folds.

The flop comes low and dry. Everyone checks. There's a good chance no one has a great hand, but there could be a small pair like a four or deuce lurking out there, or maybe a pocket pair like sixes or threes.

On most turn cards, we would recommend you check again due to your many opponents. But the **8♥** is a perfect bluffing card for this board. It's unlikely anyone has an eight since the flop got checked around. Indeed, from your opponent's perspective, you, as the small blind, would be the most likely candidate to have one, since you might very well check it cautiously into four hands of unknown strength.

So when you bet the turn, you're representing something specific: an eight that you checked the first time around. Your opponents likely didn't have much to begin with, and now they have to worry that they are drawing dead to your trips. This bluff has a good chance to succeed even in a multiway pot.

Typically, you don't bluff into four opponents because their combined hand ranges are too strong. Someone is likely to have something worth calling with. So it follows that the exception to the rule would come when your opponents happen to have particularly weak hand ranges. This hand is an example of one of the times you can know that your opponents have a far weaker collective hand range than usual. Thus, it's a good candidate for a rule-breaking hand.

Finally, a quick read of your own hand seals the deal. You could easily have checked top pair on the flop from the small blind. If you were on the button instead, a bluff wouldn't be as credible since it would be hard for your opponents to imagine that you would give four players a free card holding top pair.

You might still try the bluff from the button, but in this situation the small blind is the perfect bluffing position.

Hand 4

Effective stacks are $200. Everyone folds to the 19/17 button, who opens for $7. He is a solid player, though not too tough or tricky. He opens on the button with a wider than normal range but otherwise plays straightforwardly. You have **6♠5♠** in the small blind and reraise to $23 because a 3-bet will win the pot a large percentage of the time in this spot. The big blind folds, and the button calls.

The flop comes **Q♥7♦3♥**. You c-bet $32 into the $48 pot. The button thinks for a few seconds and calls.

The turn is the **8♦**. You check, and your opponent checks behind.

The river is the **2♣**, and you are first to act. Is a bluff worth considering in this spot?

When your opponent calls your 3-bet preflop, you think his range is QQ-22, AK, maybe AQ-AJ or KQ, and occasionally a suited connector. He would typically 4-bet with pocket aces or kings.

When he flat calls your flop bet, he could have a stubborn JJ or TT, a set, top pair, or a draw like **A♥K♥** or **9♥8♥**.

But when you check the turn and he checks behind, his range narrows a bit further. The board is quite draw heavy on the turn, so the fact that he didn't bet suggests that his hand lies in the weaker portion of his range. He is very unlikely to have a set, and slightly unlikely to have a queen.

The river is a total blank. If he has a draw, he missed. He might have you beat with a better high card or a weak pair, but he isn't going to call a big bet. If he has JJ or TT, he called the flop to see if you'd let him get to showdown, but he's probably not going to call a big bet with either of those hands. The only hands he may check the turn with and then call a big river bet are AQ or KQ. But these are just two hands, and even then he'd sometimes bet the turn.

All in all, this is a decent spot for a big river bluff. The pot is $112, and you have $161 left. Push. He will fold often.

Hand 5

Effective stacks are $200. You notice three TAGs in the game (all about 21/17), a wet noodle (22/5) in the cutoff, and another one in the small blind (27/9). Under the gun you are dealt A♥8♥. What should you do?

Examine both the make-a-hand and steal components of this situation.

A♥8♥ doesn't make strong hands often. When you make a pair of aces, your kicker is weak. When you make one pair with the eight, your equity is usually marginal. Your odds of flopping two pair or better are slim. In a typical $1–$2 game you simply won't make a strong hand and get paid off often enough to play this hand purely for showdown equity.

Tight and shorthanded games often call for planning hands mostly around stealing. But here your steal equity isn't very good either. You are under the gun, so your position is terrible. If the game were extraordinarily weak-tight, and you had very good reads on your opponents, perhaps then you might raise to take control. But with no reads and a fair possibility of decent players entering the pot behind you, forcing a steal under the gun is a bad idea.

Folding is the correct play here.

Tight play under the gun is important even in games where your primary strategy revolves around stealing. In fact, often the mark of a tough player is a big skew in the number of hands played in early position versus late position. It is not uncommon for a very good player to play three times more hands on the button than under the gun, such as 13 percent under the gun and 39 percent on the button.

If you had **A♥8♥** in the cutoff, and the first two players folded, then you would almost certainly raise. But under the gun, against possibly decent opponents, folding is the best play.

Hand 6

Effective stacks remain $200. Everyone folds to you in the small blind. You open for $6 with **A♠9♠**. The big blind calls. He is a smart regular with stats of 27/24 and a 3-bet percentage of 6.

The flop comes **Q♦9♥3♠**. You bet $8 into the $12 pot. He calls. His range is pretty wide at this point. It's a blind versus blind battle, and from experience you know that he likes to float.

The turn is the **K♠**, giving you the deceptive backdoor nut flush draw to go along with your pair of nines. You decide to check for a couple of reasons. You want to give your opponent a chance to bluff with his weak hands. And you don't want to get blown off your draw in case he flopped or turned a strong hand.

You check, and your opponent bets $20 into the $28 pot. You call.

The river is the **9♦**, giving you trips. The pot is $68, and you have $166 left. What should you do?

Against a weaker opponent you might make a value bet, but here checking is a little better. This opponent will bet hands that he will not call with. Complete air is still very much in his range, and he'll obviously fold that to a bet. Furthermore, your hand probably looks weak from his point of view. After all, you checkcalled an overcard turn and then checked the river. From his perspective, it's a good spot for him to launch a river bluff. Also, if he has a king, he's probably going to bet it again anyway for the same reasons. So you don't have to worry about losing value there. He may even bet a good queen if you check the river. But he might fold that same hand if you lead out for a big bet.

When most players checkcall the turn then lead out strongly on the river, they are rarely bluffing. And smart players will often recognize the strength in that line and fold a lot of hands to the river bet. Therefore, sometimes your best play on the river when heads-up out of position against a decent player is to check, for the simple reason that your opponent will bet a lot more hands than he'll call with.

Hand 7

In the big blind in a $1–$2 game with $200 effective stacks, everyone folds to the small blind, who opens for $6. His stats are 19/17, and he has a Fold To 3-Bet percentage of 81. In position in a blind versus blind battle, you have a profitable 3-bet here with a wide range. You make it $18 with **9♣7♣**. He calls.

The flop is **J♥9♦2♦**, giving you middle pair. Your opponent checks. You decide you are not committed because your opponent will almost never get all-in without good to excellent equity against your hand. Given that you are not committed, betting this flop can work against you. While betting denies your opponent a free card, it opens you up to a semibluff. The board is fairly draw-heavy, and the pot would be fairly big after a flop bet, so a bet-fold would be too risky. Checking the flop keeps the pot more manageable, gets you closer to showdown, and gives you more options on the turn to use your position.

You check. The turn is the **J♦**. Your opponent bets $24 into the $36 pot. What should you do?

This is a great spot for the freeze play. A minraise to $48 forces your opponent to define his hand. If he comes back over the top, you have an easy fold. And if he calls, you often earn yourself a free showdown on the river. Plus, you force hands like **A♥Q♦** or **7♦7♠** to either put more money into the pot or fold. That's good because you get value while you have the best hand, and you minimize your chances of making a mistake on the river. Just make sure you occasionally minraise with strong hands too, or you'll be telegraphing your modest hand strength.

Hand 8

Stacks are $200. The button raises first-in to $7 with **J♠9♠**. A solid pro in the big blind calls. The pot is $15. The flop comes **K♥7♠6♥**. The big blind checks. The button bets $12. The big blind calls. The pot is $39. The turn is the **J♣**. It is checked through. The river is the **3♥**. The big blind bets $45. What should the button do?

A typical decent $1–$2 player usually folds, with the occasional suspicious call. The flop call followed by the big river bet suggests the big blind either hit his draw or flopped two pair or better and on the turn tried to checkraise or induce a bluff. A tougher opponent might also do that with ace-king or king-queen. Of course the big blind could be bluffing, but at first glance it seems unlikely.

Now let's look at it from the big blind's perspective. The button raises first in. That means a wide range of hands. The big blind calls. On the flop, the button c-bets. That means the same wide range of hands. The turn goes check-check. What is the button's range now? By far his most likely hand is nothing or a weak pair. If he had two pair or better he would normally bet the turn. He might have a king, but if you count up all the hands he plays, a king is less likely than a busted hand. Further, suppose the button frequently semibluffs with his flush draws on the turn. Then once he checks the turn, he is less likely to have a flush when the flush draw completes on the river. In that situation, the big blind can profit by overbetting the pot on the river regardless of whether the flush draw completes.

The big blind sees the profit in the line "call preflop out of position, checkcall flop, then bomb the river if the turn is checked." He can't do that every time though or the button will catch on. To preserve the play's effectiveness, he uses it less than half the time and also bets big with made hands. Against weak-tight opponents he can do it more often.

The button should adjust by defending or disrupting the line. Defending the line means playing it with hands that can win on the river. For starters, he might check the turn with any king then call the river. He might also call sometimes with his pair of jacks with a nine kicker. This is why you sometimes see excellent high-stakes pros make unexpected calls with third pair. They know their opponents understand the inherent profitability of that big river bet, so they call down with weaker hands. Top high-stakes pros also occasionally reraise on a bluff. However, on average they lose a lot when they attempt the steal reraise. The benefit comes in the future, when the big blind must make some thin calls himself and is discouraged from making the profitable river bet.

The button can also disrupt the line. Disrupting the line means letting fewer hands get to that point. How can the button accomplish this? There are several ways. He can tighten up preflop. He can check the flop more. And, after c-betting the flop and getting called, he can bet the turn with nothing more often. Should he do those things?

It depends. The button wants to pick an overall strategy that maximizes profit. Raising first-in from the button is quite profitable for him, so he doesn't change that. C-betting the flop 80–90 percent of the time also works well for him, so he doesn't change that. He decides to bet the turn with nothing more often and to call the river with weaker hands more often.

This hand illustrates critical differences between online $1–$2 with several decent players and online $10–$20 filled with strong pros. In $1–$2 most players don't take full advantage of the profitable line. They might occasionally bluff the river, but they do it infrequently enough that the button doesn't have to make hero calls. In $10–$20 the big river bet is a normal part of the game. Most players understand the line, and they adjust. These adjustments can lead to crazy hands, like the nut flush getting called down by second pair. In aggressive high-stakes games, if you don't look like an idiot sometimes, you aren't calling enough.

So what's the take-home message? At $1–$2 (and any other stakes where the regulars are reluctant to make big calls), exploit the big river bluff. When you are out of position and call a preflop raiser, then checkcall the flop and see the turn checked through, consider bombing the river.

Do it about a fourth of the time that you miss and work up from there if your opponent doesn't adjust. Don't try this against players who call with anything. And don't forget to make some big bets with your made hands too. But don't be afraid to deploy the big river bluff. Many of your regular opponents won't handle it effectively. It can be an enormously powerful blunt instrument with which to crush any online $1–$2 6-max game.

PART 3: 7 EASY STEPS TO NO-LIMIT HOLD'EM SUCCESS

At this point, your mind may be reeling with advanced strategies. Excellent poker involves adjusting to current conditions, but sometimes the adjustments can obscure the original strategy. The basics still need to be there. They are the foundation that all the adjustments stand on.

So, to refresh your mind on the fundamentals of solid play, we've adapted the following section from a series Ed wrote for his website. This section is meant to be a breather—a little easier to read and understand than the parts before and after. It's a good section to reread in the middle of a downswing when you're feeling like you just can't seem to do anything right.

Step 1: Play Tight

It's hard to find simple, unconflicted no-limit hold'em tips. Most advice contains the phrase "it depends" about twelve times. And it's for good reason: no-limit is a complex game with more exceptions than rules.

Having said that, I've recently been thinking, "If I had one week to teach someone no-limit, what topics would I cover?" I wouldn't try to be 100 percent precise or go into the details of the game. There wouldn't be time.

But that's not what most people want. Most people just want to be able to beat their regular small stakes game. I think I can help you to achieve that goal through some simple, straghtforward principles. This is what I've come up with, the 7 Easy Steps To No-Limit Hold'em Success. The goal is to hit the high points, avoid complexities when possible, and generally get you on the winning track. Let's do it.

Here are the parameters. You're playing in a full-ring (9- or 10-handed) $1–$2 no-limit game at a local cardroom. The maximum buy-in is $200, and that's how much you play with. The players are typical for $1–$2 games at local cardrooms, namely, they aren't particularly good.

Play Tight

Playing tight is the easiest and most important step you can take to improve your game. Yes, I know you saw Phil Ivey raise with 93 offsuit last week on the Ultimate Professional Mega Super-Duper Poker Showdown and pull off some sick bluff.

Nevertheless, playing tight is the cornerstone of good no-limit hold'em play. It's the rule. Loose is the exception. You have to know the rules backward and forward before you can learn to break them.

Play tight. What does it mean? Basically two things.

Don't Play Trash

Fold your trash hands. Most hands are trash. It's easier to define what's *not* trash, so I'll do that. The "Not Trash" list:

- All pocket pairs.
- Two suited cards jack or higher (e.g., **K♥J♥**).
- AK, AQ, AJ, and KQ offsuit.

Okay, it's not quite that simple. I have another list, the "Sometimes Trash" list:

- Suited connectors (e.g., **8♣7♣** or **J♥9♥**).
- AT and KJ offsuit.
- Suited aces (particularly the big ones like **A♦T♦**).

Everything else is trash. Don't play trash. (I'm not going to say this over and over, but I'll say it once here. These are the rules. Good players can and do break them. But you have to learn the rules before you start breaking them. Furthermore, don't let anyone tell you that following these rules will keep you from winning, because that's a load of hooey.)

Most of the trash hands look like trash. **J♦4♣**. Clearly trash. So is **8♠2♠**. Some trash hands masquerade as not trash. Here are some notable "It's Really Trash, I Promise" hands:

- Unsuited aces (e.g., A♠7♥).
- KT offsuit (yuck).
- Suited barely-connectors (e.g., 9♣6♣).
- Unsuited connectors (e.g., 9♦8♥—this will no doubt ruffle some feathers, but in general you really don't need to be playing these hands).

In no-limit, the headliner hands are pocket pairs, AK, and AQ. The rest of the Not Trash and Sometimes Trash cast plays a supporting role. They make money in their own right, but they also mix it up a bit so your opponents won't know that you always have a headliner. In other words, the supporting cast makes a little money on its own and also helps you to make extra money with your headliners.

So what's the difference between the Not Trash and Sometimes Trash hands? It's the second part of playing tight.

Play Extra Tight Against A Raise

Lots of people tend to play roughly the same mix of hands for a limp as they would against a raise. It's a big mistake. A raise dramatically changes the math of a hand. It's a very different thing to call $2 in a $10 pot with $200 stacks than to call $10 in a $50 pot with $200 stacks. In the $10 pot, you probably won't get all-in until the river, and most hands you won't get all-in at all. In the $50 pot, just one pot-sized bet and a raise will get all-in.

Because hands get all-in faster in raised pots than in unraised ones, favor hands that make something *quickly* when playing against a raise. The Not Trash hands listed above (pocket pairs, big suited cards, and really big offsuit cards) all make hands quickly. The pocket pairs flop sets, and the big cards flop top pair. Generally you'll know by the flop whether you "got there" or not.

The Sometimes Trash hands take a little longer. Suited connectors flop draws, not made hands. Likewise for suited aces. (Obviously, the aces can flop top pair of aces, but with a weak kicker, that doesn't necessarily constitute getting there in a raised pot since you might be against a better ace.) The longer the hand takes to materialize, the worse it plays in raised pots.

When calling a raise, tend to fold everything except the hands I listed above as Not Trash. When no one has raised in front of you, generally you can play the Sometimes Trash hands also.

Here's an example. You're four off the button. The player two to your right, a normal player in your game, makes it $10 to go. You have **T♥9♥** . Fold. Your Sometimes Trash hand is no good in this circumstance. You're facing a raise, and five players are left to act behind you. You'd also fold **A♣7♣** and **A♠T♥**. You could call with **7♠7♣** or **A♦Q♦**.

The other thing to watch out for when calling a raise is being dominated. If someone who's really tight raises, don't call with KQ offsuit. Your tight opponent will have AK or AQ a lot, and you'll end up losing your stack too often when you flop top pair. But if your opponent is not so tight, you can call with AJ and AQ and the other Not Trash hands.

The main message, though, is fold your trash. If you play this way, you'll notice that you're folding most of your hands. That's right. By playing only the best hands, you give yourself the best chance to win each hand you do play. This natural advantage you'll have over your looser opponents is the first step to no-limit hold'em success.

Step 2: Don't Play Out Of Position

Playing out of position is the number one mistake I see. I probably make more money from chronic out-of-position players than from anyone else. Here's an example of the problem. Our Hero limps in for $2 up front with A♣5♣. Another player limps, and then a tough player raises to $10. Everyone folds to our Hero who calls. It may look routine, but it's not. Limping in early with a weak ace and then calling a raise will get you in trouble real fast. Why is it so bad to be out of position?

The Problem

Being out of position hurts you in every aspect of the hand. It makes it harder to read your opponents' hands, it makes it harder to bluff successfully, and it makes it harder for you to make money on good hands and get away from bad ones. Basically, it puts you at a big fat disadvantage.

If you're going to make money playing poker, you need advantages, not disadvantages. If you start out of position—a big disadvantage—then you need serious advantages to compensate. Being God's gift to poker isn't enough. You also need a good hand.

The Good

If you're out of position, you generally need an extra-strong hand to play. This is doubly true if your in-position opponents are aggressive and often raise after you enter.

Pocket pairs play okay out of position, because they are binary hands: they either flop a set or they don't. If you flop a set, you're gunning to get all-in. If you don't, you're probably folding whether you're in position or not. So it's fine to play pairs out of position.

The really big cards—ace-king and sometimes ace-queen— also play okay out of position. Again, they're sort of binary. They either flop a strong hand or they miss.

The Bad

Suited connectors and suited aces really suffer out of position. You usually flop draws or weak pairs with these hands. That means you often have to play out all five cards before you know whether you've got something good or not. Every betting round where you're still on the draw is a round your opponents can use their positional advantage against you.

The Ugly

Getting raised by someone who has position on you is ugly. Oftentimes, if you're in there with a borderline hand and someone raises behind you, you need to fold. Getting raised represents a triple whammy:

1. It makes the pot bigger, escalating the betting and forcing you to make a hand earlier to stay in.
2. It gives your opponent the initiative, making it harder for you to pull off a credible flop bluff (among other things).

3. It forces you to bet more money while you're at a disadvantage.

Some Examples

In each example, you're playing $1–$2 with $200 stacks in a 9-handed live game.

Example 1. You're four off the button in your local $1–$2 game. Your opponents are typical, but a little more aggressive than usual. Everyone folds to you. You have A♦6♦. Fold! Don't play this hand out of position against an aggressive crowd. If you limp in, and someone raises behind you, you're in bad shape. You're not in great shape even if you get to play the hand for one bet. Your suited ace isn't good enough to jump in out of position.

Example 2. You're under the gun with 6♥6♠. You can play this hand. Pocket pairs are great hands, and they play okay out of position. Making a small raise and limping can both be fine depending on the particulars.

Example 3. You have 9♥8♥ in the big blind. An aggressive player opens for $8 from middle position and everyone folds to you. Fold! You're out of position against an aggressive raiser. Suited connectors are not made for these situations. It doesn't matter that you have $2 in already; it's not a good situation.

Example 4. You open for $7 with A♥J♠ from four off the button. A fairly good player one off the button makes it $25 to go. Everyone folds to you. Fold! You're out of position with what is now a marginal hand, and the money is getting big already.

The Bottom Line

You don't make money playing no-limit by playing fair. You make it by insisting on playing with an advantage. One way you can get an advantage is by playing only good hands. Another way is by playing only when you have position (or an excellent hand). Refuse to play so-so hands out of position, and your results will automatically begin to improve.

Step 3: Don't Overcommit In Small Pots

No-limit decisions revolve around pot size. More to the point, they revolve around the balance of risk versus reward. How much risk you should take depends on what the reward is. For instance, you'd probably never run across a major highway to pick up a dollar bill lying on the other side. But you just might decide to chance it if it was a brick of hundreds. You're naturally willing to take bigger risks for bigger rewards.

No-limit is the same way. What's in the pot and your opponents' stacks is your potential reward, and what's in your stack is what's at risk. When the pot is tiny compared to what's in the remaining stacks—like on the flop after two or three players limp in—that's a small pot. When the pot is relatively large compared to what's in the remaining stacks—like on the river after there's already been a lot of betting—that's a big pot.

Big Hands Deserve Big Pots And Small Hands Deserve Small Pots

Every pot starts small. Most of them stay that way. Every once in a while, a hand escalates into a huge all-in affair between two or more players. The point in a hand where small pots become big ones (or don't become big ones)—that is, the point where you need to choose whether to commit your stack to this pot—is a critical one in no-limit. Playing well at these critical moments will put you well on your way to being a solid winner.

There's one guiding principle: Big hands deserve big pots,

and small hands deserve small ones. If you have a super-strong hand like a set, then you want to get all the money in. If you have a weak or vulnerable hand, then you want to avoid a big confrontation. It sounds simple, but many no-limit players go wrong here again and again. Step 3 is about avoiding one of the most common problems, overcommitting in small pots.

Don't Overcommit In Small Pots

In an absolute sense, there are no good hands and bad hands. In some situations, it's worth going all-in with just ace-high, and in others, you should fold a set or flush. Hands get their value in relation to two things:

1. The hands you think your opponent could have.
2. The size of the pot (compared to the remaining stacks).

A♥Q♠ looks like a good hand on a Q♦9♦8♣ flop. But it's obviously not a sure thing. If you have a $20 stack in a $50 pot, then the potential reward is well worth the price of the risk and the chance you'll get burned. If you have a $1,000 stack and the pot is $10, though, you'd be foolish to push all-in with just top pair. You won't lose too often, but the price is way too high when you do lose. It's like crossing the highway for the dollar bill. You probably won't die, but for just a dollar, is it worth the risk?

Control The Pot

If you have $20 and the pot is $50, then you can just push all-in with your top pair. But what if you do have the $1,000 stacks in the $10 pot? Do you fold?

Of course not. Top pair is a good hand, and there's a solid chance you can make some money with it. The key is simply to keep control of the pot. Feel free to make a bet or two, but don't let things get out of hand. Don't let the betting escalate to the point where your stack is on the line. If you let things get out of control, you'll end up with two bad choices: folding or getting all-in against a likely better hand. Make sure it doesn't get to that point.

In practice, what does that mean? Say you have **A♥Q♠** on a **Q♦9♦8♣** flop. You raised preflop on the button and one player called. The pot is $10, and you have $200 left. You usually want a reasonable amount of money to go in the pot, maybe $40 to $80 more (depending on your opponent). If things get crazy and your opponent makes a big raise or threatens to play a big pot, then you're probably in bad shape. You want to stay in control and ensure that doesn't happen.

How to proceed depends on how your opponent plays. If he's loose and passive, such that he'll call with a lot of hands, but will generally raise only with a hand that beats your pair, then make some modest-sized bets. Maybe bet $10 on the flop, $25 on the turn, and $40 on the river.

If he's aggressive and tricky, though, and he likes to bluff a lot, then you can't just plow ahead and bet-bet-bet, because that's how you lose control of the hand. This flop offers a lot of draws, which means a lot of chances for your opponent to semibluff raise you. If you bet and get raised, you'll be in a sticky situation because your opponent will threaten you with a big pot. You may want to check the flop or turn to keep the pot the size where you want it to be.

To be sure, checking gives your opponent a free card to draw out on you. You may have heard that it's important to "protect your hand" with bets. But you don't actually protect a hand, you protect the pot, because that's what you're trying to win. And you also need to protect your stack, because that's what you're trying not to lose. How hard to protect depends on how big the pot is. Just like you wouldn't protect a loose dollar bill with your life, you shouldn't always protect a small pot just because you have a decent hand. Sometimes you need to protect your stack instead.

The Bottom Line

It's all about risk versus reward. With hands like top pair, how you play depends strongly on how that balance plays out. When the pot is already big, then the reward is worth fighting over, and you should bet to protect the pot. When the pot is small, but your opponent is too weak to put you to the test, then bet your hand for value. But when the pot is small and your opponent is a real threat, don't overcommit. Checking once on the flop or turn will allow you to keep control of the hand. If your opponent draws out on you in a $10 pot, no big deal. It's even okay if he occasionally collects $40 or $50. But if he takes you for $200 because you overcommitted with top pair, then next time you need to be more careful.

Step 4: Big Pots For Big Hands

Big pots and small pots require very different mindsets. When the pot is small and you're in a precarious position, you should be cautious and control the pot so things don't get out of hand.

When the pot is big, the reward is big, and you should take extra risks to win it. Creating big pots for your big hands is a key no-limit skill.

Big hands may come up only once per night, but that single hand can make all the difference. If you average a $200 win with your big hands, you might be a big no-limit winner, while if you average only $50, you could really poke along. Always remember, big hands deserve big pots.

Swing For The Fences (Europeans: Shoot For The Goal)

Many people flop a set and think, "Well, I'd better make sure I win a little something with this hand." That's wrong, Wrong, WRONG! Sets don't want to win a little something. They want to win huge, enormous pots that take ten minutes to stack. Sometimes you're going to scare your opponents out early and win nothing. So what? Play for the big pot anyway. After all, which is better: winning three $40 pots, or winning two $10 pots and one $200 pot? (For the arithmetically challenged, the second one is a lot better.) No-limit math generally supports swinging for the fences with your big hands, so put yourself into that mindset.

Chunk It Up

Okay, you flopped a set and you want to get all the money in. What's the first step?

Chunk it up. Look at the remaining stacks and mentally break it up into bet-sized chunks. For instance, say the pot on the flop is $15, and you have $200 left. One bet would be about pot-sized, $15. After that bet, the pot would be $45 (the original $15 plus the $15 bet and call). So maybe bet another $40 chunk. After that, the pot would be $125. There's $145 left, so you could make that the final bet. In this case, you came up with three chunks: $15, $40, and $145.

Sometimes you might want to make the bets a little smaller. So perhaps start with a $10 chunk. That bet (and call) makes the pot $35, so maybe next bet a $25 chunk. That bet makes the pot $85, so maybe next bet a $50 chunk. That bet makes the pot $185 with $115 left, so that's the final chunk. This process leaves you with four chunks: $10, $25, $50, and $115.

As you can see, you can chunk up a stack in many different ways. Oftentimes, you will have two major choices: three (give or take) big chunks or four (give or take) smaller chunks. Keep these options in mind for the next step.

Plan Your Attack

Now's the tricky part. You have to look at the exact flop, think about what hands your opponent might have, and think about how he might play them. After you do that, you have to decide which chunking style and what betting line will be most likely to build the monster pot you crave.

You're in the big blind with 6♥6♠. You're playing $1–$2. Someone open-raises to $7 from a few spots off the button, and you call. The pot is $15, and the stacks are roughly $200 (just like in our chunking exercise).

The flop comes Q♣6♣5♥. You flopped a set, and there's a flush and straight draw on board. Let's talk about some different opponent types for a second.

First, let's say your opponent is loose and a little too aggressive, especially early in the hand. But he doesn't run a lot of bluffs for big money, and he will fold if his hand is weak. If you check the flop, he's likely to bet with almost anything. You can take advantage of that fact and the fact that he's a little loose, but not crazy, by breaking it up into the four smaller chunks. Your plan is to check and let him bet. Then you'll raise, but not a huge amount: depending on how much he bets, it could be a minraise or maybe a half-pot to two-thirds pot raise. You want to make sure he calls with some of his weakish hands like AK or 88.

That puts two chunks in the pot. If he calls, you then bet chunk #3 on the turn and chunk #4 on the river.

Now say your opponent is really loose and crazy, almost a maniac. If you bet the flop, you expect him to raise with a lot of hands, even some not-so-great ones. Here the three chunk option is perfect. You bet, let him raise, and then move all-in for chunk #3. You're getting all-in early on this one. Or as a possible alteration, you can just call the flop raise, check the turn, and then checkraise all-in. Which one you choose depends on how likely he is to call your flop all-in and how likely he is to bet the turn if checked to. But either way, you should take the betting to him early with a large-sized lead.

Now say your opponent is weak and passive. He folds often, he rarely bluffs, and he almost never raises without a big hand. If you check the flop, he may well check behind, even if he's got a fairly decent hand. You don't want that to happFurthermore, you're unlikely to get more than three chunks in, since he's probably not going to raise. So I like the three chunk option with a bet-bet-bet plan. If he folds, so be it. This guy folds a lot, so it's going to happen. But bet-bet-bet is your best chance to win a big pot from him.

No Slowplaying Allowed

Slowplaying has its place. But it's almost always a bad idea when you flop a set. Big hands deserve big pots, and you don't build a big pot with checks and calls. Come out swinging, especially on the flop. Letting the flop get checked through can mean the difference between winning a $120 bet on the end and a $50 bet. In the above examples, we played the hand three different ways against three different opponents. But on the flop in each case, we either bet out or checkraised. In this situation, checking and calling is not where it's at.

Playing big hands well is an important no-limit skill. Remember the three basic principles:

1. Swing for the fences.
2. Mentally divide up the stacks into bet-sized chunks.
3. Think about how your opponent plays and choose the betting line most likely to build a monster pot.

Step 5: Pull The Trigger

Bluffing is the most mystical aspect of no-limit. It captures the imagination of everyone, not just poker players. Indeed, it seems the less people know about poker, the more they think poker is all about bluffing.

Bluffing isn't the be-all-and-end-all, but it's a very important no-limit skill. This article will hit the high points.

The Guidelines

A lot of bluffing in no-limit is "smallball." You throw out a modest bet to try to pick up a pot no one else wants. A continuation bet after the flop can be an example of such a bluff. So are position bets, bets from the blinds after a checked flop, and so forth. If no one else seems to want a pot, often you should toss something out there and see if you take the pot down.

This article concentrates on big bluffs. I can't tell you when your opponent will fold, but I can give you some general practical guidelines for getting the most out of your bluffs.

Be In Position

Having position makes bluffing a lot easier. It gives you extra information about the strength of your opponent's hand, and it puts your out-of-position opponent in a vulnerable situation. It's like having the high ground in a battle. Your adversary is likely to give up without a fight if he's gazing uphill at an imposing fortress. If instead he has the high ground, he may decide to take more chances. Bluffing is partly about making your opponent feel at risk and vulnerable, and he's more likely to feel that way if he's out of position.

If you do bluff from out of position, you tend to want both a fairly strong draw and the bluff to be naturally all-in (or close to it). For instance, say you're in a $20 pot with $100 behind. You flop the nut flush draw. If you check and your opponent bets $20, you could move all-in for $80 more. Since you're all-in, your opponent can't put you to a tough decision by reraising you (or calling and betting the turn). And since you have a good draw, you still have a good chance to win even if your bluff fails.

Of course, since you're reading this book, you don't play many pots out of position anyway.

If you're in position, you have more latitude. You often don't need as good of a hand or need to be all-in. All you need is the right situation.

Make The Bluff Enough

A while ago, a friend of mine played the following hand. He and his opponent both had about $120 in a $1–$2 game. His opponent opened for $7, and he called on the button with T♣8♣. The flop came 9♥7♠2♣, giving him a straight draw. His opponent bet $20, and he called. The turn was the 2♥. His opponent bet $50, and he raised $43 more all-in.

His opponent hemmed and hawed, and then eventually called and turned over K♠Q♠. The river was a blank, and king-high won.

As my friend was telling me about the hand, he kept saying, "King-high. Can you believe that fish called me with king-high? What was he thinking?"

Unfortunately, my friend's bluff wasn't large enough. By the time he got around to trying to push his opponent off his hand, the pot was $200, and it was just $43 more to call. Since the pot offered nearly 5–to–1, the player with king-high likely figured that, despite his weak hand, he had pot odds to call.

If you want your big bluffs to work, make sure you don't offer such good odds to your opponent. Good odds make your opponent think "What the heck?" and call with weak hands. If you and your opponent are nearly all-in and you can't bet at least two-thirds the pot, often you shouldn't try the bluff at all.

Try To Leave Something Behind

Bluffs tend to be more effective if there's a threat of an even bigger bet on the next round. It's one thing to call $100 with your weak top pair. It's another thing to call it staring at another $300 that might get bet on the river. Naturally, to make that threat, you need two things:

1. More money (preferably at least twice the size of your present bluff).
2. Another betting round.

Say the pot is $50, and you suspect your opponent may have top pair (and be willing to lay it down). Your best chance is if you are in position, you have at least $150, and you're on the flop or turn. You can bet $50 now, threatening a $100 all-in bet later. Or you can bet $35 and threaten a $115 all-in bet. There's leeway in how you bet it, but you'll have a lot more success with money behind than without. Sometimes you'll actually follow through with the second bluff, and sometimes you won't. But you'll always threaten it.

If you don't have enough money for a future bet, you're generally better off having a decent draw to go with your bluff. If you have the nut flush draw on the flop or a flush and straight draw combo on the turn, you don't necessarily need money behind to make the bluff, because you're in decent shape if you get called. In fact, money behind can be a bad thing in that circumstance if you'll have a tough call if your opponent moves all-in on you.

But the general rule is that bluffs with money behind are more likely to work than bluffs without.

A Standard Bluff

You are playing $1–$2, and you have a $400 stack. A loose-aggressive, but decent player opens for $7, and you call on the button with **6♦5♦**. The flop comes **J♥T♣5♠**. He bets $15, and you call. The turn is the **K♦**. He bets $30. Some players wouldn't bet the turn on a board this scary without at least a king. Not this one, though. He's aggressive, and he likes to keep betting until he meets resistance. After your call, the pot will be $107, and there will be $348 left in each stack. Let's run down our bluffing checklist:

♦ You're in position.
♦ There's another betting round after this one.
♦ If you raise, you'll have left in your stack at least twice the size of the raise (a pot-sized raise would be $107 and leave you with $241, more than twice as much).
♦ There's a solid chance your bluff will succeed.

This is a fine opportunity for a bluff. You could raise the pot, $107, but that's probably not necessary to get your opponent to fold most hands. When choosing a size, the first rule is to bet as little as necessary to get the job done. Here, a $70 raise is probably enough, so you might make it $100 to go.

Watch Your Opponents

While every player I've ever seen has been bluffable to some extent or another, some are obviously more bluffable than others. Before you launch the bluff, consider your opponents, the hands they might have, and which of these hands they might call with. And, obviously, the fewer opponents you have, the more likely your bluff is to succeed.

Pull The Trigger

The final guideline is to pull the trigger. Don't chicken out! It's a lot easier to talk yourself out of trying a big bluff than it is to talk yourself into it. To play no-limit well, you have to make big bluffs when the situation calls for it. Don't back down; just go for it.

It may seem like a lot of money, but really the math is not much different than betting a decent hand. If you follow the guidelines listed above, your opponent will fold quite often. In our example, we were betting $100 to win $77, so we were laying odds of roughly 4–to–3. If our opponent folded at least 57 percent of the time, the bluff would make money. It may feel like $100 is a lot to risk on nothing, but we have a chance to win $77, and with bottom pair we may even win the pot if we get called. Some bluffs will work, some won't, but if you do it well, over time your bluffs will make you a lot of money.

While I don't want you to run around being reckless, I think it's better to err on the side of taking a risk and going for it. As I said before, it's easy to talk yourself out of a good bluff, and good bluffing opportunities do arise frequently, particularly in tight games. Like learning to roller skate, you have to fall flat on your face a few times before you get it right. If you aren't willing to wipeout some while you're learning, you'll simply never learn. So play at stakes where you're comfortable, and start busting out the big bluffs. Once you get the hang of it, you'll be a real no-limit terror.

Step 6: Adjust To Your Opponents

Steps 1 through 5 have given you some easy-to-apply, basic rules of thumb for good no-limit play. Steps 6 and 7 are a little different. They require a little more interpretation from you, the reader, but if you master them, you'll use them for the rest of your no-limit career.

This section is about adjusting to your opponents. All players have weaknesses. In your local $1–$2 game, you'll find most of your opponents have huge, glaring weaknesses. Winning poker is about playing tight and staying in position and pulling the trigger, but more fundamentally it's about attacking your opponents' weaknesses. Every dollar you win comes from an opponent. Every opponent plays well in some situations and poorly in others. If you want to win the most money, you need to find the situations where your opponents give their money away and create them again and again. That's what adjusting is all about.

Player Classification

You are probably familiar with the "standard" player classes: loose-aggressive, weak-tight, loose-passive/calling station, tight-aggressive, and so forth. While I often use these classifications, they can be overly general. Three players might all play a lot of hands and raise a lot, thus falling under the loose-aggressive umbrella, yet play very differently and have very different weaknesses. Players aren't defined just by how many hands they play and how often they raise. You also should look for what kinds of hands they play, how often they slowplay or checkraise, how often they like to bluff and in what situations, which hands they take to showdown, how deeply do they think when reading hands, and much more.

Nevertheless, I will use the umbrellas listed above for this article. Don't take them too literally; weaknesses can show up large and small, and you want to exploit them all. But since you're probably most familiar with those categories, we'll talk about how to adjust to exploit them.

Exploiting Weak-Tight Players

Weak-tight players fold decent hands too often after the flop, and they don't raise often enough—either as a bluff or with good made hands. They tend to play tight preflop as well.

Whenever someone doesn't raise often enough, you can bet more hands. Betting puts pressure on your opponents, and if you tend to play in position (as you should), relentless betting is hard to defend against. The best defense is a checkraise, but weak-tight players don't use it often enough. So they end up as sitting ducks.

Their strong point is in playing big pots. Since they fold all but their best hands, it's hard to win a big pot off of them because they will always show up with an excellent hand in the big ones. So don't try to win a big pot. Win lots of small and medium pots instead.

Here's the basic strategy. When the weak-tight player enters the pot and you have position (preferably on the button or in the cutoff to discourage interference from others), raise. You don't need a great hand; more important is that you can isolate the weak-tight player. Though avoid really bad hands until you get comfortable changing gears.

This is an exception to the Play Tight rule from Step 1. If you can count on your opponent to fold without an excellent hand after the flop, it doesn't much matter what you have. Try to ensure you end up playing against only the weak-tight player, though. If others slip into the pot, you're just playing a bad hand.

The goal of the preflop raise is two-fold:

1. Isolate the weak-tight player.
2. Get more money into the pot.

You want to get more money in the pot because you want to win more when your opponent folds. Just make sure that you have left enough money behind to launch credible bluffs on the flop and turn. After your opponent calls and checks the flop, make a modest-sized bet. If your opponent calls, look at the flop and try to figure out what hands he might have called with and if he'd fold them to a turn bet. Follow up with a turn bluff when you think it has a good chance to work.

If you're new to adjusting to opponents, you don't have to go crazy at first. Just make the occasional extra button raise when a weak-tight player enters. Follow up on the flop and turn and watch what happens. Then try it again a few times. Learn what works and what doesn't, and do more of what works. Learning poker is largely a trial and error process, so be prepared to make your share of errors.

Beating Loose-Passive Players

Loose-passive players don't bet and raise often enough and call too often after the flop. Because they don't raise often enough, you can respond by betting more often. Unlike the weak-tight player, they call too often, so big pots are their weakness. Simply put, the goal is to make a good hand and win a big pot from them. Also, you can generally win medium pots against them with hands too weak to bet against a solid player.

Preflop, you should generally stick to playing tight. You can loosen up a bit when you have position and you can isolate the loose-passive player with a raise. Raising preflop is often more for isolation than building the pot, as loose-passive players will build the pot after the flop by calling with weak hands.

Postflop, you bet your good hands. Play for the big pots when you flop excellent hands like two pair or a set. You can also play for big pots with top pair/good kicker. Solid players typically won't call off their stack with a hand that can't beat top pair/good kicker, but loose-passive players often will. Since their calling standards are lower, you can push some marginal hands harder. If you flop top pair with ace-king, you should often look to get all-in against a loose-passive player.

You can even bet some weaker hands. Hands like K♠4♠ on a K♥9♦6♦ flop and Q♥T♠ on a K♠T♣2♦ flop can be worth a couple value bets against a loose-passive player. You don't want to play for all-in (unless the stacks are short), but you'll tend to have the edge as long as your loose-passive opponent doesn't raise you.

Don't launch big bluffs. You can try some smaller bluffs when it looks like the loose-passive player really has nothing. But the basic strategy is to play in position, flop a decent hand, and bet it.

Beating Loose-Aggressive Players

Loose-aggressive players frustrate a lot of people. They play "crap," but they are aggressive and can put pressure on you. Their fundamental weakness is that they put too much money in the pot with too weak a hand. You exploit it this way:

Step 1: Play Tight

Step 2: Don't Play Out of Position

Step 3: Don't Overcommit in Small Pots

Step 4: Big Pots for Big Hands

Step 5: Pull the Trigger

It may sound glib, but what you've learned in the first five Steps is the recipe for beating loose-aggressive players. They put too much money in with weak hands, so they are vulnerable to losing big pots against strong hands and to getting bluffed out. You want to avoid big confrontations with them when you are vulnerable. And if you play tight and play in position, you'll have the edge on them. The same recipe beats tight-aggressive players too; you'll just start with less of an edge because they are playing tight and in position as well.

Wrapping It Up

Adjusting to your opponent is a critical aspect of no-limit. If you play the same way against everyone, you will miss some of the most profitable opportunities. Look for the weaknesses in your opponents' play and then create situations that take advantage of them.

Aggression is the primary no-limit weapon, and passive players don't use it very well. You can exploit that weakness by betting more hands. You bluff more against weak-tight players, and you bet more hands for value against loose-passive ones.

Loose-aggressive players use aggression, but they can be reckless with it. They put too much money at risk without the goods to back it up. You exploit that fact by keeping the pot small when you're vulnerable, but making big bluffs and value bets when you have a good situation. That way you'll tend to lose small pots and win larger ones.

Most of your opponents won't fit nicely into any category or pigeonhole. Don't try to jam them in where they don't fit. Examine how each of your opponents plays, think about all the things they do wrong, and tailor your strategy to create and exploit those situations.

Step 7: Keep Your Head In The Game

Most good poker players fail. Or, at the very least, they fall well short of their potential. Even when they have mastered the small games and can easily play profitably at the medium levels, they tend to end up back at the bottom time and again, looking for a stake or rebuilding their roll at the $1–$2 game.

There's no shame in it. Fulltime poker is a grueling endeavor, even for the talented and experienced. But the problem most of these players have is they don't keep their heads in the game. It's not that they're playing in games that are too tough for them. It's that they consistently make mental errors and errors in judgment that keep them from getting where they want to go.

It's impossible to have no-limit hold'em success without tackling the mental side of the game. I can't cover all the bases in this article, but I'd like to share a few tips with you.

You're Going To Get Stacked Sometimes

My first mental roadblock when I switched from limit to no-limit was getting stacked. Frankly, I was afraid of it. It didn't matter how much money was involved. I played in limit games where $300 was a run-of-the-mill loss on a hand that went to showdown. These losses didn't phase me a bit. I'd lost over $5,000 in a session and went back in and played the next day.

But it was a whole different story in no-limit. I protected my $100 stack like it was my baby. I wasn't afraid of losing the money; I was afraid of getting stacked. To me, getting stacked in no-limit meant getting outplayed. It meant getting tricked. It meant being had. I had visions of some Doyle Brunson-like Texas rounder from the 1950s stacking my chips cagily reassuring me, "Son, you win some and you lose some."

It's all nonsense. Getting stacked doesn't mean any of that. It's a normal part of the game. In fact, if you play no-limit regularly and you don't get stacked, you're either buying in for a million dollars or you're playing like crap.

Good no-limit means putting your stack on the line when you have the edge. And having the edge is nothing like having a sure thing. You may have the edge with a big all-in bluff, but sometimes you'll get unlucky and get called. You may have the edge by getting all-in on the flop with the nuts, but sometimes you'll get drawn out on by the river.

If you have top pair against a really loose player, you often play to get all-in. It's a winning play because they'll call with even worse hands. But naturally they'll call with better ones too. If you're playing right and taking the right risks, sometimes you're going to end up all-in with top pair against a bad player with a set. And you'll get stacked.

Leave Your Ego At Home

Think about that last scenario. You make a big all-in bet with top pair. A terrible player you've been targeting all night calls— and rolls over a set. Would you feel foolish? Be honest.

Most people would. I sure would have when I started playing no-limit. Where does that feeling come from? It comes from your ego. Most poker players lose a lot due to their egos. Either they make unsound plays with bad hands because they have undue confidence, or they avoid taking sound risks to protect their ego from the bruising of an unlucky outcome.

The ego needs to go. It doesn't belong in your decision-making at all. If your opponent is bad enough to call an all-in bet with middle pair, then moving in with top pair is the right thing to do. Who cares what he showed up with this time? Don't feel foolish just because you got unlucky—not even if he needles you about it. Who cares? Your job is to make the best decisions you can, and if that's what you are doing, you should feel proud no matter who is stacking the chips.

Grousing about bad beats is another symptom of overactive ego. In fact, if you're grousing about bad beats, you have an especially acute ego problem. After all, if you lose to a bad beat, everyone can see perfectly well that you played your hand fine and got it in with an advantage. And with the release of everyone knowing you should have won, your ego is still bruised? What about when you get it all-in against a better hand? I can only imagine the internal mushroom cloud that scenario must generate.

It's ridiculous. Every poker player wins, and every poker player loses. No one cares whether you're winning or losing today, for the month, or for your life. No one cares whether you got your money in with the best of it or not. They may pretend they care, but they don't. Losing a hand doesn't make you lose face. It's all in a day's work.

If you feel anger, despair, or embarrassment at the poker table, chances are your ego is making your decisions instead of your poker brain. Tell your ego to stay out of it.

Every Session Is A Learning Experience

No one has completely mastered no-limit. Everyone has more to learn. Even the best players in the world need to keep learning, or soon someone else will take their place.

You're going to make a mistake in virtually every session. Sometimes you'll make several. Sometimes you'll make a whopper. It's natural, and if you let it get to you, then you're making another mistake.

Why are you playing today? Are you playing to show everyone how good you are? I hope not. I think playing to learn promotes the healthiest mindset. If you are learning, then it's okay to lose. It's okay to make mistakes. And it's okay to get stacked. You're just learning, and tomorrow you'll be better for the experience.

That's how I see the game—as a perpetual learning experience. And it's the method I've used to gain control over the tilt monster. Tilt is a problem for every player, but when you leave your ego out as much as possible and you permit yourself to make mistakes because you're still learning, playing poker will be a happier experience, your decisions will improve, and your results will eventually show it.

Keep The Stakes Comfortable

To have no-limit hold'em success, you need to risk your stack when the situation calls for it. After you've lost four buy-ins, you still need to risk your stack when the situation calls for it. If you can't—if you play in fear of losing—you simply won't play well, and you should quit.

Take the money out of it as much as possible. Play for stakes where you can lose 10 buy-ins and still be willing to risk the 11th. Some people say, "I can't play at those stakes because the money isn't meaningful. I just don't care anymore." You do need to keep the game meaningful, but playing high stakes isn't the only way to do it. One trick I use when playing for small money is to focus on one player and try to learn everything I can about how they play. Then I try to find situations where I can use what I've learned to win something extra that I'd normally have missed. It turns into a game on its own; I'm not worried about the money so much anymore, and I start playing better.

The bottom line is, if winning money is what motivates you most to play (or losing money what scares you most), you're likely to end up in some very negative mindset situations at some point down the line as variance carries you one way or the other. Try to find non-monetary reasons to play, to keep you interested. If you don't, you won't have anything to cushion the emotional impact when the results roller-coaster begins speeding downhill at top velocity.

Losing is as integral a part of poker as winning is. You don't necessarily have to love losing to succeed, but you do have to make peace with it. Whenever you lose, just remember that you start again tomorrow, totally afresh. The only thing different is that you'll be better prepared.

Congratulations

You've made it through all 7 Easy Steps to No-Limit Hold'em Success. Steps 1 and 2 will keep you out of the trouble many players get themselves into. By sticking to strong hands and refusing to play out of position, you'll start every hand with the advantage.

Steps 3 and 4 give you the basic fundamentals for postflop play. With small hands, avoid major confrontations, but with big hands, build big pots.

Step 5 outlines the principles of bluffing and tells you to go for it, because you'll never learn to do it well if you never have the heart to try.

Step 6 stresses the importance of adjusting to your opponents. After all, you win money not from your brilliance, but from their mistakes. If you tailor your play to take advantage of what they do wrong, you'll make a lot more money.

And Step 7 tackles some of the mental demons that haunt nearly every no-limit player. We've been taught that losing is something to be ashamed of, but in poker that couldn't be more wrong. You flat-out cannot win at poker without also losing as well. Your ego belongs well outside the equation. Learn to enjoy taking smart risks, and accept the sometimes unlucky consequences with indifference. If you treat every session as a learning experience, then unless you let your ego get the better of you, each day you are guaranteed to succeed.

Now go out and crush that local $1–$2 game. They'll never know what hit 'em.

PART 4: BEYOND $1–$2

This section features slightly more advanced material aimed at readers who are looking to take their games to the next level. Some of the concepts are complicated and require you to put on your thinking cap. But if you're looking to move beyond $1–$2 and eventually play at higher and higher stakes, you will find this section to be extremely valuable.

Understanding Fixed Bet Sizes

Fixed bet size means when you bet, you always bet the same amount or percentage of the pot. Most successful online players used fixed bet sizes before the flop, especially when open raising. Many also use fixed bet sizes on the flop. If you face tough opponents who read hands well, you should too.

When you use fixed bet sizes, you are betting a range, not the actual hand. For example, suppose one player's opening range is AA-TT, AK-AQ under the gun in a 10-handed $1–$2 game. When he gets one of these hands, he bets 4bb. Otherwise he folds. It does not matter which hand of his opening range (AA-TT, AK-AQ) he has. If he has AA he bets 4bb. If he has AQ he bets 4bb. This is a fixed bet size. Every hand in the range is bet the same.

Fixed bet sizes make hand reading tougher. When our example player raises to 4bb under the gun, you can guess he has AA-TT, AK-AQ. However, you have no idea which of those hands he has. Now suppose instead he typically raises to 5bb with AA-KK and 4bb with QQ-TT and AK-AQ. These variable bet sizes give you information. When he raises to 5bb, you know he probably has AA-KK. His varying raise size allows you to read his hand more easily.

Variable raise sizes give up information that opponents can exploit. Here is a practical example. A weak player raises in front of you, and you call in position. Suppose his range is roughly AA-22, AK-AJ, KQ. The flop comes ace-high. He bets the pot. Some time later the same situation comes up. This time he bets half the pot. After a few thousand hands against him, you realize that he usually bets the pot when he hits top pair and half the pot when he misses or flops a set. You now have a huge edge. A few hands later a similar situation comes up. You have 55 and miss an **A♠9♥8♥** flop. He bets half the pot. What does he have? You know he is unlikely to have top pair. That makes AK-AJ unlikely. His range is probably AA-22, KQ. It's very likely he missed.[19] So you play to steal: raising the flop or calling the flop to steal on the turn.

When To Use Fixed Bet Sizes

Use fixed bet sizes when your opponents pay attention. For example, if you are under the gun against tough regulars in an online $2–$4 game, you should always open raise for the same amount regardless of your specific hand. Betting and raising a fixed portion of the pot disguises your hand range. It makes hand reading harder.

When Not To Use Fixed Bet Sizes

That said, don't fall into the trap of always using fixed bet sizes. Fixed bet sizes disguise information, but often *at the cost of value*. Many times the trade-off is not worthwhile, and you should vary your bet sizes to exploit weak opponents. This comes up most often in live games. For example:

You are in a loose live $2–$5 game with $1,000 stacks. Your opponents aren't paying attention, don't adapt, and don't care about calling sizable raises preflop. One player makes it $20. It means little. Two players call. You have **K♠K♦** on the button.

---

[19] Of the range AA-22, KQ, nine combinations make him a set, 60 combinations make him an underpair, and 16 combinations make him king-high, one of which is the K♥Q♥. He is 76-to-9 against to have a set. Even with a small chance he bet half the pot with top pair, he is still a substantial dog to have top pair or better.

What should you do?

You could use a fixed bet size like "raise the pot," which is a raise to $67. However, these opponent don't use information well, and kings is a strong hand. It may sound crazy, but in some games you can make it $150 and still get called by several weaker hands.

Even against astute opponents, you can vary your preflop raise sizes if your opponents can't or won't use that information to reduce your hand range. For example:

You are playing in a loose aggressive $10–$20 online game with $4,000 effective stacks against astute opponents. They use information well. However, preflop many players are making huge raises with marginal hands in late position. The cutoff opens for $60, and the button calls. The small blind folds. You have A♥A♦ in the big blind. What should you do?

Ordinarily you'd just raise pot. But this time you decide to raise bigger, for several reasons. One is that the game has been playing very aggressively over the past hour. Everyone is 3-betting and squeezing left and right, so a big 3-bet will be viewed suspiciously even though you yourself haven't been involved in the shenanigans. Also, you are 200bb deep, so you'd like to get a lot of money in preflop with aces. This cuts a caller's implied odds to hit a better hand and may get him to stack off with KK/QQ or even less.

Sometimes within a game you can pick and choose which opponents to vary your raise sizes against. In a tough game, say you have a good hand against the one weak player, a calling station. Against any other opponent at the table, you would use a fixed bet of two-thirds pot. But this opponent will call much more. Take advantage. Bet as much as you think he will call.

If your opponents won't notice, or won't change their actions even if they do notice, vary your bet size and make the more profitable play. Otherwise, use fixed bet sizes to disguise your range.

Fixed Bet Sizes Should Vary With The Situation

Fixed bet means you always bet the same amount in a given situation. Many players take "situation" to mean something like "on the flop." But poker is more complicated than that. For example, betting the flop after opening from under the gun with a narrow range is not the same as betting the flop after opening from the button with 60 percent of your hands. They are vastly different situations, and they deserve different fixed bet sizes.

Fixed bet sizes conceal information. But some information cannot be concealed. For example, you cannot hide your position. If you raise under the gun, opponents know you are under the gun. So feel free to use a different fixed bet size under the gun than on the button.

Many other factors are also known to all. Everyone can see the board, so you are free to choose a different fixed bet size based on what cards are showing. Everyone can also see the stack sizes, the pot size, each player's position, and which opponents remain in the hand. Good opponents will also know something about how each opponent plays. You can use different fixed bet sizes as these factors change. "Fixed" means that when you bet *in a given and specific situation*, you always bet the same amount regardless of which hand in your range you happen to hold.

The best fixed bet size for a given situation depends on your range, position, stack sizes, opponent tendencies, and board texture. You also have to consider your opponents' ranges and playing styles, implied odds, how much aggression you may face, and most of the other factors that go into poker. It sounds complicated, but in practice it's not hard to do. Let's get to it.

Sizing Fixed Bets

Choosing a fixed bet size starts with your range and what you are trying to do. Is your range small and skewed toward made hands? Or is your range large and full of air? Are you playing primarily to make the best hand or to steal? Many other factors can come into play, such as stack sizes, the pot size, which opponents are in the hand, and implied odds.

We're going to go through hand situations and give general recommendations for fixed open-raise sizes for different positions, ranges, and stack sizes. These recommendations are just suggested starting points. The modern online game is too tough for cookie-cutter poker. In some cases, we give the theory recommendation and then immediately tell you that something else works better in practice. Similarly, if you find a suggested starting raise size does not fit well with your game situation, you'll have to adapt.

The starting point for choosing a fixed bet size for preflop and flop play is:

Match your bet size to the average strength of your range.

Strong ranges merit bigger bets. Suppose you are raising preflop with AA-99, AK-AQ, KQ. This strong range profits most from making the best hand, not from stealing. When you play to make the best hand, you like bigger preflop pots. So preflop, you do better by making a larger raise. If the standard preflop open-raise is 3bb, you do better with a 4bb raise provided your opponents will still call or reraise.

With strong ranges, instead of a preflop open-raise to 3bb, try 4bb. Instead of a flop bet of half the pot, try two-thirds the pot or more.

Weak ranges demand smaller bets. Suppose you open-raise on the button with 50 percent of your hands. You range is huge and contains many weak hands. Most often you will flop nothing or a weak pair. You are not playing primarily to make the best hand. You are playing to steal. When you steal, you normally prefer to bet the smallest amount that will get your opponent to fold if he will fold. If the steal succeeds, you win the same amount whether you bet 3bb or 20bb. But when the steal fails, you lose less when you make a smaller bet. With a weak range, small bets usually work better.

With weak ranges, instead of a preflop open-raise to 3bb, try 2.5bb or 2.25bb. Instead of a flop bet of half the pot, try a third of the pot.

Put another way:

> If your range is strong and the profit comes from having the best hand, use a larger fixed bet size as your starting point.

> If your range is weak such that the profit comes from stealing, use a smaller fixed bet size as your starting point.

We say starting point because range strength isn't the only

factor. Sometimes game conditions or opponents will push you to make larger or smaller bets. For example, if no one folds to your 2.25bb button raises, make a larger raise.

Remember, we are talking about fixed bet sizes. When you bet, bet the same amount regardless of which hand in your range you happen to have.

Let's go through some specific scenarios. We'll start with a few from 10-handed games to better illustrate some key points.

Hand Situations

In the following situations, you are in a relatively tough online $1–$2 game.

Situation 1: Open-Raising Under The Gun

Players at the table: 10
Effective stack size: 100bb
Your position: Under the gun
Your range: AA-TT, AK

Preflop. Most players open for 3bb or 3.5bb under the gun, regardless of how tight their range is. However, we contend that if you are playing a very tight range like this one, you should consider choosing a larger fixed bet size.

First, a larger raise size does not cost you. Big pairs and AK can call or reraise typical 3-bets. Since you won't fold preflop, there is no immediate penalty for raising to 4bb or 4.5bb instead of 3bb. Compare this with a steal attempt. If you open-raise with a wide range on a steal, you will fold to 3-bets fairly often.

When you raise to 4bb instead of 3bb on a steal, you lose an extra 1bb each time you fold to a preflop 3-bet.

Second, many opponents are almost indifferent to a 4bb raise versus a 3bb raise. You do not mind calls preflop since you have premium hands. You especially do not mind being called by weak aces and kings, because so often when they hit top pair you will have them beat. If raising to 4bb instead of 3bb won't cause opponents to fold many of the weaker hands in their 3bb raise calling range, you prefer the 4bb bet.

Third, stack-to-pot ratio issues do not affect a decision between 4bb and 3bb in 100bb games unless 3-betting is common. You cannot get to a low SPR without a 3-bet unless stacks are short. If loose 3-bets aren't common, ignore SPR when choosing a fixed bet size. If instead loose 3-bets are common, and the 3-bettor is indifferent between a 3bb and a 4bb raise, raising to 4bb is superior. A 4bb raise yields better SPRs for top-pair and overpair hands.[20]

What if the stacks are shorter? With 40bb stacks, it is criminal to raise to just 3bb with your strong range if your opponents will also call or 3-bet a bigger raise. For example, a 4.5bb raise yields an SPR under 4 heads up, whereas a 3bb raise yields far less attractive SPRs of 5–6.

Overall, with AA-TT, AK, raising under the gun to 4bb or 4.5bb is superior to raising to 3bb. If opponents will still play with you if you raise to 5bb, do it.

What if they just fold every time you raise to 4.5bb? Smile!

---

[20] With 100bb stacks, an open-raise of 3bb followed by a positional two-thirds-pot reraise to 8bb yields a pot of 17.5bb and an SPR over 5. If you instead raise to 4bb, these positional two-thirds-pot reraises yield a pot of 22bb and an SPR of 4 with 100bb stacks. An SPR of 4 is often easier and more profitable for playing a top-pair hand than an SPR of 5.

You are making money. You win 1.5bb every time this happens. However, you can probably improve. You might raise to just 4bb instead, or exploit their tightness by adding a few hands to your opening range.

Conclusion: Raise to as much as you can get away with. Experiment with increasing your standard raise size. If you normally open for 3.5bb, try 4.5bb or 5bb. If you don't get action, tinker some more. And remember, winning 1.5bb in blinds is never a bad result.

Flop. Let's say one or two opponents call your 4bb raise. What fixed bet size should you use on the flop?

Your range of AA-TT, AK is heavily weighted toward strong hands on the flop. You will not be bluffing often. So bet big. Here we recommend a default bet size between two-thirds of the pot and the pot. Start with betting three-fourths of the pot and see how it goes. If they fold too often, lower the bet size. If they play back at you constantly, increase it to a pot-sized bet to take advantage.

Does it matter if you hit the flop? Yes, but not for choosing a fixed bet size. It only matters for deciding whether to check or bet. For example, you might check more often when you miss the flop. However, when you do bet, use the same bet size regardless of whether you hit the flop.

Does it matter which opponent you face? Absolutely. Feel free to use different bet sizes against different opponents. For example, suppose your opponent calls with a wide range preflop then bluffs often postflop. His wide preflop range and frequent postflop bets mean he is bluffing and semibluffing a lot.[21] His range is weighted toward weak hands. Meanwhile, your range

---

[21] We are assuming you have enough experience with this opponent to know that he didn't just hit a good run of cards.

is weighted toward top pair and overpairs. Take advantage by doing whatever extracts the most. If he will bluff at pot-sized bets, bet big. If not, consider a smaller fixed bet size, like half the pot or even less, to encourage him to bluff.

Should you ever stray from your fixed bet size? Yes, if it will create favorable action. This is especially true against unobservant opponents. Remember, we use fixed bet sizes to disguise our ranges. If our opponent isn't paying attention, we don't need the disguise. For example, suppose an aggressive opponent reads small bets as weakness. He is not very observant, in part because he chats frequently while 12-tabling. This is a good situation for mixing up your bet sizes. When you hit, you might bet half the pot or less to induce a bluff-raise or a float. Fixed bet sizes are only a default. If you have good reason to vary your bet sizes, do it.

Situation 2: A Wider Range Under The Gun

Players at the table: 10
Effective stack size: 100bb
Your position: Under the gun
Your range: AA-22, AK-AJ, KQ

Preflop. Your opening range here is wider than in Situation 1. Should your standard bet size be higher or lower?

Lower! Adding 99-22 and AQ-AJ, KQ to the range changes things. Here is the breakdown:

Big pairs AA-TT: 30 combos (21%)
Other pairs 99-22: 48 combos (34%)
AK-AJ, KQ: 64 combos (45%)

This range is far weaker than the previous range. By our rule of thumb, weaker ranges deserve smaller bets. This is a medium-strength range, so in general we recommend a medium-sized fixed bet of about 3bb. But you may want to get rid of part of this range. Here's why:

Your average equity with pairs 99-22 is much lower than with premium hands. With these pairs, you would like to steal the blinds as cheaply as possible, play a multiway pot for a small bet to maximize set value, or—barring that—get it heads-up against someone who will let you steal postflop. Overall, you don't want much money to go in before the flop.

Big card hands AQ-AJ and KQ also have problems under the gun 10-handed. First, if they hit top pair or better, they often won't be against another top-pair hand. And even if they do end up against a weaker top-pair, they won't necessarily win much money. You want weaker top-pair hands to come in. A smaller raise size may encourage that. Second, like all big card hands, AQ-AJ and KQ miss the flop most of the time. If you cannot steal effectively when they miss, you often want less money in the pot preflop and prefer a smaller preflop raise size. Third, if a tight player 3-bets in this 10-handed game, often you will have to fold AQ-AJ, KQ. When the risk of being forced to fold preflop is high, you prefer smaller raise sizes or to avoid the hands. All this suggests a smaller raise size.

If you are curious how often you will be dominated when you hold a big card hand or big pair, check out the following chart.

Table 1. Percentage chance of various hands being dominated.

Number of Opponents Remaining

	9	8	7	6	5	4	3	2	1
K K	4.4	3.9	3.4	2.9	2.4	2.0	1.5	1.0	0.5
Q Q	8.6	7.7	6.7	5.8	4.8	3.9	2.9	2.0	1.0
J J	12.6	11.3	9.9	8.6	7.2	5.8	4.4	2.9	1.5
T T	16.5	14.8	13.0	11.3	9.5	7.6	5.8	3.9	2.0
A K	4.4	3.9	3.4	2.9	2.4	2.0	1.5	1.0	0.5
A Q	16.8	15.0	13.2	11.4	9.6	7.7	5.8	3.9	2.0
A J	27.8	25.1	22.2	19.3	16.3	13.2	10.0	6.8	3.4
A T	37.7	34.2	30.5	26.6	22.6	18.5	14.1	9.6	4.9
K Q	24.4	21.9	19.4	16.8	14.1	11.4	8.6	5.8	2.9
K J	34.5	31.2	27.8	24.2	20.6	16.7	12.8	8.7	4.4
K T	43.5	39.6	35.5	31.2	26.6	21.9	16.8	11.5	5.9
Q J	40.8	37.1	33.1	29.0	24.7	20.2	15.5	10.6	5.4
Q T	49.0	44.8	40.3	35.5	30.5	25.2	19.4	13.3	6.9
J T	54.1	49.7	44.9	39.8	34.3	28.3	22.0	15.1	7.8

This chart shows the percent chance a big card hand will face one or more dominating hands given how many players are left to act preflop. It assumes everyone up to that point has folded. For this chart, we define a dominating hand as one that has you beaten badly preflop or that often has you in deep trouble if you flop top pair. So AK is dominated by AA and KK, TT is dominated by AA-JJ, and KJ is dominated by AA-JJ, AK, AJ, and KQ.

As an example, suppose you are under the gun in a 6-handed game. Five players are left to act, so TT is dominated 9.5 percent of the time, and KJ is dominated 20.6 percent of the time.

There is no cookie-cutter way to use this chart. If you expect to play the hand out of position against good opponents, then as a starting point you might fold any hand that has a 20 percent or greater chance of being dominated. Under the gun 10-handed, this limits you to AA-TT, AK-AQ. Under the gun 6-handed, this would limit you to AA-TT (lower pairs are not considered here), AK-AJ, and KQ. However, as you approach the button, your chances of picking up the blinds with a raise increases. When the blind stealing equity is significant, it largely compensates you for the risk of being dominated.

We recommend you ignore this chart on the button. There is too much money to be made stealing blinds to worry about preflop domination.

Returning to the bet-sizing discussion, the hands 99-22, AQ-AJ, KQ comprise two-thirds of the new range. These additions work best with smaller open-raises. Therefore, the wider range in Situation 2 may work better with a smaller fixed raise size than in Situation 1. Also, you should consider dropping the weaker portion of this range in some games.

Try raising to 2.5bb or 3bb and see what works best.

Flop. Your range is much weaker than in Situation 1. Most of the time you will miss the flop. Consider betting smaller on the flop, like half the pot or a little less. The smaller bet size reduces your cost of c-bet bluffing.

This is only a starting point. Poker requires adaptation. If you find some opponents attack your small c-bets too often, adjust by betting half to two-thirds the pot instead. If that doesn't work, consider tightening up from early position.

The only difference between Situations 1 and 2 is your opening range. Your range is the most important factor in determining a fixed bet size against thinking opponents. We considered the best preflop raise size for each hand in the range then took roughly the weighted average. This works fairly well for approximating the "best" fixed preflop raise size for a range. To repeat:

> Match your bet size to your range's average strength. Then adjust it for the other factors.

Situation 3: A Shorter Stack Under The Gun

Players at the table: 10
Effective stack size: 30bb
Your position: Under the gun
Your range: AA-22, AK-AJ, KQ

Preflop. Your range is the same here as in Situation 2, but your stack size is different. How does that affect things?

First, as we said above, in tough 10-handed games you should probably drop some hands from this range.

Are you playing primarily to make the best hand with this range? With 30bb stacks, often yes. First, your opponents may mistakenly 3-bet you with a wide range. With a short 30bb stack, you are happy to see a light 3-bet so you can push. Second, if you can get all-in reasonably when you hit top pair or better with AA-22, AK-AJ, KQ, you profit significantly from making the best hand.

When stacks are small, stack-to-pot ratios play a major role in choosing an optimal fixed preflop raise size. Here the effective stacks are 30bb. If you raise to 3bb, heads-up pots will have SPRs around 4. If you instead raise to 4bb, heads-up pots will have SPRs around 3. This larger bet size can substantially increase expectation, even if opponents fold more often to the 4bb bet. When you are playing primarily to make the best hand and can achieve a good SPR *against weaker ranges*, raise enough to get there.

Your ranges in Situations 2 and 3 are identical. The only thing that changed was the effective stack size. With 100bb stacks in Situation 2 we recommended starting by open-raising to 2.5bb or 3bb. In Situation 3, effective stacks are 30bb. With 30bb stacks it is far easier to play for commitment with top pair hands. This dramatically changed our strategy. With 30bb stacks, we recommend playing for commitment and raising to 4bb.

When your range is weighted toward top-pair hands and stacks are short, SPR is the driving factor for choosing a fixed preflop raise size.

Let's look at 6-handed games.

Situation 4: A Tight Range Under The Gun In 6-Max

Players at the table: 6
Effective stack size: 100bb
Your position: Under the gun
Your range: AA-TT, AK

Here your range is the same as in Situation 1, but you are at a 6-handed table instead of a 10-handed one. Does that affect things?

Yes. This range is way too tight. Add more hands. If you raise only these premium pairs and AK, then as with Situation 1, aim for a larger fixed bet size. But in general, if this is you, stop being a wuss and widen your range.

Situation 5: A Wider Range Under The Gun In 6-Max

Players at the table: 6
Effective stack size: 100bb
Your position: Under the gun

Your range: AA-99, AK-AJ, KQ, and occasionally a lesser pair, suited connector, or small suited ace

Preflop. This is a strong range with a good balance of premium and non-premium hands. Let's talk about choosing a fixed bet size.

First, how often will someone 3-bet? Suppose you expect many 3-bets. What will you do if that happens? If you will fold a good percentage of your range, in general you should open-raise for less or drop some hands from your range. (Sometimes a larger bet will deter some of the 3-bets and work better.) Smaller fixed raise sizes reduce the cost of folding to 3-bets. If you won't fold to 3-bets often, feel free to make larger raises.

Second, how often will you take down the blinds? This can play a significant role in 6-handed games. For blind stealing, you want to raise just enough to get the job done. For example, a raise to 3bb or 3.5bb might be plenty.

How about postflop stealing? If you can steal many pots postflop, you like more money going in preflop and so might raise more. However, under the gun against tough opponents, most players cannot steal enough postflop pots to justify a larger raise.

Overall, we recommend raising to 3bb for starters, then adjusting from there.

Flop. This works similarly to Situation 2.

Situation 6: Open-Raising From The Cutoff

Players at the table: 6
Effective stack size: 100bb
Your position: Cutoff
Your range: 30 percent of hands

22+, A2s+, K9s+, Q9s+
JTs-87s, J9s-97s
A2o+, KTo+, QTo+, JTo

Preflop. Choosing an opening bet size from the cutoff can be tough because it depends so much on how the button and blinds play. If they are tight, you play to steal the blinds. Here your range is 30 percent of starting hands. It's a good start for a stealing range. You might widen or narrow it depending on how tight the three players to your left are.

As usual, when your range is wide and weighted toward steal hands, aim for smaller fixed bet sizes. Bet just enough to get the job done. If you match your bet size to your range's average strength, a raise to 2bb or 2.5bb would be best. But that is only a starting point, and it can break down here. In the cutoff, you're trying to get three players to fold, and the button has a major incentive to play. In general, in current online $1–$2 games, raising to 3bb or 3.5bb from the cutoff works better.

If the button plays a lot of hands well against you, tighten up. If he 3-bets frequently, ask yourself how often you will take it down postflop. If the answer is "often," you want more money in preflop. If the answer is "not often," you want less money in preflop.

Situation 7: Open-Raising From The Button

Players at the table: 6
Effective stack size: 100bb
Your position: Button
Your range: 51.4 percent of hands

22+, A2s+, K2s+, Q8s+, J7s+
T9s-54s, T8s-53s, T7s-85s
A2o+, K9o+, Q9o+, JTo-54o, J9o-75o, J8o-85o

Opening on the button is a special situation requiring a multi-pronged approach. Here is the key question: Will most of your profit come preflop or postflop? Typically most profit comes from taking the blinds preflop. When that's the case, bet the smallest amount that gets the job done. If instead most of your profit comes postflop, you don't mind building the pot and should raise more.

Preflop. Let's say the blinds play roughly AA-22, AK-AT, KQ-KJ, some suited connectors, and the occasional suited ace, suited one-gapper, and unsuited connector. This is about 20 percent of hands. Preflop, stealing is extremely profitable. You might be used to making a pot-sized 3.5bb opening raise on the button, but you want to bet the smallest amount that will get these tight blinds to fold. In practice this is typically 2.5bb or 2.25bb.

Small open-raises lay the lowest price to win the blinds. They also reduce the cost of folding to 3-bets.

When the blinds play only 20 percent of their hands, you should open-raise half your hands or more from the button. This assumes that the blinds don't loosen up and that you won't spew money postflop. If they don't and you won't, you have found a gold mine. You can expand your button open-raising range up to 100 percent of hands if the blinds don't adjust. It's free money. Don't be afraid to open-raise 60 percent or more of your hands from the button, especially against tight blinds.

Against looser blinds that play, say, 30 percent of their hands and 3-bet with 10 percent of them, you must take down a few pots postflop or tighten up preflop. Against blinds who play 30 percent of their hands, you steal the blinds roughly half the time you raise. If you are open-raising for 2.25bb or 2.5bb, you usually only have to take down a modest percentage of the postflop pots to show an overall profit. This assumes you don't spew for stacks or routinely pay off when your opponent hits.

Flop. Say you open-raised preflop to 2.25bb from the button. One of the blinds called. The flop comes, and the blind checks. Most of the time you will c-bet here. How much should you bet?

Your range is strongly weighted toward weak hands. Most of the times you bet, you will be bluffing. The best c-bet size here is the smallest bet that will get your opponent to fold frequently. You might start with betting a third to half the pot. Amazingly, some opponents fold about the same number of hands to a third-pot bet as they do to a half-pot bet. Against such an opponent, it is foolish to bet half the pot. The smaller third-pot bet achieves the same result at lower cost.

If you are lucky enough to face an opponent who will fold frequently to even smaller c-bets, bet less.

Against tough opponents in $1–$2, larger flop bet sizes tend to result in the most profit. Consider c-betting two-thirds the pot and adjusting from there. Rounded off, after open-raising to $4.50 or $5 and getting called by one blind, this means betting $7 or $8.

Elasticity Of Bluff Sizes

Here's a question for you. Suppose a half-pot bluff takes down the pot a third of the time. How often does a pot-sized bluff have to win to be equally profitable?

Most people intuitively answer two-thirds of the time. The correct answer is half the time. Say the pot is $10. A half-pot bluff is $5. The bluff creates a pot of $15. If you win that $15 one-third of the time, your expectation is $5. Subtract the $5 the bluff costs you and you break even. Similarly, a $10 pot-sized bluff creates a $20 pot. Win that half the time, and you break even on your $10 bet.

Now say a half-pot bet wins half the time. To have the same expected value, a pot-sized bet must win just 62.5 percent of the time.

Don't let intuition fool you. When you are stealing, bigger bets must succeed more frequently to be superior to smaller bets. But over the size ranging from one-third the pot to the pot, and with success rates in the range of 30 to 70 percent, the bigger bets don't have to succeed that much more often.

In other words, it usually doesn't cost that much to bet more on a bluff. It just feels that way.

Situation 8: Open-Raising The Button Against Looser Blinds

Players at the table: 6
Effective stack size: 100bb
Your position: Button
Your range: 60.2 percent of hands

22+, A2s+, K2s+, Q5s+, J5s+, T5s+
98s-32s, 97s-53s, 96s-63s, 95s-73s
A2o+, K5o+, Q8o+, J7o+, T9o-54o, T8o-64o, T7o

Preflop. Let's say the blinds play roughly AA-22, any broadway, Axs, suited connectors to 54s, and about half of their suited one-gappers and connectors to 54 (about 25 percent of hands). They 3-bet about 3 percent of hands. These opponents play a fair number of hands but are tight with reraises, especially considering you are opening 60 percent of your range. Such players are becoming less common as the online game evolves, but you will still find plenty of them in smaller-stakes games.

Your opening range here is 60 percent. Is that too loose?

No. Stealing the blinds remains a major source of profit. You will take down the blinds 56 percent, get called 38 percent, and get reraised 6 percent of the time. Every time you open-raise from the button, you have 0.84bb in immediate expectation from stealing the blinds. This is so high that blind stealing becomes your main goal. Since your profit comes mainly from stealing, choose a small fixed bet size. Start by raising half the pot, to 2.25bb. If the blinds fail to adjust by playing more hands and 3-betting more, try minraising to 2bb. If they instead start playing more hands or 3-betting more, raise to 2.5bb.

Flop. On the flop the same rule applies. Your range is weak, so start by betting small, say one-third pot. If they won't fold frequently to this bet size, bet half the pot instead. If they do fold often to a one-third-pot bet, consider betting less. In the unlikely circumstance that your opponents will fold often for 1bb, consider betting 1bb. Choose the amount that makes the most profit.

As an aside, even against sticky postflop players, you might throw the occasional 1bb c-bet at them. It will look very suspicious, like you are trying to induce a checkraise, and you might induce a mistake. But don't overdo it. Also, keep in mind this entire section is about fixed bet sizes *when you bet*. You can also check.

Situation 9: Adjusting Bet Size For Different Blind Opponents Postflop

Players at the table: 6
Effective stack size: 100bb
Your position: Button
Your range: 60.2 percent of hands

22+, A2s+, K2s+, Q5s+, J5s+, T5s+
98s-32s, 97s-53s, 96s-63s, 95s-73s
A2o+, K5o+, Q8o+, J7o+, T9o-54o, T8o-64o, T7o

Let's step back a moment and review a key point about fixed bet sizes. We use fixed bet sizes to conceal information. Your opponents are known to all, so you give up no information by using a different fixed bet size against different opponents.

Say you open-raise to 2.25bb on the button, because on average you find 2.25bb works best against this pair of blinds.

Here is an example of how you might use different postflop bet sizes against different opponents:

Suppose the big blind plays about 20 percent of his hands preflop and plays weak-tight postflop. He is a classic weak blind defender. When you raise and he calls, the pot becomes 5bb. If you c-bet 1.5bb, he folds often. This is a fantastic blind opponent. He folds too often both preflop and postflop. When he is the caller, take advantage by making those small 1.5bb continuation bets.

In contrast, the small blind also plays about 20 percent of his hands, but he gets sticky postflop. When he calls your 2.25bb preflop raise, the pot becomes 5.5bb. But when you c-bet 1.5bb, he is all over you, calling and checkraising far more often than the big blind. You find when you c-bet 3.5bb, he folds much more. So you adapt. When the big blind calls, you c-bet 1.5bb. When the small blind calls, you c-bet 3.5bb.

Feel free to use different fixed bet sizes against different opponents when the situation calls for it.

Situation 10: A Button Open-Raise Against A Dream Opponent

Players at the table: 6
Effective stack size: 100bb
Your position: Button
Your range: 60.2 percent of hands

22+, A2s+, K2s+, Q5s+, J5s+, T5s+
98s-32s, 97s-53s, 96s-63s, 95s-73s
A2o+, K5o+, Q8o+, J7o+, T9o-54o, T8o-64o, T7o

Preflop. In this scenario, one of the blinds plays about 20 percent of his hands. The other is on call-tilt. He calls anything that looks remotely playable, around 60 percent of his hands. He 3-bets premium pairs and AK-AQ. When he calls, he plays fit-or-fold, checkfolding the flop if he misses. If he flops a gutshot straight draw or better draw, he calls the flop then checkfolds the turn if the draw misses. He usually raises the flop if he hits second pair or better. You have found a dream opponent. How do you exploit him?

Much of your profit will come postflop, so raise more. Start with raising to 4bb. If this were heads-up, you would happily raise to 5bb or more if he will still call. But here the second blind can wake up with a hand, so you don't want to raise to 5bb.

Flop. Say your dream opponent calls your flop bet. Your opponent is checkfolding when he misses, and your range is very weak. You should make a small bet. If a third-pot bet is enough, bet that. If not, bet half the pot.

If he calls your c-bet, fire a second barrel on the turn. This opponent tends to raise the flop with big hands. Therefore, when he calls a flop c-bet, he is usually weak.

It takes a pretty bad opponent for most of your profit to be made after the flop. Normally when open-raising from the button, the profit comes from stealing blinds, and smaller bets work better.

Situation 11: Open-Raising From The Small Blind

Players at the table: 6
Effective stack size: 100bb
Your position: Small blind
Your range: Varies

This one is tough, because matching your bet size to your range's average strength doesn't work. Too much depends on the big blind's habits. There are two major decisions. First, how many hands should you play? Second, given this range, what should your raise size be? Here are some suggestions.

Weak-Tight Opponent. Suppose the big blind is truly weak-tight. Against such a player, you should raise many hands from the small blind. Your strategy shouldn't change much from raising the button against tight blinds. Blind stealing is still the major source of profit, and you want to raise as small as will get the job done.

Start by playing lots of hands, like the 60 percent range you opened from the button with.

Test the big blind. If he keeps folding, keep raising.

As a starting point against a weak-tight big blind, open-raise to 2.5bb or 3bb. Adjust from there.

Solid Opponent. Against a decent big blind defender who won't lay down for you, tighten up. You might start by raising with 30 percent of your hands or less.

The big blind will have position, so make him pay for playing the hand. Play around with bet sizes of 3bb-4bb to start. Some otherwise solid players play pretty much the same selection of hands regardless of whether the raise is 3bb or 4bb. Since your goal is to steal the blinds, you prefer the smaller raise size if that will work.

Tougher opponents will make you earn their money. In practice, a raise to 4bb may work better against them. This charges them to play and makes it easier for them to lay down. After all, you are laying a stiff price to take the pot. If they are really tough, you may have to play fewer hands.

A Special Case. Occasionally you will find a big blind who sees lots of flops but plays weak-tight postflop. Call it see-a-flop tilt. Against him, start by open-raising to 4bb or 5bb preflop. On the flop, start with c-betting frequently for half the pot or perhaps a little more. Adjust from there.

Flop. On the flop, the ideal fixed bet size depends a good deal on your range. If you open-raised with a tight range, betting two-thirds pot works in most situations. With a wider range, betting half the pot works better if it is enough to get the big blind to fold. But be flexible. A cookie-cutter approach rarely suffices for blind-on-blind play between thinking opponents. You will have to fight for the pot and get creative.

Summary Concepts

To choose a fixed preflop bet size, start by betting your range's average strength. If your range is strong and the profit comes from having the best hand, use a larger fixed bet size. If your range is weak such that the profit comes from stealing, use a smaller fixed bet size. Adjust as needed.

Preflop, when choosing a fixed bet size consider the following concepts:

♦ Fixed bet means when you bet, you bet the same amount regardless of which hand in your range you have.

♦ One size does not fit all. Fixed bets are chosen for a specific situation, such as "out of position against Tom in a 3-bet pot with an ace-high flop." Fixed bet does not mean you use the same bet size for broadly defined situations like "on the flop."

♦ Feel free to use different fixed bet sizes against different opponents. For example, against a habitual bluffer, smaller can be better if smaller fixed bet sizes will encourage more bluffing.

♦ If you are playing primarily to make the best hand, meaning you have a strong range, start by raising more. Adjust from there.

♦ If you expect substantial profit from stealing the blinds, start by raising less.

♦ From the cutoff, you are opening a loose range, so you might think a small raise will work best. In practice, usually a larger bet size of 3bb or 3.5bb works better.

♦ Most players in the blinds fold to 2.5bb almost as often as they fold to 4bb. This makes it far better to pay only 2.5bb to steal the blinds from the button.

♦ If you are playing primarily to make the best hand and stacks are short, watch your SPRs. Against shortstackers, SPR plays a huge role in choosing an optimal fixed preflop raise size. For example, suppose effective stacks are 40bb. If you raise to 3bb, heads-up pots will have SPRs of 5 or more. If you instead raise to 4bb, heads-up pots will have SPRs around 4. This can substantially increase expectation, even if opponents fold more often to the 4bb bet.

♦ You can usually ignore SPR when choosing a fixed bet size if the effective stacks are 70–100bb. You still use SPR concepts for postflop play, just not for choosing a fixed preflop bet size.

♦ If you expect substantial profit from stealing *after* the flop, you might raise more preflop. Bigger preflop bets make for larger postflop pots, which in turn usually result in greater profit if you are taking down most postflop pots. As a rule of thumb, if you think you'll take down significantly more than your share of pots *that see a flop*, you want more money in the pot preflop. For example, consider those times you raise, get 3-bet, and call. Two see the flop. If you expect to win, say, 70 percent of these types of pots, you have reason to raise more preflop.[22]

For postflop play, when choosing a fixed bet size, start with these concepts:

♦ When your preflop range yields more made hands than missed hands on the flop, start by betting bigger on the flop. Adjust from there.

♦ When your preflop range will be strongly weighted toward missed hands and weak pairs, start by betting smaller on the flop. Again, you will have to adjust from there.

---

[22] This is just a rule of thumb. It can fail because it does not consider implied odds. For example, say you expect to win 70 percent of the pots. The rule of thumb says get more money in. But suppose the average pot you win is small, as it usually is with successful c-bet bluffs. If the pots you lose are a lot larger, say after unsuccessful c-betting, overall you can lose money postflop even though you're winning 70 percent of the pots.

Choosing the right fixed bet sizes requires extensive estimating. Our suggestions for starting points are just that: starting points. You will have to adapt your fixed bet sizes to your game conditions. Try our recommended starting points out first, but don't be shy about changing them if they aren't working.

Planning Big Bluffs

Big, multi-street bluffs are relatively uncommon in most no-limit games. But the threat of a big, multi-street bluff hangs over nearly every hand and plays a role in many decisions. No-limit would be a much simpler game if big bluffs didn't exist. For instance, say you have top pair and you're out of position. If you can somehow know for sure that your opponent will never bluff all three streets, then you can adopt a very simple strategy. Just check and call the flop and turn and then check again on the river. If your opponent bets, it's for value, and you're beaten and can fold.

But if your opponent sometimes bluffs the river, everything changes. Now you can't necessarily just call the flop and turn because sometimes you'll put all that money in, only to get bluffed out on the river. Or you'll sometimes pay off a better hand on the river. The mere threat of a big bluff forces you to reexamine your strategy for the entire hand.

So even though big bluffs actually occur in only a small percentage of all no-limit hands, the *threat* of a big bluff will alter correct strategy on many hands. Thus, it's critical to learn how to launch those big bluffs when they're appropriate.

Big bluffs play a much larger role in shaping no-limit strategy than their frequency would suggest.

Two Keys To Big Bluffs

Opportunities to run big bluffs arise fairly commonly. But to run bluffs effectively, you need to figure out which opportunities are good and which ones aren't. There are two keys to identifying good situations for big bluffs:

1. Be aware of your opponent's hand range and which hands out of that range you would expect him to call a big bet or get all-in with.
2. Be aware of what your hand range looks like to your opponent, and know when you can plausibly represent a hand that would justify a big bet.

Here's an example of using the two keys to identify a good bluffing opportunity:

You're in the big blind of a $1–$2 6-max game with $200 effective stacks. A relatively tight player in the hijack opens for $6. A bad player calls on the button, and you call with 8♥7♥. The flop comes 9♣6♥2♦ giving you an open-ended straight draw on a rainbow board.

You check, and the preflop raiser bets $14 into the $19 pot. The button folds, and you call. The turn is the 2♥, pairing the board but giving you a flush draw to go with your straight draw. You check, and your opponent bets $30 into the $47 pot.

You call. The river is the 9♠. You missed your draws entirely, and the board has now double paired. There's $107 in the pot and $150 left in the stacks.

What is your opponent's hand range in this situation? He's a tight player who raised preflop from the hijack, so high card hands and pocket pairs are the most likely starters for him.

You checked the flop, and he bet more than 2/3 pot into two players on a dry, raggedy board. He might have an overpair or possibly just two overcards. Far less likely, but still possible, is that he flopped a set.

Would your opponent bet overcards into two players? It's possible, depending on how aggressive the player is. Most decent players realize that continuation betting tends to be more successfully on uncoordinated flops than coordinated ones. So your opponent might assume that he's more likely than usual to get folds from both opponents and try it.

Now an innocuous-looking card comes on the turn, and your opponent bets again. A second bet tends to carry more implied strength than the first one, as your opponent might check through the turn with some of the overcard hands in his range. So he could easily have an overpair. He could also have decided to fire again with overcards, hoping that you called the flop with a weak pair that you'll now release to the bigger show of strength. He may have decided to fire again particularly if his overcards were suited hearts like **A♥K♥** or **K♥J♥**.

He could also have some less likely hands. He might hold a nine with a hand like **A♦9♦** or **T♦9♦**. He might have 99, 66, or 22. He could hold a straight draw with a different combination of 87. It's also possible (but quite unlikely) that he holds a deuce.

Overall, however, the most likely hands in terms of the number of possible combinations and consistency with the betting so far are overpairs and overcards (possibly suited hearts) with nines and sets less likely.

The river puts a second pair on board. Which hands in your opponent's turn range would he now like to get all-in with? Likely he would be comfortable getting all-in with only the hands that contain a 9 (A9s, T9s, 99, etc.) and 22. Overcards, overpairs, and even 66 now have to worry that you hold a 9 and therefore a stronger hand.

So the hands that made up the bulk of the opponent's range on the turn—overpairs and overcards—now don't want to get all-in. Only a relatively small percentage of that turn range will now want to get it in.

Let's re-examine the hand from your opponent's perspective. What hands can he put you on?

You called a standard-sized preflop raise out of the big blind after a poor player entered the pot. You could hold quite a wide range of hands. Your opponent can probably discount the strongest hands, as you may have reraised with hands such as pocket aces, kings, queens, or ace-king.

You checked and called on a raggedy, rainbow flop. With so few draws available on the flop, your opponent would rightly assume that most of your range consists of made hands rather than draws: mostly pairs with the occasional set or two pair hand thrown in. If he thinks you're loose, he could also include unimproved overcards like A♦J♥ in your range.

After you check and call the innocuous-looking turn, your opponent would narrow your range further. If you perhaps called the flop with overcards or a small pocket pair like fours, you would likely have relinquished them to the turn bet. So, given that you checked and called the turn, your most likely hand in your opponent's eyes is probably a nine. You could also hold a deuce or perhaps a pocket pair like tens or eights that you may not have reraised preflop but that might now still be best. You could also possibly hold 99, 66, or 22.

On the river, if your opponent indeed has an overpair, he is likely cursing his luck. After checking and calling the turn you were marked with a likely nine, which would give you either two or five outs against an overpair. While your opponent was way ahead of your range on the turn, he's well behind it on the river because of the significant chance that you hold nines full.

Let's go back to the two keys and summarize the discussion thus far:

Your opponent most likely has an overpair or overcards, and he's unlikely to want to get all-in with either hand.

From your opponent's perspective, you are fairly likely to hold nines full. Other possible hands for you are deuces full or a pocket pair like tens or eights.

This is a good opportunity for a big bluff. Your opponent is unlikely to want to get all-in, and you have a very reasonable, obvious hand to represent. If you move all-in for $150, you have a good chance to win the $107 pot.

But before you shove the money in there, consider two more points.

Even if your opponent doesn't like getting all-in with an overpair, will he actually fold it, or will he make a crying call? This is an important question and will vary for different opponents. Some will lay the pair down quickly without thinking much about it. Some will hem and haw and say something like, "Aces get cracked every time," and then call. And some will think long about it and behave unpredictably. Obviously the bluff will work better against the players who will lay down the pair.

If you choose to bluff, how large a bet should you make? When bluffing, particularly on the river, you typically want to make the smallest bet that's likely to get the job done. In this case, to "get the job done," you want your opponent to fold hands like pocket queens. A small bet could be suspicious and may not be enough to suffice. In this circumstance, an all-in overbet is probably your best chance to sell the story that you hold a nine and to get an overpair to fold. But an all-in bet won't always be your best option.

Before moving on, think one more time about how the hand you actually hold fits into your opponent's perception of your hand range. You hold the only hand that made a legitimate draw on the flop. And of the 16 different possible combinations of eight-seven, you hold the only one that also picked up a flush draw on the turn. As far as your opponent is concerned, your hand is an anomaly. You'd be more likely to hold quads on the river (two hand combinations—99 and 22) than your actual hand. Indeed, you ended up playing the flop and turn very passively, perhaps making quads more likely in his mind.

In other words, the hand you actually hold is by far the weakest of all the hands in your range on the river. And it makes up only a tiny percentage of your overall range. Whenever that is the case, whenever the hand you actually hold is both unlikely and much weaker than your other possible hands, you will often have a profitable bluffing opportunity.

Big Bluff Practice

The thought process outlined above is essentially all you need to start bluffing with power and precision. Now we'll walk through the same process with some more example hands and see which bluffs make sense and which ones don't.

Hand 1. You're on the button with **9♥8♥**. An aggressive player opens under the gun for $6 in a $1–$2 6-max game with $200 stacks. You call, and the blinds fold. The flop comes **Q♦7♥6♦** giving you an open-ended straight draw. Your opponent bets $10 into the $15 pot, and you call.

The turn is the **3♣**. Your opponent bets $24 into the $35 pot, and you call.

The river is the **J♣**, and your opponent checks. Should you bet as a bluff, and if so, how much should you bet?

First, what's your opponent's range? He raised preflop and bet a queen-high flop twice. Since he's an aggressive player, he could do that with a fairly wide range of hands. Most obviously, he could hold a queen or an overpair. He could also have a hand like an unimproved pocket pair. The higher pairs like tens are most likely (assuming he would have bet jacks on the river), but some aggressive players will plow ahead with many pocket pairs.

Another possibility is a hand with a jack in it such as ace-jack or king-jack. He bet the flop and turn as bluffs, but then he checks the river now that he has showdown value.

He could also have flopped a flush or straight draw and have bet both streets as a semi-bluff. His river check could represent simply giving up on his bluff.

Other possible hands are a flopped medium pair with a hand like **8♠7♠** or **K♦7♦**, a flopped monster (set or two pair), or total air.

That's a fairly wide range, but most of it is composed of hands that have some showdown value. Only the missed draws and total air hands have no showdown value.

Second, what does your range look like to your opponent? You called preflop on the button and then called twice on a queen-high and draw-heavy board. Your most obvious possible holdings are a queen with a marginal kicker or a flush or straight draw. With a strong hand like ace-queen, two pair, or a set, you likely would have raised either the flop or turn. You could also hold a pocket pair like jacks or tens and be calling this aggressive player with position, refusing to give him credit for top pair or better.

Out of that range, which of those hands would you legitimately bet for value on the river? Except for pocket jacks, you would likely check the pocket pairs down. You might bet a queen.

So a river bet here represents a fairly narrow range of legitimate hands—primarily queens with at least a decent kicker and pocket jacks.

On the other hand, every draw has missed, and most of the drawing hands in your range are potential bluffing candidates. So if you bet the river, you're representing a relatively narrow range of legitimate value betting hands while at the same time having many busted draws in your range. From your opponent's perspective, a river bet is fairly likely to be a bluff, so this is a poor bluffing opportunity.

Indeed, if your opponent is a sharp player, he might well check a fairly good hand on this river specifically hoping to induce a bluff. He knows that busted draws comprise a large percentage of your range. You'll fold those hands to a bet, but you might bluff with them if checked to. Your overall range looks fairly weak, and you have a weak hand. Check it back.

If the river had been a diamond, completing a possible flush, then the dynamic would have changed considerably. Now your overall range is much stronger, since flush draws comprise a large portion of your turn calling range. Say the river were the **A♦**. Against many players (excluding calling stations obviously), a nearly pot-sized river bet would be a good bluff. The bet is large enough to discourage a crying call from a weak one-pair hand, and you are representing a very plausible holding given your play thus far.

Without the ability to bluff some scary river cards, calling the turn with your straight draw is no better than a roughly break-even proposition. Calling $24 in a $37 pot, you're getting just shy of 2.5–to–1 direct odds. You're about 4.75–to–1 to hit your straight. If you catch a non-diamond straight card, you'll hold the nuts, and you'll likely win a river bet a good percentage of the time. So your implied odds are probably enough to just about break-even on the call, but really no more than that.

Fortunately, you also have some good bluffing outs, which add extra value to your hand. When deciding whether to call the turn with a draw, consider in advance which river cards will present good bluffing opportunities and which ones won't. Also consider a turn raise.

Hand 2. You open for $7 in a $1–$2 game with $200 stacks from two off the button with **A♦Q♦**. The button, a solid aggressive regular calls. The blinds fold.

The flop comes **T♣9♦4♦** giving you two overcards and the nut flush draw. You bet the pot ($17), and your opponent calls. This player likes to call the flop with a wide range of hands to either make a hand or to steal the pot on the turn when he perceives weakness.

The turn is the 4♥. Because your opponent likes to try to steal against turn weakness, you check with the intention of inducing a bluff and checkraising. Your opponent disappoints you by checking as well.

The river is the 6♣. Is this a good opportunity for a bluff?

What is your opponent's range? So far he's called preflop on the button, called a draw-heavy flop with medium-sized cards, and checked back the turn when the bottom card paired. His range for these actions is fairly wide.

Preflop he could call with small and medium pocket pairs (likely reraising the big ones). He could also call with two big cards, suited aces, suited connectors, and perhaps some weaker hands as well.

On the flop he called with position on a draw-heavy board that's relatively unlikely to have hit a preflop raiser too hard. He could do this with nearly every hand he called with preflop. He would perhaps fold hands that missed the flop entirely such as 7♠5♠, but a large portion of his range will have at least some sort of pair or draw on this flop. He might raise some of his stronger hands such as ace-ten, ten-nine, a big combo draw, or a set. But he might flat call with those hands sometimes also. So his flop call doesn't narrow his range much.

The turn misses his range almost entirely. If he called the flop with a hand with virtually no value such as 6♣5♣ hoping to attack turn weakness, then he would likely have bet the turn. And if he called the turn with a strong hand, he also likely would have bet. So his turn check suggests that his hand has some value, but that he wants to avoid being checkraised. He could have a straight draw or flush draw. He could also have some showdown value with a modest one-pair hand or even a decent ace-high.

The river card again misses that range almost entirely. All the draws missed except for eight-seven. Pocket sixes are also in his range. Aside from those hands, however, the river will likely be a disappointment for him. So his most likely hands at this point are either busted draws or weak one-pair hands. Only a small portion of that range will want to call a big river bet.

What does your range look like to your opponent?

You raised preflop from two off the button. As an aggressive player, you could have various hands: principally pocket pairs, two big cards, and suited connectors. You bet a draw-heavy flop from out of position. Your opponent would have to consider that you might bet the flop with any hand you raised preflop. However, this flop hits your opponent's range fairly hard by making him many one-pair and drawing hands, so you would expect to get called more often than usual. Therefore, your opponent might conclude that you would check some of your worst hands and that your bet suggests that you may have connected with the flop in some way.

The turn card is almost certain not to have improved you. Your turn check could obviously represent unimproved overcards. If you held an overpair or top pair, this board would be a somewhat scary one on which to offer a free card. So your check means that your opponent can discount those holdings somewhat. However, if he knows that you know that he likes to call flops light, he could anticipate that you would check some of your good hands on the turn hoping to induce a semibluff.

In other words, your turn check shows some weakness, but big hands like full houses and overpairs are still plausibly within your checking range.

The river is also unlikely to have improved you. So you likely have whatever hand you checked on the turn. This range has medium-level strength. You likely checked many of your unpaired hands, and you could also have checked pairs and full houses as well.

Because your range is semi-weak, the stars are not aligned for a perfect bluffing opportunity. Nevertheless, the opportunity doesn't need to be perfect to be profitable. Your opponent's range is generally quite weak. Rarely will he hold a hand stronger than top pair with a marginal kicker, and often he'll hold a busted draw or a small pair. A pot-sized bet will confront your opponent with a very tough decision, and most opponents will simply fold rather than call the large bet with a weak hand hoping to pick off a bluff. You should get a fold often enough for the bluff to show a profit.

Of course, you do have ace-high, and therefore your hand would beat some of your opponent's range in a showdown. The problem with checking for a showdown is that sometimes your opponent will value bet the top of his range (top pairs and the occasional bigger hand) and will also bluff with some busted draws to balance. If your opponent balances well here, you can't call profitably with ace-high, and you'll have ceded a significant portion of your equity to him by allowing him to bluff.

A pot-sized bluff in this situation will frequently get your opponent to fold a better hand, and it also preempts him from bluffing you off the best hand.

Overbetting The Flop

An overbet on the flop can be a very effective weapon, and many novice players don't utilize it enough. It requires a solid understanding of the range war (your opponent's range and his perception of your range).

Say you are in a 6-handed $1–$2 game with $200 effective stacks. Everyone folds to the cutoff, who opens for $7. The button calls. You make it $30 in the small blind with black kings. The big blind folds, the cutoff calls, and the button folds.

The flop comes **Q♥9♥3♥**. The pot is $69, and you have $170 left. This is a good spot for an overbet.

With an overpair and an SPR of about 2.5, you are almost always committed in this spot. The board is extremely coordinated, and you are out of position. Pushing all-in protects the pot and leaves you with no decision to make on the turn.

When we suggest a line like this to players, they sometimes say things like "But, better hands aren't folding, and worse hands aren't calling."

This way of thinking leads to errors. Don't think in dualities: "My hand is *better* or *worse* than my opponent's hand." Think in terms of ranges and equity.

If you are playing the range war correctly, your opponent *will* fold hands that he should call with, and he *will* call with hands he should fold.

For example, what is 7♥7♠? Is that a "better hand" or a "worse hand"? Currently it might be behind your pocket kings, but with 11 outs and two cards to come it has more than enough equity to get all-in. And yet, your opponent will sometimes fold it to your all-in.

What about A♠Q♠? You are way ahead of that hand. Will your opponent fold it? He cannot correctly fold it in this spot, because your range includes hands that he has more than enough equity to call against.

When overbetting, just like with any other line you take, the wider and more balanced your range is, the less your opponent can make correct decisions against you.

Go all the way back to the preflop action. Your opponent opened from the cutoff, and the button flat called. That puts you in a perfect spot to squeeze from the small blind. Your range for 3-betting should be wider than just pocket kings.

Here's another example.

Same game, same stacks. Cutoff opens for $7, and the button calls. You make it $30 from the small blind with 7♦5♦. The big blind folds, the cutoff calls, and the button folds.

The flop comes Q♦9♥3♦. The pot is $69, and you have $170 left. Once again, this is a good spot for an overbet.

Your preflop 3-bet was designed to win the pot outright. Unfortunately, the cutoff called your squeeze. You flopped a flush draw, you have 2.5 times the pot left in your stack, and you are first to act. Of course you should push!

Your opponent will fold a lot of hands to your all-in. What will he do with any medium pocket pair like JJ, TT, 88, and 77? Probably fold. What will he do with A♠K♠? Probably fold. AJ? KJ? AT? Fold. Fold. Fold.

When he does call, you have two cards to come and often 9 outs to hit. Occasionally you'll have as many as 15 if your pair outs are good (like if he called with jack-ten).

These are just two situations where an overbet on the flop will yield a substantial profit. You usually want to try it on coordinated boards where equity is more likely to be evenly distributed between opposing ranges. But occasionally you might try it on a dry board.

As always, a solid understanding of your opponents' ranges, as well as their perceptions of your range, is crucial.

Underbetting In Multiway Pots

Players tend to play more straightforwardly in multiway pots than in shorthanded pots. You can use that fact to your advantage. When you have a medium strength hand, making a smaller than normal sized bet can serve the purposes of getting value from worse hands, gaining information, and controlling the pot to your liking.

Say you are in a 6-handed $1–$2 game with $200 effective stacks. A loose-passive player opens under the gun for $7, a decent player on the button calls, and a tight player in the small blind calls. You are in the big blind with J♠T♠. Against tighter opponents you might consider a reraise squeeze. Against very tough opponents you might consider folding. But here you are comfortable calling even though the preflop pot is a fairly awkward size for a hand that can flop dominated top pairs.

The flop comes J♥8♣3♠. The small blind checks, and the action is on you.

This is a good spot for an underbet. Your hand is too weak to commit to. But at the same time, you are susceptible to overcards, so giving a free card to three opponents is dangerous.

The pot is $28. Betting an amount like $9 or $11 accomplishes the same tasks as betting a two-thirds pot amount like $19. You charge weaker hands to continue (you may get calls from hands like weaker jacks, pocket tens or nines, ace-eight, straight draws, and overcards), and you gain information. Since information tends to be purer in multiway pots, you can get reliable information cheaply.

The smaller bet also benefits you in several ways. You keep the pot small with a hand that prefers to play a small or medium pot. Compare these two lines. If you bet $9 on the flop and get one caller, the pot is $46 on the turn with $184 behind. You can make another bet on the turn and still get away from your hand if raised. Or, you can call a bet on the turn and fold to a big bet on the river if you think you're behind. If instead you bet the full pot on the flop and get one caller, the pot is $84 with $165 behind. Your next betting decision is a commitment decision.

Other benefits of the small bet are that you keep initiative and avoid having to call a bigger bet. If you check the flop and the button bets two-thirds pot or full pot, you are back in the commitment predicament, but the situation is even worse because he has initiative, and his range is unknown. He could be betting a strong hand like ace-jack or a set, he could be semibluffing with a draw that has decent equity, or he could be purely bluffing. You are left playing guessing games on the turn and river.

If your bet is raised on the flop, you can usually fold. You are betting into three players and leading into the preflop raiser on a dry flop. That's a show of strength, so anyone who raises is probably strong.

To balance your range for making this play, you can also use this line to set up bluffs. For example, if on this same flop you were on the button with a hand like **T♣7♣**, and three players checked to you, you might make a small bet with the plan of possibly continuing your bluff on later streets. Also, for balance, you can sometimes underbet with monster hands.

Underbetting can be a sneaky weapon in multiway pots.

Balancing Your Lines

Let's talk defense.

Bill is a semiskilled $1–$2 player. In a 6-max game, he raises to $6, second to act. Only the button calls. The flop comes K75 rainbow. Bill bets $10. The button calls. The turn is a deuce. Bill checks and folds to the button's $12 bet.

Over the next four hours, this situation comes up many times. Bill raises in early position, gets called by the button, c-bets the flop, and is forced to fold on the turn. It doesn't happen every time, but overall he is getting killed. Bill has a major playing flaw and needs to figure out what it is. That's the bad news. The good news is it's pretty simple to do.

Read your own hands.

Let's pretend we're Bill and try reading our hand. Bill's big problem (our problem now) is the betting line "raise preflop and get called by the button, bet flop, check turn." So what is our opening range? Second to act in a 6-handed game, Bill raises with

22+, A2s+, KTs+
QJs-65s
ATo+, KJo+, QJo.

Once the next player folds, the button calls about two-thirds of the time. On the flop, Bill bets around 99 percent of the time when he hits top pair or better. He occasionally checks with a set and rarely checks with top pair. When he flops second pair or less, he c-bets about 90 percent of the time. On the turn, he bets again with top pair or a set most of the time. Otherwise he checks.

Let's start with the flop. What does Bill have when he c-bets? Naturally this depends on the flop. So pick a couple flops. In the opening example, we used K75 rainbow. How often does that flop hit Bill? It breaks down like this:[23]

Preflop Range:

22+, A2s+, KTs+

QJs-65s

ATo+, KJo+, QJo

Line: Raise Preflop Get Called
Board: **K♠7♣5♦**

Flop Holding	Percent
Three of a kind	4.0
Overpair	2.7
Top pair	17.5
Weaker pair	31.0
No pair	44.8

Category	Percent
Top pair or better	24.2
Underpair/Nothing	75.8

Now Bill bets the flop. What does he have? He bets the flop about 99 percent of the time with top pair or better, and bets about 90 percent of the time with an underpair or no pair. It breaks down like this:

---

[23] We show how to determine these numbers toward the end of the chapter. Or you can use a software package called Flopzilla (available freely at http://www.stoxev. com/flopzilla/flopzilla.htm) to calculate these numbers.

Preflop Range:

22+, A2s+, KTs+
QJs-65s
ATo+, KJo+, QJo

Line: Raise Preflop Get Called, Bet Flop
Board: **K♠7♣5♦**

Holding	Adjusted Percent[24]
Top pair or better	26
Underpair/Nothing	74

What does the button know about Bill's range? He knows two things. First, almost three-fourths of the time Bill has less than top pair. Second, Bill is about to give him a huge hint about his hand's strength. If he checks the turn, he's probably weak. If he bets the turn, he's probably strong. The button starts salivating and calls the flop c-bet.

Say the turn is the **2♥**. Rarely, this will give Bill a set of deuces, so we need to adjust the numbers:

Holding	Adjusted Percent
Top pair or better	27.4
Underpair/Nothing	72.6

Bill checks. What does his range look like now? Recall that on the turn, Bill bets top pair or better most of the time. Say he bets that 75 percent of the time. He rarely bluffs or bets weaker pairs, so when he bets again on the turn, he has top pair or better over 90 percent of the time.

---

[24] We say "Adjusted" because some of Bill's starting hands were checked on the flop and therefore have dropped out of his range.

What about when he checks? On the turn, he checks about 25 percent of his top pair/overpair/set hands, and about 99 percent of his weaker pair and no-pair hands. It breaks down like this:

Preflop Range:

22+, A2s+, KTs+
QJs-65s
ATo+, KJo+, QJo

Line: Raise Preflop, Get Called, C-bet Flop, Check Turn
Board: K♠7♣5♦2♥

Holding	Adjusted Percent
Top pair or better	8.7
Weak pair/Nothing	91.3

Bill's turn check range is heavily skewed toward weak hands. The button has figured this out. He knows Bill's turn check means weakness, so he bets the turn to steal. Usually, Bill will fold. The button is killing Bill when he checks the turn, because Bill's betting line narrows his range to over 90 percent weak hands.

This an unbalanced line. A line is unbalanced when the line's range favors strong hands or weak hands so heavily that it is easy to exploit. Unbalanced lines are common, even for solid $1–$2 players.

You almost certainly have a number of unbalanced lines in your play. Against bad opponents it doesn't matter, because they won't take advantage. But against astute opponents, you have a major problem. You need to balance the lines.

Balancing A Line

Bill has already done the hardest step. He realizes he has a problem, and he knows the problem is his unbalanced line "raise preflop, get called, c-bet flop, check turn." What can Bill do to solve the problem?

Whenever you have an unbalanced line, there are two main corrections you can make:

1. Play some of the hands in the unbalanced line's range differently.
2. Add hands to the unbalanced line's range.

You can do either or both. Let's explore these options.

Playing Hands Differently

When Bill checks the turn after c-betting the flop, 91 percent of the time he has a weak pair or nothing. One solution is to play some of those weak hands differently. For example, Bill can bet some of his weak hands on the turn. This has two advantages. Not only does it help balance the "c-bet flop, check turn" line, it also helps balance his "c-bet flop, bet turn" line. Let's try it out. Suppose Bill bets a third of his underpair or worse hands on the turn. What does that do to his turn-check range?

Preflop Range:

22+, A2s+, KTs+
QJs-65s
ATo+, KJo+, QJo

Line: Raise Preflop, Get Called, C-bet Flop, Check Turn
Board: K♠7♣5♦2♥

Turn Holding	Adjusted Percent
Top pair or better	12.4
Weak pair/Nothing	87.6

This is an improvement, but not a big one. The range is still too unbalanced, because an astute opponent can still exploit it easily by betting whenever Bill checks the turn. What else can Bill do?

He could avoid the line. For example, suppose Bill checked the flop more often with his weak hands. Then there would be fewer "c-bet flop, check turn" hands, and the button would have fewer opportunities to exploit this unbalanced line. Avoiding lines can work well, but a word of caution is in order. Those weak hands have to go somewhere. If Bill starts checking weak hands frequently on the flop, he creates a new unbalanced line. Namely, his new "raise preflop, get called, check flop" line would heavily favor weak hands. To compensate, he must also check good hands more often on the flop.

Let's go back to the turn-check line. Bill can reduce the number of weak hands in this line by playing tighter preflop. Whenever an unbalanced line favors weak hands too strongly, tighter preflop play usually improves the situation. In tough aggressive online games when you are out of position and don't play as well as your opponents, this is often a decent solution. But in a way, tightening up is a crutch. Once you become more skilled, playing too tight preflop can hurt your bottom line. Don't get pigheaded about your masterful skills though. If a certain button is killing you, just tighten up until you figure him out.

Overall, among the ways he can play hands in his range differently, Bill's best choice to balance the line is betting the turn with more weak hands. However, this only reduces the problem. It does not eliminate it.

Playing Other Hands The Same Way

This is the other way to balance a line. In Bill's case, he has too many weak hands in his "raise preflop, c-bet flop, check turn" line. He needs to add some strong hands to his range. Let's try it out. Bill has been checking 25 percent of his good hands on the turn. What happens if he instead checks 40 percent of his good hands? He still checks 99 percent of his weak hands. His new range looks like this:

Preflop Range:

22+, A2s+, KTs+
QJs-65s
ATo+, KJo+, QJo

Line: Raise Preflop, Get Called, C-bet Flop, Check Turn
Board: K♠7♣5♦2♥

Turn Holding	Adjusted Percent
Top pair or better	13.2
Weak pair/Nothing	86.8

This has a similar small effect, because he only adds a few good hands to the range. The line is now more balanced, but not by much.

Putting Them Together

Let's review. Whenever you have an unbalanced line, there are two main corrections you can make:

1. Play some of the hands in the unbalanced line's range differently.
2. Add hands to the unbalanced line's range.

You should do both. Here are the main corrections for you to consider when balancing a line:

Add whatever is missing to the unbalanced range. In Bill's example, his "bet flop, check turn" range has only 8.7 percent hands that are top pair or better. He needs to add more good hands to the turn-check range.

Play some of the overrepresented hands differently. In Bill's case, we started betting more of his weak hands on the turn.

Consider avoiding the line. By changing your actions on a prior street, you can reduce the percentage of hands that lead to the bad line. Be careful with this. When you avoid one line, others occur more often. Make sure these other lines are balanced.

Tighten up preflop to avoid lines that heavily favor weak hands. We list this last because it is a bit of a crutch. Crutches work, but they can slow you down. Similarly, tightening up preflop usually works to balance weak lines, but it can hurt your bottom line.

When you find an unbalanced line in your game, try the first two corrections initially. If the unbalanced line favors strong hands, add weak ones, and vice versa. Second, play some of the hands in the unbalanced line differently. Here is what happens when Bill uses both adjustments, checking 40 percent of his top pair or better hands and betting a third of his weaker hands.

Turn Holding	**Adjusted Percent**
Top pair or better	18.4
Weak pair/Nothing	81.6

This is much better. It's still over 4–to–1 weak hands, but there's not much Bill can do about that. Bill only flops top pair or better 24 percent of the time. He then bets the flop with almost all of his hands. His opponent has called the flop bet, so Bill has not folded any hands to get to the turn. Because of this, he cannot have top pair or better much more often than the 24 percent he flopped. Anything close to that 24 percent is reasonable.

Punishing The Exploiter

This is another way to think about line balancing. Someone is exploiting your unbalanced line, so you figure out how to punish him. The biggest problems come in two forms:

1. Your unbalanced line heavily favors weak hands, so your opponent bets or raises.

2. Your unbalanced line heavily favors strong hands, so your opponent folds.

Let's take the weak hands first. Bill's button opponent exploits his weak "raise preflop, bet flop, check turn" line by betting the turn when checked to. Bill can make it tougher for the button by balancing the line. He can also take punitive action. What does the button have when he bets after Bill checks the turn? Usually, the button is weak and just taking advantage of the unbalanced line. Bill can punish him by checkraising the turn. The button puts extra money in on a steal, then is forced to fold.

In general, when an opponent takes advantage of your weak unbalanced line by betting or raising, you can and should punish that opponent by checkraising or 3-betting. This can be done with strong hands or as a bluff. Either is effective.

What about strong unbalanced lines? Suppose in a 6-max $1–$2 game the cutoff raises to 3bb, you 3-bet preflop from the small blind to 9bb, and the cutoff calls. You bet 14bb on the flop, get called, and then bet 30bb on the turn. What do you have?

If you are like most amateur $1–$2 players, you have top pair/good kicker or better about 90 percent of the time. So what does your pro opponent in the cutoff do? He folds anything worse than top pair/top kicker without a thought. Think about how much this costs you. Suppose you have kings and your opponent has JTs. He raises preflop. You 3-bet. He knows you're a tight 3-bettor out of the blinds, so he does not 4-bet. He flat calls. Now you hit a wonder flop, J75. This is the best possible situation for your kings against JTs, but the wily cutoff folds on the turn anyway.[25] How do you punish him for folding?

Bluff! Your unbalanced line heavily favors strong hands. So, add some weak ones. 3-bet from the small blind with a wider range of hands, then bet the flop and turn sometimes even when you miss. This punishes the cutoff for laying down his JTs on the turn when he flops top pair. Secondarily, you should play some of the strong hands differently. Sometimes you should check the flop with an overpair of kings. And sometimes you should check the turn. Adding bluffs and occasionally checking the kings makes it much harder for the button to lay down his JTs when he hits top pair.

Remember, we only do these things against observant opponents. If your foe is clueless and does not realize your "3-bet from the blinds preflop, bet flop, bet turn" line means you have a strong hand, just fire away. Line balancing is defense. Reserve it for thinking opponents.

---

[25] The cutoff might instead raise the flop. We're ignoring that here to focus on the unbalanced line "3-bet from blinds preflop, bet flop, bet turn."

When Is A Line Balanced?

Let's take the extreme case. Suppose we balance a line to game-theoretic perfection. For example, say we start with Bill's preflop range of

22+, A2s+, KTs+
QJs-65s
ATo+, KJo+, QJo.

We raise preflop and get called. On the **K♠7♣5♦** flop we have:

Flop Holding	Percent
Three of a kind	4.0
Overpair	2.7
Top pair	17.5
Weaker pair	31.0
No pair	44.8

Suppose we c-bet 80 percent of these hands. What does a perfectly balanced c-betting range look like?

It mirrors what we flopped. We bet 80 percent of our sets, 80 percent of our overpairs, and so on all the way down to no pair. This perfect balance exposes the least amount of information. Our opponent learns nothing new about our actual hand. He knows only that we bet 80 percent of the time. This approach reduces our decision-making to checking or betting, and picking a bet size if we bet.

Nobody balances lines perfectly. There is no need to do so, especially in $1–$2. Instead, the goal is to balance a line sufficiently that your opponent cannot easily exploit your lack of balance. The better the opponent, the more balanced you want your lines to be. Against terrible opponents who won't exploit your unbalanced lines, line balancing is a waste of money.

So the real question isn't "When is a line balanced?" Instead ask "When is a line *sufficiently* balanced?" That answer depends on the opponent. A line is sufficiently balanced when your opponent cannot or will not exploit the remaining imbalance in it.

How Far Should Bill Go?

How far does Bill need to go to fix his unbalanced line? Unfortunately, there is no math answer to this problem. Too much depends on opponents, game conditions, and what street you are on. However, there are a few guidelines to follow.

The more unbalanced a line, the more profitable it is for your savvy opponent. An 80%/20% line gives your opponent an exploitable situation.[26] A 90%/10% line gives him a sledgehammer. To start, make sure you don't have any 90%/10% lines.

On the flop, the proportion of good hands in a line should be within several percentage points of the proportion of good hands you expect to flop. For example, say you expect to flop top pair or better 25 percent of the time. (Flopzilla calculates these numbers for you.) When you check the flop, you should have top pair or better around 15 percent to 35 percent of the time. Similarly, when you bet the flop, you should have top pair or better 15 percent to 35 percent of the time. This is just a guideline. We chose these margins because they work well

---

[26] By "80%/20%" we mean 80% of the hands are either strong or weak. Sometimes you won't have a good hand much more often than 20% of the time. So be it. At least it's not a 90%/10% line.

against most $1–$2 opponents. Against a tougher opponent, you may have to balance further. But for starters, just make sure to check enough good hands on the flop that an opponent cannot assume you missed when you check. Also, bet enough weak hands on the flop that an opponent cannot assume you have a good hand when you bet.

After the flop, the proportion of weak hands in a balanced line typically decreases. Many hands get folded on the flop. Most of these folded hands will be weak, so your range becomes stronger on average if the hand reaches the turn. However, if you have not folded many hands by the turn, then little changes. This is the case with Bill's turn-check line above, so the proportion of good hands in that line should still be within several percentage points of the proportion of good hands he expected to flop.

However, if you have folded many hands, we use a different guideline. As a general rule for the turn and river, lines are reasonably balanced for $1–$2 if at least 25 percent or so of the hands in the range are weak and another 25 percent or so are decent made hands. The remaining 50 percent is the middle ground for you to work with. This can still be exploitable, but it plugs the big leaks.

The more unbalanced a line is, the easier it is to recognize and exploit. Above all, avoid 90%/10% lines against thinking opponents. After that you can work on your 80%/20% lines if you find opponents are exploiting them. Again, you don't want to balance lines perfectly. You just want to balance them enough that your opponents cannot exploit you easily.

A great deal of line balancing is just mixing up your play. You may have heard advice like "Don't always bet the flop when you hit top pair with an ace," or "Sometimes you should check the nuts on the flop." These simple strategies help you avoid unbalanced lines. But each of those strategies addresses only a single situation. Thinking in terms of line balance can help you address all your lines systematically.

Strong And Weak Are Relative

We want to emphasize that for balancing purposes, strong hands and weak hands are relative. For example, sometimes your range will be heavily skewed toward powerful made hands. Say you 3-bet from the button, and two saw a flop of A♥Q♦7♣. You c-bet and get checkraised the pot. You call. The turn is the 7♥. Your opponent pots it. If you call or raise, you will have an ace or better most of the time. Yes, occasionally you will have less, but most of the time in $1–$2 you'll have at least aces and sevens. When you think about balancing this line, your strong hands are now full houses and occasional trip sevens. Your weak hands are aces up and lower. Make sure you can still have these strong or weak hands some of the time. Earlier in the chapter, we use top pair or better as our definition of a strong hand. But strong and weak are relative.

As an aside, your turn line from the last paragraph can easily be unbalanced. From your perspective, the line is "3-bet from button, call a checkraise on flop, call or raise on turn." How can that line be unbalanced? As an example, say you nearly always 3-bet the flop with a set on an uncoordinated board. But in this line, you just called the flop checkraise. Your astute opponent can figure out you didn't flop a set. Therefore, you become quite unlikely to have a full house on the turn. To balance this line, when you flop a set on an uncoordinated board, you must flat call the flop checkraise a fair percentage of the time.

The Limitations Of Line Balancing

Unfortunately, you only have so much to work with. On that

K♠7♣5♦ flop, Bill flops top pair or better only 24 percent of the time. No matter how well Bill balances his lines, he is in a potentially difficult spot. An opponent can fire away with nothing and make life hard for Bill.

This is one reason online games get more aggressive as stakes increase. For example, take a $10–$20 online game. A pro raises on the button with 40 percent of his hands. Another pro calls from the big blind. The flop is 5♣4♦4♥. Both players understand that a loose button raising range hits two pair or better less than 1 time in 4 on a 5♣4♦4♥ board. So they don't give up easily. For example, instead of c-betting then folding to a checkraise, the button might reraise or float the checkraise with nothing. It becomes a game of high-stakes chicken. And this is how it should be. When the preflop pot is 10bb and there is less than a 1 in 4 chance your opponent has two pair or better on a 5♣4♦4♥ board, you should be willing to risk a lot more than 10bb to win the pot, even if you have nothing. But this is true only against an opponent who also understands this.

A typical $1–$2 player does not get this concept. He won't risk a lot more than that 10bb to win the pot even though there is less than a 1 in 4 chance you flopped a modest hand or better. If he does put in, say, 25bb more, he has a good hand so often that you can safely fold. You should exploit this fact by not paying him off. In general in $1–$2, when you hit strong resistance, it is okay to give up your bluffs. But be wary. The game is getting tougher. At some point you will move up in stakes or come across a few $1–$2 players who won't give up so easily. Then you must fight harder for pots when no one is likely to have anything.

When Do We Care About Unbalanced Lines?

The answer is, "When your opponents are observant." Line balancing is defense. If you opponent is clueless, drunk, or on serious tilt, you don't have to worry as much about unbalanced lines.

Why Do We Care About Unbalanced Lines?

We care because we like money. Unbalanced lines are terribly expensive when your opponents are clever. Is your range too skewed toward weak hands? Thinking opponents just raise or float and force you to fold. Some of these lines, like "raise preflop, get called, c-bet flop, check turn" come up often. Say an opponent steals just one extra time every 500 hands against you because this line is unbalanced. That can easily cost you 10bb per 500 hands, or 2bb/100. This is in a game where a solid winning pro might earn 4–5bb/100. And these numbers can easily understate the problem.

What about when your range is too skewed toward strong hands? Thinking opponents just fold. It's as simple as that. Take the line "call raise preflop, checkcall flop, checkraise turn." For many amateurs, that lines means they hold a strong hand 90 percent of the time or more. A good player folds top pair or worse to your checkraise without a thought. This comes up less frequently, but the penalty is severe. In a game where a 2bb/100 winrate provides a good living wage, having an opponent routinely fold top pair to your 30bb turn checkraise is a disaster. Say he folds one extra time per 1000 hands. That's still 3bb/100. So much for making a living.

Unbalanced lines don't matter much against bad players. But against tough competition, you must balance or fall.

Exploiting Transitions

Say you have found an unbalanced line in your game. An opponent is taking advantage. You go through your lines and figure out what adjustments you need. Should you make those adjustments right away?

No! Take Bill's problem with the line "raise preflop, c-bet flop, check turn." His wily button opponent sees the flaw. He uses it against Bill by betting the turn whenever Bill checks. Bill has figured out that to balance his lines, on the turn he needs to check more good hands and bet some weaker hands. But he should not do this right away. Instead, it's time to turn the tables.

The button is conditioned to bet when Bill checks the turn. So, the next time Bill gets a good hand, he should checkraise the turn. This punishes the button. Note that when Bill first checkraises the turn, the button may well think Bill is full of it and just checkraising out of irritation. So it is best for Bill to have a good hand when he first checkraises.

What should Bill do next? This depends on how long it takes his opponent to figure out what Bill is up to. Some opponents won't be paying too much attention. If you guess this is the case—say because your opponent is 18-tabling—then you might checkraise most times on the turn for a few cycles until he figures it out. Then, and only then, do you switch to the balanced line.

Transitions are opportunities. Your opponent expects you to do one thing and will act accordingly. Punish him. Do whatever costs him the most. Here checkraising works well, because it extracts extra money out of the button.

What About Other Flops?

Did you notice we only went though Bill's lines on a K75 rainbow board? What happens on an ace-high flop? What about a highly coordinated middle board like **T♣8♣7♥**? The proportion of strong and weak hands in Bill's range changes quite a bit. For example, on an ace-high board, Bill will hit top pair or better over 30 percent of the time, since he plays many more hands with an ace than hands with a king.

Flops are perfect information. Everyone can see them. It's a minor point but important for line balancing, because your lines may be unbalanced only on certain flops. As a common example, a line can be balanced on an ace-high board but not on other board types. Also, when boards are coordinated, drawing hands enter into your ranges, adding another dimension.

When adjusting an unbalanced line, ideally you should work through three or four different flops. At a minimum, test an ace-high board, a coordinated board with a face card, like **Q♥T♦2♥**, and a low flop. Your thinking opponents know you are less likely to hit a **5♣4♦4♥** board than an **A♥J♥T♣** board. If you want to survive in the modern game, do your homework and check your balance across multiple board types.

Some Typical Unbalanced Lines

Chances are early in your career you had many severely unbalanced lines, but they didn't cost you much. Your opponents probably weren't good enough to realize your lines were unbalanced, or they didn't know how to exploit your flaws. To survive in the modern game past $1–$2, you must eliminate most of these severely unbalanced lines. There are too many strong opponents not to.

We're going to go through several common unbalanced lines. We'll give suggestions for correcting the problem after each. If you feel a twinge of recognition, make the general corrections we suggest. You can fine tune later.

For example, here is a betting line that is terribly unbalanced for most $1–$2 amateurs:

"Bet flop, bet turn, bet river."

Imagine yourself doing just this. You bet the flop, turn, and river. What do you have? If you are like most amateurs, your range consists of big hands and big hands alone. You might be a really frisky amateur and once in a while do this with a flopped flush draw, so instead of a 100%/0% range you proudly have a 95%/5% range. Good for you, but you're still dead. We crush you by folding. What happens when we fold to your big hands, but you pay off ours? We win, and you complain about running bad.

If ever there were an argument for a three-barrel bluff, this is it. You very much want freedom to bet your big hands across three streets. To protect that freedom, you must balance your "bet flop, bet turn, bet river" line by bluffing sometimes. What is sometimes? If you're not bluffing at least 10 percent of the time you make that third bet against tough opponents, you might as well get a day job. You should be bluffing on the river more like 15–20% of the time against skilled opponents.[27] Keep in mind you can "bluff" with top pair. The point is you should be trying to get a better hand to fold a fair percentage of the time.

Don't take this the wrong way. We are not advocating randomly firing three barrels. Rather, when you make a flop

---

[27] We are not going for game theoretic bluffing frequencies here. That would be foolish against a typical $1–$2 player who calls too much and overestimates opponents' bluffing frequencies.

semibluff, sometimes you should follow through on the turn and river. Alternatively, when you c-bet with a gutshot draw and one opponent calls out of position, think again before checking the turn. A half-pot or two-thirds-pot turn bet can be quite powerful. If that bet gets called and you miss, don't be shy about firing a third barrel a fair percentage of the time.

Also, remember that flops are perfect information. What happens when you "bet flop, bet turn, bet river" on an uncoordinated board? Are you an overwhelming favorite to have a huge hand? If so, it's time to fire a few turns with second pair or a gutshot, and follow through with a river bet more often than you might be comfortable with. If you don't, good players fold to that river bet unless they have a huge hand.

Another way to help balance the bet-bet-bet line is to bet a wider range of made hands all the way. As with bluffing, this makes it harder for an opponent to fold correctly.

Once you attempt to balance the bet-bet-bet line, take a few minutes with your favorite tracking software to see how you did. Isolate the hands that followed the line and see for yourself. How often was that third bet a bluff? If your answer is less than 10 percent, you are going to get eaten alive by skilled opponents.

Here's another typically unbalanced line:

"3-bet preflop out of the blinds."

What do you have? Many amateurs have only strong hands such as a range of AA-QQ, AK. This is way too tight. Blind stealing is a huge source of profit in online games. You want to make it at least a little expensive for the thieves to steal from you. The most potent way to punish a blind stealer is to 3-bet. At a minimum, you should 3-bet with a much broader range such as most of AA-99, AK-AJ, KQ, and some suited connectors. The suited connectors help because they form the bulk of your bluff hands and make it possible for you to hit any flop.

How about this line:

"Raise preflop, bet an ace-high flop."

At first glance this doesn't seem like much of an unbalanced line. But it is amazing how many weak players bet that flop 90 percent or more when they have an ace or three of a kind, yet check it half the time they don't. If their preflop raising range is heavily skewed toward ace hands, such as AK-AT, KQ-KJ, AA-TT under the gun, then on an ace-high flop with lower cards they have:

Preflop Range: AA-TT, AK-AT, KQ-KJ
Line: Raise Preflop, Bet An Ace-High Flop
Board: A♠9♥8♥

Flop Holding	Percent
Three of a kind	2.8
Top pair	44.9
Weaker pair	22.4
No pair	29.9

Suppose this player also has a common amateur habit. He habitually checks KK-TT when he hits second pair on an ace-high flop. This results in him checking when he has an underpair or no pair half the time. Since he also bets the flop around 90 percent of the time when he hits top pair or better, his flop check range looks something like this:

Flop Check Range	Adjusted Percent
Top pair or better	15.4
Underpair/No pair	84.6

See the problem? When he checks the flop, a skilled opponent will bet to steal. The line is too unbalanced. For example, say the pot is 10bb and an opponent bets 6bb every time when checked to. If the checker folds all but top pair or better, the bettor wins 84.6 percent of the time for an immediate 7.5bb in expectation.[28] If the checker also calls with KK-TT, then he folds 48.3 percent of the time, and the 6bb bet returns an immediate expected profit of 1.7bb for his opponent.[29] Either way, it's easy money for the opponent.

This can go the other way if you check top pair of aces too often. On an uncoordinated ace-high flop, it can be optimal to check when you hit top pair. This check shows weakness. It works best against opponents who like to bluff or call light on later streets once they sense such weakness. Suspicious opponents often won't believe you when you bet the turn and river after checking the flop. But if you overdo it, say by checking top pair of aces and sets 90 percent of the time, then your c-bet line becomes unbalanced:

Preflop Range: AA-TT, AK-AT, KQ-KJ
Line: Raise Preflop, Bet An Ace-High Flop
Board: A♠9♥8♥

---

[28] He bets 6bb, making the pot 16bb. He wins 84.6 percent of the time. 0.846×16bb=13.5bb. Subtract the 6bb wagered to get the profit of 7.5bb.

[29] We say immediate because that is his expectation from winning the pot right then. Usually his overall profit is higher than that. This is because when he is called, the skilled bettor can sometimes win more by betting again on later streets or by showing down the best hand.

Flop Bet Range	Adjusted Percent
Top pair or better	15.4
Underpair/No pair	84.6

These are the same numbers we saw before, but this time they are for when you bet, not check. In this scenario, an astute opponent just raises whenever you bet an ace-high flop.

There is no excuse for poorly balanced flop bets and flop checks. Early in the hand it is easy to balance ranges. For example, just by betting 80 percent with top pair instead of 90 percent, these lines become reasonably balanced for $1–$2. All you have to do is make sure the percentage of good hands in a line is within several percent of the percentage of good hands you expect on a given type of flop. This is not perfect, but it's tough to exploit.

Hunting For Unbalanced Lines

How do you find your unbalanced lines? In principle, it is simple:

Read your own hands.

Put yourself in your opponent's position and ask, "What do I have?" If you don't habitually read your opponents' hands, this will be tough. But stick with it. Reading your own hands is a tremendously valuable exercise for defeating thinking opponents. It will also help you read others' hands.

Using Brute Force/Counting Ways

We skipped the arithmetic when we talked about Bill's "raise preflop, bet flop, bet turn" line. Let's get your hands wet. Here is a recap of the problem:

Usually, when Bill raises preflop, the button floats the flop. Postflop, the button seems to know when to raise and when to fold. How? That's not an easy question to answer, since it depends on Bill's opening range, his betting tendencies, and the flop and turn. It is so complicated, in fact, that most successful high-stakes players analyze the problem intuitively rather than mathematically. From experience and memory, they develop a keen sense of their opponents' betting lines. Once a weakness is found, they exploit it. They also analyze their own play to avoid the same problem.

But what do you do if you don't have that intuition? Count the hands. A program like Flopzilla is the easiest way. But for old schoolers, you can find an Excel version for Bill's "raise preflop, bet flop, check turn" line on a K75 rainbow flop at

http://smallstakesnolimitholdem.com/SSNLHE_K75_Line_Balancing_Example.xls

This is brute force counting. The chart lists every hand in Bill's opening range. It gives the preflop betting action or range of actions for each hand. Namely, Bill raises to 3bb with every hand he plays. Then, on a given flop, it shows what Bill has and what he does with each hand.

From these columns, you can add up the ways Bill can have, say, top pair or better when he takes a particular line. Divide that by the total number of combinations for that line and you have the percentage of the time Bill has top pair or better.

This chart tells only part of the story. To better understand his weaknesses, Bill will have to repeat the exercise for other flop types, such as an uncoordinated ace-high flop like A♣T♥4♦, low boards like 6♥6♣4♦, and perhaps a couple other board types. He should look for 90%/10% lines first and correct those right away. Then he should ask whether he needs to tweak his 80%/20% turn lines against certain opponents.

Summary

Line balancing takes time. First you have to find unbalanced lines, then you must figure out how to fix them. Further, if the flop and turn change dramatically, you could end up with a quite different set of betting and checking frequencies. It gets complex quickly. But the value in doing the exercise remains. You'll find leaks and plug them.

Any time a betting line results in an easily exploitable frequency of good vs. bad hands, mix it up. We recommend that when you find a common hand situation that causes you trouble against your tougher opponents, do this exercise and see if the problem is an unbalanced line.

Bankroll Requirements

You need way more than you think you need. You need way more than the successful pros say you need. You need way more than the statisticians say you need.

You need a lot.

Let's talk basic stats first. Pretend you are Seo Awsum, a solid poker pro. Seo plays online $1–$2 6-max for a living. He plays eight or nine tables at a time, buys in for a full stack of $200, reads stack sizes for every table before entering a pot, knows the regulars, analyzes stats, does not play too many hours at a time, and rarely tilts. Seo played a million hands last year and averaged $12 per 100 hands with a standard deviation of $200 per 100 hands.

If Seo plays another million hands this year and plays the exact same way in the exact same game conditions, he can expect (with 99 percent confidence) his total winnings at the end of the year to be anywhere between approximately $70,000 and $170,000. That is a difference of $100,000 due purely to randomness. And Seo's winnings over any given 80,000 hand sample—about a month's worth of work—could be anywhere between approximately –$5,000 and $25,000 (again using a 99 percent confidence interval). His monthly income can vary by as much as $30,000. That's a monthly difference of 150 buy-ins due to chance alone.

Now let's talk reality, because you are not Seo Awsum. If you are an online poker pro, your situation is likely worse. For starters, your winrate may be lower than $12 per 100 hands. Also, you may not have the stamina to play a million hands in a year. And most importantly, we haven't yet discussed one of the biggest threats to bankrolls.

We calculated Seo's variance numbers using basic Stats 101 formulae. To predict bankroll requirements, statisticians have traditionally taken this approach of using a player's historical winrate and standard deviation and plugging them into these formulae. Some also then make estimated adjustments for stepping down and other factors. These adjustments tend to be optimistic in that they typically assume you won't tilt and will step down when you should. But there is a far bigger problem. Stats 101 calculations assume that in the future you will play in similar games. This is called sampling from the same distribution. Reality is vastly different. Games change.

Games change. It's as simple as that. Past results do not dictate future performance. Or, in statistics terms, the underlying distribution can change quickly. One day you're playing against Andy, Bill, Caroline, David, and Eric with a 3bb per 100 hands winrate and a standard deviation of $200 per 100 hands. The next day, two major events happen that lower your winrate. Andy figures out that when you raise the turn, you are more likely than an average opponent to have a real hand. He exploits your flaw by folding more frequently when you raise. It's a subtle difference, maybe one extra correct fold every 600 hands, but if that fold costs you 12bb you now win 2bb per 100 less. Meanwhile, Eric is replaced by Felicia. Felicia reads hands a little better, which impacts you in a few ways. She is less likely to lose chips to David, the weak player in the game. Also, she occasionally makes a thin value bet against you that Eric would not have. Again it's a subtle difference that costs you 2bb per 100 hands.

Overnight your win rate has gone from 3bb per 100 to –1bb per 100, while your standard deviation remains around $200 per 100 hands. You are now a loser. You just won't figure it out for tens or hundreds of thousands of hands.

The fact is, games can change quickly, and small changes can kill your expectation. This fact dramatically increases bankroll requirements.

You will, as a professional player, experience downswings you probably never thought were possible. In preparation for this book, Sunny played several hundred thousand hands of $1–$2 6-max. He took the gig seriously, regularly analyzed his play, tilted minimally, and achieved an excellent winrate. Yet, at one point he suffered a downswing of 40 buy-ins. Forty! That's $8,000.

You may have read stories about successful pros who rose to the top on 30- or 40-buy-in bankrolls. Well guess what? It's selection bias. They got lucky. Literally hundreds of players who could have been just as successful did the same thing and went broke. If you play on 30 buy-ins, it's only a matter of time before you too bust out.

So what can you do? First, assume solid 6-max pros almost never suffer 30 buy-in downswings due to chance alone. This is not true, but it's a great assumption. If you find yourself in a big downswing, ask how much you are tilting and stubbornly sticking to tough games. Then ask whether the game has changed. And don't forget collusion. This is one of those delicate topics that all the "in" people don't like to talk about. But the fact is, if Andy and Danny get on instant messenger and play best-hand against you, you will take a major hit right in the winrate.

The best way to deal with a small downswing is to tighten up a little while you determine whether you have played well. Run hands by your poker friends, your coach, or the online forums. Review stats like VP$IP, PFR, 3-Bet Percentage, and C-Bet Percentage, and analyze them by position—not just as averages—to help figure out if you are making consistent mistakes.

The best way to deal with a big downswing is to take a few days off. Relax, exercise, sleep, and get your head back in the game.

After a few losses, you should step down. There comes a point in a downswing where you may be playing badly and not know it. In general, after losing 20 buy-ins, not only should you take a break and analyze your recent game, you should also seriously consider dropping down a limit or two.

So how big a bankroll do you need? Clearly—and perhaps surprisingly—it is more than 40 buy-ins. But what is the magic number for an online pro who doesn't have much room to move down and still make a good living? This number depends on a great many factors, such as how much you think games might change, how aggressive you are, your risk tolerance, your winrate, your living expenses, how much you tilt, and how good you are at stepping down. It also assumes you don't have a job or a trust fund to replenish your bankroll. No matter how you slice it, it's just an estimation. No one can know your true number.

But who are we to deprive you of our recommendation? If forced to give you a specific bankroll number, ours is:

100 buy-ins

You may not like that recommendation. That's okay. Our goal with this book has been to challenge you to see situations in new ways—to see all 64 squares if you will—and to help you survive and thrive in the online poker world. If this recommendation sways you to keep 60 buy-ins in your bankroll instead of 30 buy-ins, then we have done our job. We have increased your chances of survival dramatically, and even more importantly, we have made you think.

Best of luck to you!

Ed, Sunny, and Matt

Other Books from Dimat Enterprises, Inc.

Texas Hold'em Odds and Probabilities: Limit, No-Limit, and Tournament Strategies

By
Matthew Hilger

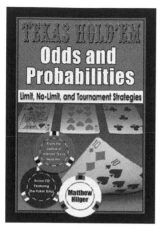

How often does each starting hand win against a specific hand or random hand?

What are the odds of your opponent holding a pocket pair when he raises?

What is the probability that an over-card will flop when you hold JJ?

How do you determine if drawing is profitable or not?

Texas Hold'em Odds and Probabilities answers all of these questions and more. Every single decision you make at the poker table is in some way related to odds and probabilities. Whether you are deciding to bet, call, fold, raise, or even bluff, odds and probabilities are an integral part of the decision-making process.

Texas Hold'em Odds and Probabilities covers all forms of the game, including limit, no-limit, and tournament situations. This book does more than just show you how to calculate the odds—it focuses on how to *apply* odds to make better decisions.

My approach shows that you do not need to be a math wiz to be successful in poker. Simple concepts and strategies that anyone can learn will have you matching wits with the top players in no time.

Some of the topics include: raising draws for value, backdoor draws, facing all-in decisions before the flop, protecting your hand, the impact of stack sizes, and much more. In addition, the most comprehensive collection of Texas Hold'em charts and statistics ever printed is provided as reference.

Poker is a fun game, but it is even more fun when you win. Expert players understand the simple math behind every decision they make – now you can, too.

Winning Poker Tournaments One Hand at a Time

By

Eric "Rizen" Lynch, Jon "PearlJammer" Turner, and Jon "Apestyles" Van Fleet

Want to win poker tournaments? Now you can learn exactly how consistent winners REALLY do it.

Meet "PearlJammer", "Rizen", and "Apestyles". These top guns of tournament poker are frequent winners in today's highly competitive online scene, as well as in live tourneys. Their collective experience and track record is staggering: more than 35,000 tournaments played, more than 1,000 final tables made, over 200 major wins, and more than $6,000,000 in cashes. They regularly outplay fields consisting of other top professionals—victories that are documented by detailed online hand histories

Are you ready to learn winning ways from today's *true* tournament experts?

The authors are not only consistent winners, but powerful teachers as well. Step-by-step, they reveal their decision-making processes, using hands drawn from actual play—not examples contrived to fit a particular poker theory.

Reading this book is like attending a master class in tournament poker.

You'll see the way cutting-edge pros use their wisdom and incredibly extensive experience to analyze almost every poker situation imaginable. Deep-stacked or short-stacked, against single or multiple opponents, you'll learn the skills that will make you a winner including:
- When and how to play aggressively or tightly
- When to make moves
- When to make continuation bets and when to hold back
- How to induce and pick off bluffs
- How to accumulate chips without constantly risking your tournament life

Poker is a fun game, but it's even more fun when you win.

If you want to become a great tournament player, shouldn't you be learning from the best? NOW You can!

Winning Poker Tournaments One Hand at a Time Volume2

By

Eric "Rizen" Lynch, Jon "PearlJammer" Turner, and Jon "Apestyles" Van Fleet

YOU'RE IN THE MONEY...NOW WHAT?

You've put in the time, you've built up your stack, and now, at last, you're inching ever closer to serious tournament payoffs. At this stage, playing smart is more crucial than ever, and who better to give you the edge than three of modern poker's greatest tournament pros?

THEY'LL TAKE YOU FROM THE BUBBLE TO THE FINAL TABLE

Volume 1 of this series shed new light on the fundamentals, and now in, Volume 2, Pearljammer, Apestyles and Rizen—players whose collective stats include, more than 1,800 final tables made, over 300 major wins, and more than $10,000,000 in cashes—return to show you how to crush the final table.

When deep in a tournament, the ability to analyze opponents' play is more than an advantage—it's a necessity. In this exciting follow-up, you get to sweat the best as they walk you through the key hands of actual tournaments: what they did right, what they did wrong, and what you need to do to win, including:

- How to use the changing dynamic of stack size to your advantage as the field narrows
- The unique strategies and tactics of Final Table play
- How to dominate weak players and outthink strong players
- How to take maximum advantage of your table image to confound your competition
- How hand selection changes in short-handed and heads-up play

Poker is a fun game, but it's even more fun when you win. Online or live, you need to keep your cool and make the right moves to enjoy big-money finishes. If you've gotten this far, these top professionals will help you go all the way.

Internet Texas Hold'em:
Winning Strategies for Full-Ring and Short-Handed Play

New Expanded Edition

By
Matthew Hilger

A Complete Course in Playing Winning Limit Hold'em

No Limit Hold'em has become the glamour game of poker. Yet today's savvy pros know that some of the best low-risk money-making opportunities exist in Limit Hold'em. This complete manual will show you how to consistently beat today's Limit Hold'em game, whether you play on the Internet or in live games. **Revised, updated and expanded with over 100 pages of all-new material and over 250 sample hands to bring the lessons to life**, this classic text shows you how to win again and again. Step- by-step and hand-by-hand, you will learn:

- Which starting hands to play Pre-Flop
- How to turn sound poker theory into winning play
- Traps to set and minefields to avoid
- How to play through the Flop, the Turn, and the River
- The odds and probabilities every successful player must know
- How and when to bluff and how to pick off habitual bluffers
- ...and much more

Plus detailed new chapters that include a complete strategy for conquering short-handed games and the keys to playing in multi-way pots.

Poker is a fun game, but it is even more fun when you win. With poker professional Matthew Hilger's *Internet Texas Hold 'em* as your guide, you can master in hours what most players take a lifetime to discover.

Pot-Limit Omaha Volume I:
Small Ball and Short-Handed Play

By
Jeff Hwang

The Game of the Future has arrived!
Are you ready to be its next big winner?

What would the ideal poker game look like? Big pots, lots of action, and a game where you know *way more* than your competition. Master *Advanced Pot-Limit Omaha*, and this poker dream can become a money-machine reality.

You'll learn all there is to know about:

- ♠ **Floating:** An advanced bluffing technique, and the key to advanced play
- ♠ **Advanced Concepts:** The Stack-to-Pot Ratio (SPR), deep stack leverage, the positional disadvantage/advantage, and more
- ♠ **Advanced Skills:** Check-raising, the bluff raise, 3-betting after the flop (without the nuts), value-betting the river, and picking off bluffs
- ♠ **Small Ball:** An advanced strategy for exploiting our opponents in short-handed pots
- ♠ **3-Betting Before the Flop:** A situational loose-aggressive (LAG) tactic
- ♠ **Short-Handed Play:** How to play in games played six-handed or less utilizing the Small Ball and 3-Betting strategies.

And more!

With over 200 hand examples and walkthroughs to reinforce the advanced skills, concepts, and strategies presented in this book, *Advanced Pot-Limit Omaha* successfully breaks new ground and takes Omaha strategy to the next level. For those in the know, Pot-Limit Omaha will be a bonanza of riches, but you must act now if you want to get an extra jump on your opponents.

Poker is a fun game; it's even more fun when you *win*. And with Jeff Hwang as your guide, you will win more than ever before.

Peak Performance Poker:
Revolutionizing the Way You View the Game

By
Travis Steffen

A NEW ERA OF POKER IS DAWNING

As a poker player, you have a great deal in common with today's professional athletes: You've dedicated serious time to learning the fundamentals; you practice regularly; you strive to improve by analyzing every move; you use psychology to hone your winning edge—and, if you don't take care of yourself both mentally and physically, you'll lose your winning edge...

CAN YOU COMPETE WITH THE BEST?

Learning to treat poker like the competitive endeavor it is—and yourself like the sportsperson you are—will give you the best chance at success every time you play. Packed with solid research and feedback from top pros, PEAK PERFORMANCE POKER will show you how to prepare your body and your mind to achieve optimal results during that next big tournament or cash game.

Being in peak physical condition sharpens every aspect of your play, whereas poor diet and neglect of your emotional life undermine your game at every turn. Just ask Daniel Negreanu, Phil Hellmuth, and the other top pros featured in this book, all of whom understand crucial aspects of PEAK PERFORMANCE POKER, including:

- "Flow"—what it means to top athletes and why it's equally important to you
- Chips on the table, not on your plate—eating right to improve your game
- Taking it easy—how essential rest and recovery really are
- Getting psyched—applying sports psychology to help you win
- Time management—the benefits of balancing poker with the rest of your life

The modern poker table is the domain of smart, fit, healthy competitors; let PEAK PERFORMANCE POKER seat you with the best of them.

The Poker Mindset: Essential Attitudes for Poker Success

By
Ian Taylor & Matthew Hilger

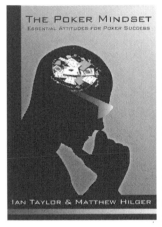

What "secret" separates top poker players from poker wannabes?

Is it zen-like mind-reading skills, a computer-like brain or thousands of hours of play? No. It is a series of established approaches and behaviors that enables these experts to bring their "A" game to the table session after session, regardless of short-term results.

In this groundbreaking book, Taylor and Hilger lay bare the secrets of the Poker Mindset: seven core attitudes and concepts that ensure you have the optimal emotional, psychological, and behavioral framework for playing superior poker.

The Poker Mindset deeply explores vital topics that most poker books only touch upon:

- Tilt: What it really is, why and when you are most prone to it, and how you can avoid it.
- Bankroll: A complete examination of bankroll management from a technical, but more importantly, from a psychological and emotional viewpoint.
- Opponents: How to determine your competitors' mental and emotional processes so that you can dominate, out think and outplay them.
- Downswings: Every poker player experiences them, but you will truly understand and be armed against low ebbs when they occur.
- Bad Beats: *The Poker Mindset* will enable you to overcome the trauma of bad beats and losing big pots.

Poker is a fun game, but it is even more fun when you win. *The Poker Mindset* may be the most valuable poker book you will ever read. Embrace its concepts and you can overcome the unseen obstacles that are limiting your success at the table.

When you make the Poker Mindset your mindset, you will take control of your game and walk away a winner.

Printed in Poland
by Amazon Fulfillment
Poland Sp. z o.o., Wrocław

62315971R00213